THE GUILD®
The Designer's Reference Book of Artists

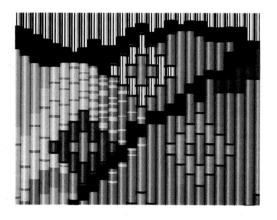

Kraus Sikes Inc.
Madison, Wisconsin

THE GUILD®

Published By:
Kraus Sikes Inc.
228 State Street
Madison, WI 53703
800-969-1556
608-256-1990
FAX 608-256-1938

Administration:
Toni Fountain Sikes,
    President
James F. Black, Jr.,
    Vice President
Susan Evans Fee,
    Associate Publisher
Karen A. Stocker,
    Circulation Manager
Darin J. Edington,
    Business Manager
Yvonne Cooley,
    Secretary

Production and Design:
Kristine Firchow,
    Production Manager
Kyle Hanson-Hanslien,
    Consultant
Fiona L'Estrange,
    Color Proofing Consultant

John Anderson, Writer
Judith Litvich, Writer
Gerri Nixon, Writer
Leslie Ferrin, Writer
Heather L. Healy, Interviewer

KC Graphics, Inc., Typographers
Toppan Printing Co., Separations,
    Printing and Binding

Regional Representatives:
Rachel Degenhardt
Susan Evans Fee
Andrea Moriarty
Cynthia Snook

Distribution:
This book is exclusively distributed
by Rockport Publishers, Inc.
Rockport, Massachusetts

ISBN (softback) 1-880140-01-2
ISBN (hardback) 1-880140-00-4
ISSN 0885-3975

Printed in Japan

Cover Artists:
Animal Spiral, art quilt by
Therese May (pg. 18), Photo: Mert
Carpenter; Cobalt lighted glass
and metal sculpture by **Michael
K. Hansen and Nina Paladino**
(pg. 205), Photo: Rick Walter;
Kwakiuti Mask by **Shawn Athari**
(pgs. 85 and 201), Photo: George
Post; *Fauna Collection: Eagle Chair*
by **Ray Lewis** (pg. 127), Photo:
Marvin Silver.

**Cover artist (Background): Joyce P.
Lopez** (pgs. 92–93), detail from
fiber and metal sculpture, North Pier
Apt. Tower lobby, Chicago, IL.
Another detail from this beautiful
piece also appears throughout the
book. Photo: Mark Belter.

Introduction

Welcome . . . to our seventh annual publication of THE GUILD and the first-ever, stand-along volume devoted exclusively to artists who create work for the wall, furniture, and accessories. Here is your definitive resource of top-notch professional artists, juried for their experience in working with design professionals.

When we began THE GUILD seven years ago as a publication that marketed hand-crafted work to designers and architects, we found ourselves in the front ranks of a design revolution. A revolution that celebrates the soaring inventive-ness of the human mind and the practiced skill of the human hand in creating one-of-a-kind solutions to design problems.

We watched with delight as increasing numbers of design professionals and art consultants began to work with artists. Meanwhile, a visually literate public also became enthusiastic about hand-crafted furniture and objects. Now, responding to a real yearning for the kind of emotional fulfillment and aesthetic pleasure that this work provides, today's clients are sophisticated and confident, ready to assess, reject or embrace what they like or don't like. They demand that the things one lives with at home and at work be fresh, challenging and, above all, well made and well designed.

The artists that we've dealt with over the years are incredibly knowledgeable about their art form and thoroughly professional about their business. They do what they say they're going to do, they do it on time, and they do it within budget. These artists are a pleasure to work with, and they are uncompromisingly honest with their client's time and money.

After seven years of working with thousands of top artists, here at THE GUILD we've discovered that the pleasure we take from their extraordinary work is nearly matched by the pleasure of doing business with them.

In a time when there's a widespread assumption that business relationships are hard-edged and adversarial, my dealings with these artists have reminded me that the virtues of competence, consideration, creativity and honesty put fun into even the most demanding projects. And I find reassurance and comfort knowing that the human spirit is still capable of creating beautiful, unique things.

To the many art lovers who have utilized the resources of THE GUILD time and again over the years, we're very proud to present an even more useful sourcebook. To see why this is so, turn the page and find out just how beneficial this new book can be for you.

Toni Fountain Sikes
Publisher

7 Great Ways to Take Advantage of THE GUILD®

1 This book begins with an assurance that these artists are professionals. All artists in THE GUILD have been juried in on the basis of experience, quality of work, and a solid reputation for working with designers, architects, and art consultants.

2 Taking your copy of THE GUILD to client meetings is highly recommended. Clients have been known to reach levels of extreme excitement upon viewing the artistic possibilities showcased here.

3 Always keep THE GUILD handy on your desktop. The hum it exudes as an idea generator will not disrupt your inspiration. In fact, it can be a powerful addition to it.

4 If something intrigues you while perusing THE GUILD -- a shape, a form, an exotic use of the commonplace -- please, *give the artist a call.* Serendipity often leads to a wonderful creation.

5 For your ease of exploration, THE GUILD is divided into three main categories: Work for the Wall, Furniture, and Accessories. But keep in mind that it's hard to put these artists in boxes, so we hope you'll see these sections as a means to begin exploring their versatile talents.

6 You can actually see the work of artists in THE GUILD at a number of galleries and showrooms in the United States and Canada. Take a look at our state-by-state listing of where to go in *Gallery Resources,* page 251.

7 Our regional index of artists in THE GUILD is found on pages 272–273. Check it out; you just never know. You could discover a wellspring of inspiration in your own backyard.

Table of Contents

Making Art
Part of the Design Package

by Judith Litvich

Many designers, consultants and clients may be quick to agree that artwork makes a difference in the way a space feels and the way people feel in that space. But too many people are quick to come up with an excuse as to why art is not a priority in the basic plan.

The designer needs to devise some considered replies to gently persuade the client to make art an integral part of the design package.

The following are six common excuses clients make for not buying art, and six responses that the design professionals can use in reassuring the reluctant or hesitant client:

EXCUSE: "I know nothing about art. Besides, I feel intimidated by galleries."
RESPONSE: "Don't worry -- very few people have an art background. Art isn't something that you learn by reading a do-it-yourself book. You just need experience in 'looking' at art -- in museums, in galleries, and at art exhibitions. It's also helpful to work with a professional you trust (designer, art consultant, art dealer) and with whom you feel comfortable, someone who can guide you in finding art that has integrity. Through the process, you will begin to define, or redefine, your tastes."

EXCUSE: "We really want artwork, but we've run out of money."
RESPONSE: "The budget has been pushed pretty far, but we're creating a fresh, new look. It's important to follow through with a finished concept; art is an integral part of the overall design." Or, "We can focus on the key areas for artwork and target other areas as circumstances allow." Or, "Some art dealers will consider payments over a period of time."

EXCUSE: "Our tastes are so different; we never can agree about art."
RESPONSE: "For personal space, everyone needs to choose pieces that strike a chord

in them. For common areas – whether in commercial or residential spaces – you'll want works that have distinction, but also a fairly universal appeal. The works may be functional or abstract; what's important is that the art suits the tone of the space and the people who will spend time there."

EXCUSE: "My sister (mother/brother-in-law/uncle) is an artist."
RESPONSE: "Great! Let's revaluate how her artwork suits the feeling of the space we're planning. Then we can decide what else, if anything, may be called for."

EXCUSE: "If I can't have a Van Gogh, I'd rather have empty walls."
RESPONSE: "If it's the concept of having an artwork for investment purposes, then perhaps you need to look at discovering the *next* Van Gogh -- an emerging artist whose work is fresh, alive, and has integrity. If it's the color or dynamics of Van Gogh's work that appeals to you, then we can seek out contemporary works that have those qualities."

EXCUSE: "We really like a clean, sparse look."
RESPONSE: "While some people enjoy a cluttered look, that certainly isn't for everyone. Every space, every wall does not have to be filled with art. We need to see how and where artwork can best help to enhance the kind of environment you enjoy."

Now, armed with these ready responses, you are ready to help your clients enjoy planning art as part of the total design package.

Judith Litvich is an art dealer in San Francisco and the owner of Judith Litvich Contemporary Fine Arts.

This book is dedicated to the artists, consultants, gallery owners, designers, architects and their clients who believe that the world should be filled with beautiful things.

Special thanks to our 1992 Review Committee:

Malcolm Holzman,
Hardy Holzman Pfeiffer Associates
Peter Mistretta,
Mistretta Designs
Charles Morris Mount,
Silver & Ziskind/Mount
Dorothy Solomon,
The Art Collaborative

American Crafts Awards

THE GUILD's 4th annual American Crafts Awards were established in 1987 to recognize the exciting new products being created for the contemporary home by North American artists. This section honors four groups of winners of special interest to the design market: Work for the Wall, Furniture, Accessories, and Sculpture and Sculptural Objects.

The distinguished jury of Robert A.M. Stern, Architect, Robert Stern & Associates; Roscoe Smith, Publisher of *Architectural Record*; Ruth Kohler, Director of the John Michael Kohler Art Center; Steve Holley, Former Senior Editor of HOME Magazine; Thomas Lehn, Associate Professor of Interior Architecture, Art Institute of Chicago; and Susan Ewing, Silversmith, Grand Prize Winner of 1st American Crafts Awards, reviewed 834 entries in these categories, and 34 were singled out as outstanding in design and execution.

From 'aerial gardens' to redwood burl vessels, these winning designs reflect a tremendous diversity of materials and techniques used by artists today.

Our thanks to these artists for providing us with beautiful evidence of the innovative and superbly crafted work being created for the contemporary home.

American Crafts Awards
Work for the Wall

Grand Prize Winner

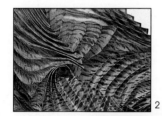

Grand Prize Winner
1. **Carol Adams,** Peninsula, OH, *Aerial Garden II: Alliance,* fabric, mylar, paints, metal, lights, Photo: Bruce Gates, The Art Factory
Merit Awards
2. **Nanette Davis,** Escondido, CA, *Sky Womb,* fiber: shibori dyed silk on metal mesh, 21" x 46", Photo: Nick Juran
3. **Donald E. Green,** Philadelphia, PA, wall chest, ebonized mahogany and bloodwood, 40" x 10" x 30"
4. **Gloria Kosco,** Silverdale, PA, ceramic and masonry, 56" x 46" x 6"
5. **Terese May,** San Jose, CA, *Prosperity,* fabric and acrylic paint with buttons, 64" x 64", Photo: Curtis Fukuda

Grand Prize Winner

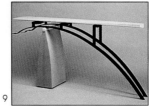

Grand Prize Winner
1. **John Larkin,** Moscow, ID, chair, steel, fiber rush, and rubber tubing, 34" x 17"

Merit Awards
2. **Jeff Hosang,** Miami Beach, FL, chair, stainless steel and salvaged fighter jet afterburner panel, 151½" x 19" x 18½", Photo: David Fields

3. **John Larkin,** Moscow, ID, stool, steel and medium density fiberboard, 25"H x 22"W

4–5. **Bruce Levin,** Washington, DC, *Semblance,* dining table, cherry, steel, 29" x 39" x 85½", and *Jules Verne,* audio cabinet, oxidized copper, analine-dyed wood, cast iron wheels, 80" x 20" x 25"

6–7. **John Marcoux,** Providence, RI, desk, basswood, stainless steel, 29" x 46" x 22', and table, newspaper, wood, 18' x 16" x 16"

8. **Peter Pierobon,** Philadelphia, PA, chest of drawers, ebonized mahogany, 63" x 22" x 20"

9. **Richard Tannen,** Rochester, NY, table, ash, curly ash, bleached, dyed and natural with lacquer finish, 83"L x 15"W x 34"H, Photo: Rick Shannon

American Crafts Awards
Accessories

Grand Prize Winner

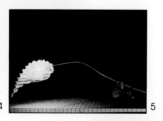

Grand Prize Winner
1. **Lin Stanionis,** Amarillo, TX, *Liqueur Cup #7,* sterling, copper, acrylic, vermeil, 8" x 2" x 2"
Merit Awards
2. **David Baird,** La Jolla, CA, table lamp, metal sheets, gold leaf covered, 13" x 4½" x 21"
3. **Stephan J. Cox,** River Falls, WI, *A Chalice with Malice,* glass, 11" x 5", Photo: Don Pitlik
4. **Carolyn A. Dahl,** Houston, TX, *Sky Fire,* vessel/basket, hand-made, hand-dyed paper, 12" x 18" x 18"
5. **Linda Fellinger,** Bryn Mawr, PA, table lamp, metal and wire, 29"L
6. **Stephen Harford,** Castle Creek, NY, halogen lamp, aluminum, copper, brass, stainless steel, 20½" x 7" x 2½"
7. **Lori Mills,** Brockport, NY, tulip holder, earthenware, 12" x 12" x 5"
8. **W. Chester Old,** Decatur, GA, *Image Reflecter,* hand mirror, removeable from base, aluminum, concrete, glass and rubber, Photo: Wayne Smith
9. **Bird Ross,** Madison, WI, *1" = approximately 16 miles,* fabric and paper vessel, paper maps, silk and cotton fabric, cotton thread, Photo: Charles Frizzel
10. **Billie Jean Theide,** Champaigne, IL, *Confetti,* beverage server, sterling silver, aluminum, 12" x 6" x 4"

Grand Prize Winner

Grand Prize Winner
1. **Ron Fleming,** Tulsa, OK, *Suspended Redwood Flora,* redwood burl, 6" x 20" x 9", Photo: Bob Hawks
Merit Awards
2. **Warren Carther,** Winnipeg, MB Canada, *Pheidias Considers 9:4,* from the Ancient Architecture Series, glass and slate, 20" x 28" x 14", Photo: James Stadnik
3. **Kevin Costello,** Amityville, NY, *Plate Series IV,* copper, patina, 3" x 18" x 18"
4. **David N. Ebner,** Bellport, NY, scallon coat rack, wood-bleached and painted ash, 69" x 12", Photo: Gil Amiaga
5. **Melissa Greene,** Deer Isle, ME, *Idluk—Fabulous Fish,* thrown earthenware, 15" x 14", Photo: Paul Liu
6. **Tom Muir,** Bowling Green, OH, vessel, sterling silver, 14 karat gold, 9½" x 3½" x 3½", Photo: Tom Muir
7. **Vincent Leon Olmsted,** Millville, NJ, *My Poor Guardian Angel,* glass, 26" x 6" x 6", Photo: Thomas Dagostino
8. **Chris and Pat Shatsby,** Lewisburg, OH, votive dish, cast bronze, patina, stainless steel, glass, 45" x 14½", Photo: Jerry Anthony
9. **Mary Kay Simomi,** Chagrin Falls, OH, *NoMo,* glass, 22" x 10" x 3"
10. **Mara and Roy Superior,** Williamsburg, MA, *Botanica,* painted wood, gold leaf, bone, porcelain, 36" x 28", Photo: Susie Cushner

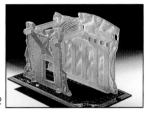

Work for the Wall

Work for the Wall

The artists who create work for the wall have grown increasingly imaginative and expansive in their choice of media, in their aesthetic sophistication and technical mastery. In this section one finds ceramics and glass, paper, tapestries, art quilts and wall sculptures in a variety of media. All are garnering new attention in art circles as a growing number of museums and galleries across the country have begun exhibiting an exciting array of new works.

An increase in visibility and status serve both artists and art buyers well -- designers have never had more choices nor artists working in craft media more opportunities.

In the words of one of the fiber artists in THE GUILD, "the public's consciousness has been raised and along with it my own inspiration." As the corporate world's interest in acquiring unique works of art grows, she and other artists are enjoying new opportunities for creating commissioned, one-of-a-kind pieces.

Not surprisingly, these artists are as concerned with the endurance of their work as those who purchase it are. They have experimented with materials, dyes, adhesives and finishes and they have mastered these materials and their craft. They have studied the masters in their fields and they have formed associations among themselves to further improve the quality of their work.

They are not only professionals at their craft but in the entire process resulting in an inspirational new dialogue with their clients. One GUILD artist spoke of getting blueprints, samples of granite, carpeting, and photographs of furnishings from a potential client to acquaint her with the client's corporate environment. Later, when the client received sketches of the artist's proposed design, he sent photos of the intended wall space with brown paper models based on the dimensions. From then on, the artist included the client in the process by sending polaroids of the work in process, including some buckets of dyed pulp!

In these pages, you'll find amazing choices. Neon sculptures that add a colorful spark, subtly woven wall pieces that bring richness and comfort to a space, whimsical mixed media sculpture that makes the environment friendly, stained glass simulations that add glorious light to a room without windows, and tapestry pictures that inspire dreaming.

Here are beautiful things to enrich the quality of our lives, and the artists who create work for the wall bring us all grand, new possibilities. We are all realizing that re-personalizing, beautifying our interior environments makes them far more inspiring places in which to live, do business and play.

See our article on pages 67–69, "The Care and Maintenance of Fiber Art," for more information on positioning, framing, installation and cleaning.

Ellen Kochansky

1165 Mile Creek Road
Pickens, SC 29671
(803) 868-9749
FAX (803) 868-4250

Ellen Kochansky's collage works depart from the traditions of quilting to humanize and soften corporate and residential settings. Original techniques involve laminating, overdyeing, transparent fabrics, airbrushed fabric dye and pigments. Fourteen years commission experience. Portman Hotels, IBM, Florida National Bank, and other collections.

Lead time averages two to three months for completed work. Proposal (10% fee) consists of actual color fabric swatches, scale color rendering, and contract confirming date of delivery, price, terms, installation arrangements and care procedure. Extraordinarily durable and light resistant for the textile medium, works may be removed for occasional dry cleaning. Easily installed mounting system. Call or write for current scheduling, price, slides, and brochure.

Shown: *Lancaster* series, *WINTER,* 12' x 12', the first of four quilted works, alternating seasonally, commissioned for the lobby of the Chemed Center, Cincinnati, OH. Hines Interests, developers. Skidmore, Owings & Merrill, architects. Installed February 1992.

Therese May

651 N. 4th Street
San Jose, CA 95112
(408) 292-3247

Therese May's quilts are made up of playful fantasy animal and plant imagery and are machine appliqued using straight stitch and satin stitch. Threads are left uncut to form a network of texture across the surface. Acrylic paint is added as a finishing touch. Her work is widely published and exhibited throughout the U.S., Europe and Japan.

Prices for finished pieces range from $1000 to $10,000. Commissions accepted; May will work with clients via drawings and samples.

More information available upon request.

Animal Spiral, detail

Animal Spiral, Convention Center, San Jose, CA, 14' x 14'

Jean Neblett

628 Rhode Island Street
San Francisco, CA 94107-2628
(415) 550-2613
FAX (415) 821-2772

Jean Neblett is a studio artist with a background in fiber arts and textiles. Her quilts evolve through an intuitive experimentation with a basic design to create change and movement. Surfaces are embellished to enhance their texture. Boundaries are defied, generating a fluidity of motion. Color engages the senses and form is derived from interaction of patterns. Her quilts are celebrations of possibilities.

She has exhibited widely, received awards and participated in travelling shows throughout the United States, Hawaii, Canada and Japan.

Her work is of varying size, and easily shipped and mounted. Production time varies depending upon size and complexity of the work. A portfolio and price list are available upon request.

Top: detail, *Primal IV*, 62"W x 47"H
Below: *Primal IV*, 62"W x 47"H

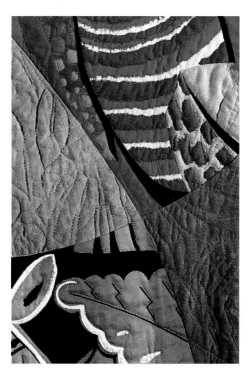

Dottie Moore

1134 Charlotte Avenue
Rock Hill, SC 29732
(803) 327-5088

Dottie Moore creates one-of-a-kind wall pieces for individual and corporate clients. Her work, known for its strong sense of color and depth, incorporates the techniques of quilting, applique, and embroidery. Her intricate quilting style has acquired, over the past twelve years, a striking sculptural dimension.

Recent projects include two pieces, 4' x 7' and 4' x 9', for C&P Telephone Company in Hampton, Virginia. She received a second grant from the Rock Hill Arts Council with funds through the South Carolina Arts Commission and the National Endowment for the Arts.

Slides and prices are available upon request.

Left: detail, *Mountain Mystery*
Right: *Mountain Mystery*, 53" x 76"

Photo: Mike Harrison

Cynthia Nixon-Hudson

Cynthia Nixon-Hudson Studio
P.O. Box 89
Pine Grove Mills, PA 16868
(814) 238-7251
FAX (814) 234-2025

Cynthia Nixon-Hudson's quilts, known for romantic realism and vibrant color, have been exhibited and published nationally and have been placed in public, corporate and private collections since 1978. Painted with textile pigments on fine cottons, the quilts are appliqued with rich and translucent fabrics, and machine-quilted for strength and texture. Quilts are displayed behind plexiglas, inside brass or enamelled wood frames.

Nixon-Hudson is experienced in working with designers and architects and in meeting the requirements of clients for small and large-scale projects. Proposals include scale color renderings. Terms and prices are available upon request.

Commissions include Baltimore Hilton (7' x 56'); Dickinson College (10' x 20'); United Federal Bank; Polyclinic Medical Center, Harrisburg, PA; Western Pennsylvania Hospital, Pittsburgh, PA.

Forest, painted and appliqued quilt, 1992, 38" x 38"

Stream, painted and appliqued quilt, 1992, 38" x 38"

Linda S. Perry

96 Burlington Street
Lexington, MA 02173
(617) 863-1107

Linda Perry's award winning quilts reflect her interest in Japanese design and classical mythology. She employs a wide range of fine fabrics including hand-dyed, hand-marbled and hand-printed cottons and silks. Perry received her training at the University of California, Berkeley, Harvard University and the School of the Museum of Fine Arts, Boston. Her quilts have been selected for numerous juried and museum shows throughout the U.S. and are included in private and public collections in New York, California, Massachusetts, Illinois, Utah and Singapore. Works range in price from $1,000–$5,000. Commissions require a minimum of ten weeks. Please contact the artist for additional information and slides.

Below: *Daybreak*, 49½" x 49½"
Opposite page: *Night Person*, 41" x 51"

Printed in Japan ©1992 Kraus Sikes Inc. The Guild: The Designer's Reference Book of Artists

Linda S. Perry

96 Burlington Street
Lexington, MA 02173
(617) 863-1107

A conversation with Linda Perry
(art quilts)

Q How have you organized your workspace?

A My studio measures 14' x 25', and one of the long walls is lined with built-in shelving. On these shelves I have 70 white, plastic laundry baskets, which I ordered wholesale from Rubbermaid in Ohio. The baskets are full of fabric, categorized by my own eccentric system. Each basket contains a particular shade or color, or a certain type of material, or maybe certain fabrics that remind me of something. For instance, I have a basket labeled "sky," which is full of different pieces of material that I think could be used to depict the sky. In the middle of this wall there is a doorway; on one side of the door I keep commercial fabric, and on the other side of the door, I keep all my hand-dyed fabric.

On one of the short walls, I have installed a material covered corkboard that takes pins easily. It's painted white and covered with a flannel sheet. Almost any kind of fabric will stick to flannel, and I can just stick a piece of fabric up and step back, and get an idea of how the colors look together, or if the pattern is working.

I also have two sewing machines in my studio. One is a more expensive, very elegant machine, which I do most of my stitching on. The other is a bottom-of-the-line machine that I use for quilting. All that tugging and turning that you do when you're quilting really strains the machine, and so I use my less-expensive machine, which has a fine stitch quality, but doesn't require me to be quite as gentle. And if it does break, it's not as difficult or expensive to fix.

Q What about dyeing fabric?

A Lately I've been using more hand-dyed fabrics in my quilts. When I began hand-dyeing my own fabric, I enrolled in a couple of workshops, but most of what I've learned has been from a fellow quilter. I usually set aside a couple of days when no one else is around, just to dye fabric. I dye about 20 yards at a time, torn into 18" x 24" pieces, and dye in one color range, say from purple to blue. It takes about two days, because the fabric must stay wet for about 24 hours to set the dye. I don't usually dye solid colors; I find that the marbled effect I get from my own dyeing adds something to my pieces that commercial fabrics often lack.

Doris Bally

420 N. Craig Street
Pittsburgh, PA 15213
(412) 621-3709
FAX (412) 621-9030

With a small color pencil sketch as a guide, the loom is the canvas. Untold hours of work give the satisfaction of improvisation and color choice at will.

Most ideas are free translations of forms found in nature and each work is a unique, individual creation.

Bally tapestries hang in boardrooms, health facilities, hotels, law offices and residential interiors in the United States and abroad.

Slides on request.

Top: *Pencil*, 32" x 39"
Bottom: *Manchuria*, 62" x 51"

Linda Denier

Denier Tapestry Studio
745 Edenwood Drive
Roselle, IL 60172
(708) 893-5854

The detailed imagery of Linda Denier's tapestries reflects her love of color. Beautifully crafted, her nationally-exhibited work blends the warmth of fiber into a durable work of art.

Denier enjoys the challenges of designing to satisfy the client, and commissions are accepted for residential and commercial spaces. Most are completed within 3–6 months of design approval. All work is installation-ready.

Finished tapestries are also available.

Slides and prices furnished upon request.

Top: *Mata Malam (Eye of the Night)*, 4' x 5'
Bottom: *Someday Isle*, 55" x 31"

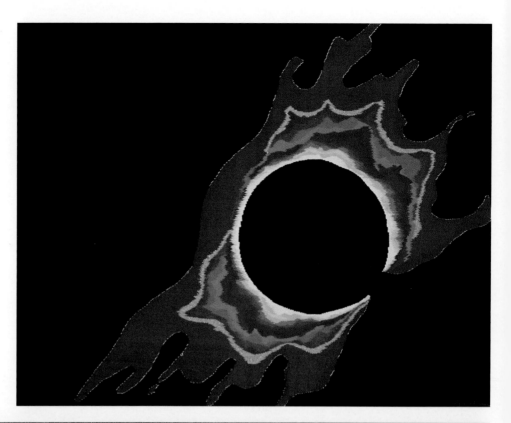

Alexandra Friedman

56 Arbor Street
Hartford, CT 06105
(203) 236-3311

Recently selected for a fellowship from the New England Foundation for the Arts, the award winning tapestries from Alexandra Friedman's Studio have been included in exhibitions internationally. They are imaginatively designed and traditionally woven to accommodate the specific requirements of the corporate or residential client. They are woven with premium quality wools which make them very durable and easy to maintain.

Scale drawings and colored yarn samples will be provided for prospective commissions. A 10% design fee is applied toward the cost of the completed tapestry. Prices range from $125 to $200 per square foot.

Further information on request.

Collections: The Aetna Life and Casualty Co., Fleet Bank Co., Connecticut Business and Industry Association, Mechanics Savings Bank and numerous private collections.

Top: *The Swim,* 65" x 44", 1991
Bottom: *Ming Vase,* 48" x 40", 1991

Logan Fry

2835 Southern Road
Richfield, OH 44286
(216) 659-3104

Noted for his use of technical imagery, Logan Fry offers a unique resource for architects and designers who serve clients in the fields of high-technology, information-processing and bio-medical engineering.

The textile pictured here is based on computer-chip iconography. Logan's other subjects have included biological micro-sensors, computer-machine language and bar-code symbology. Commissions based on plots, plans or other materials supplied by the client are encouraged.

All pieces are framed behind conservation, reflection control glass to retain crisp appearance and reduce maintenance, while assuring high UV absorption and low reflection percentage. Prices $200 to $450 per sq. ft., plus framing. Expect a minimum of two months from initial contact to completion. Further information on request.

Below: *Micro-Chip Series 2: Poly,* 37"H x 35"W

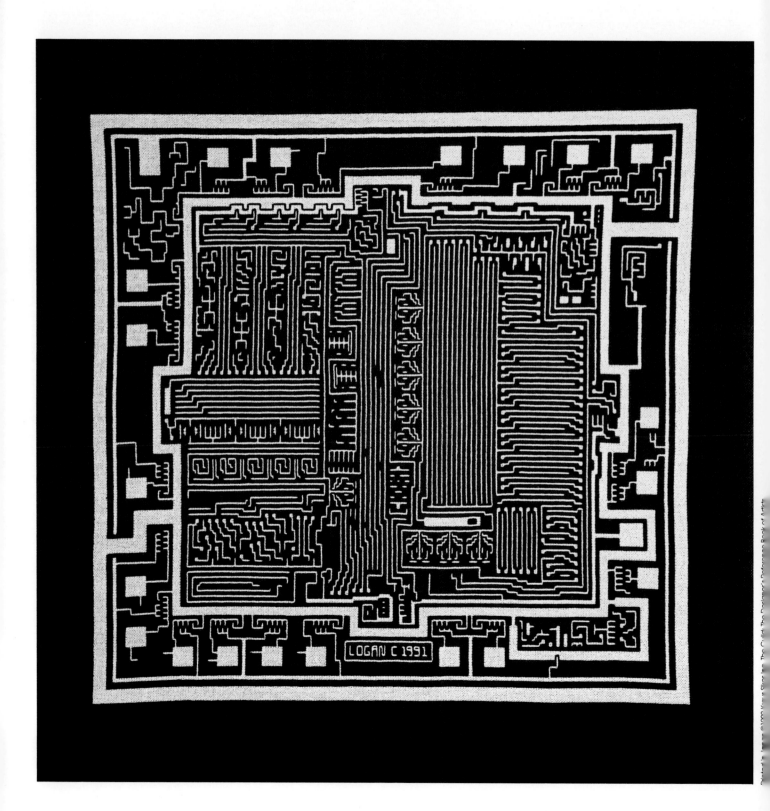

Sarah D. Haskell

30 North Main Street
Newmarket, NH 03857
(603) 659-5250

Sarah D. Haskell designs and weaves textural impressionistic tapestries in landscape and seascape themes. The tranquil balance of images and colors brings warmth and dimension to residential as well as corporate interiors.

The landscape/seascape scene can be a solo panel or extended over several panels to create a panorama. The tapestries are woven primarily in hand dyed wools, with accents in rayon, lurex, cotton, linen, and silk.

Haskell's tapestries are in the collections of IBM, Digital Equipment, Sanders Corp., and several New England Banks.

Martha Heine

7 Haggis Court
Durham, NC 27705
(919) 479-3270

Martha Heine designs and weaves tapestries that have been purchased or commissioned by private and corporate collectors. Her tapestries are installed in banks, board-rooms, and lobbies of hospitals and hotels.

The diversity of style finds expression in the abstraction of realistic images. Commissions may incorporate design elements unique to the architecture and suggestions of the client.

Prices range from $150 to $200 sq. ft. depending on size and complexity of design.

Requests for additional information are welcome.

Top: *Echoes,* 52" x 48"
Bottom: *Joy Contained,* 48" x 60"

Victor Jacoby

1086 17th Street
Eureka, CA 95501
(707) 442-3809

Using fine wools and cottons Victor Jacoby has created woven tapestries for corporate and residential spaces since 1975. Themes vary from landscape and floral to figurative.

Clients include AT&T, Kaiser-Permanente, Marriott Corporation, SEIU, and Shearson, Lehman, Hutton.

Prices begin at $175 per square foot. For further information, slides, price list and resume contact the artist.

Left: *Gladiola,* ©1990, 30" x 80"
Right: *Narrow Passage,* ©1990, 47" x 36"

Libby Kowalski

41 Union Square West, Suite 502
New York, NY 10003
(212) 627-5770
FAX (212) 989-9702

Libby Kowalski's black-and-white woven and painted pieces are delicate, yet bold, highly-patterned and hard-edged images. Although her earlier work was more constructivist in style, recent compositions reveal an exploration into symbolism. She used computers and computer imagery to design these compositions.

A professional of many years, Kowalski's work is found in the collections of IBM Corporation, UNISYS, General Motors, Kresge Corporation, Automobile Association of America and North American Communications. Her work has been exhibited in galleries and museums nationally and internationally.

Production time varies depending on size and complexity. Commissions are accepted. Price list and slides of currently available work upon request.

Top: *Altruscape*, 66" x 96"
Bottom: *The Truth We Run From is So Small Only the Promise is Great*, 41½" x 63"

Printed in Japan ©1992 Kraus Sikes Inc. The Guild: The Designer's Reference Book of Artists

Michelle Lester

15 West 17th Street
New York, NY 10011
(212) 989-1411
FAX (212) 627-8553

With twenty years devoted to tapestry, this studio has recently expanded to carpet design, murals, and watercolors. These handmade custom works complement one another, create impact and when used together in a single space can shape a total environment.

Clients include: Biosphere 2, AZ, IBM, Pan American World Airways, Bankers Trust, GE and 3M. See previous *GUILD* issues for other visuals and listings.

Interior renderings in any medium also available. Complete presentation packet, including slides, $20.

Top: design for 14' x 19' carpet, ©1987,
   Met Life, Philadelphia
Bottom: *Horse of a Different Color,* ©1989,
   tapestry, 5' x 7'

Elinor Steele

61 Weybridge Street
Middlebury, VT 05753
(802) 388-6546

Elinor Steele combines a strong sense of graphic design with meticulous craftsmanship to create contemporary tapestries for corporate and residential settings. Subjects include abstract and impressionistic images, city-scapes, and spatial geometric compositions.

Steele has exhibited nationally since 1974. Her work is included in many corporate and private collections including IBM, Prudential Insurance Co., Price Waterhouse, Vermont Technical College, and Unitil Corp.

Commissions of any size are invited and may incorporate design elements from the surrounding architecture and furnishings. Prices per square foot range from $150–$250 depending on size and complexity.

Top: *Confetti Moon,* 54" x 53"
Bottom: *Out There,* 47" x 48"
Below: detail, *Techno-Pastorale,* 22" x 48"

Printed in Japan ©1992 Kraus Sikes Inc. The Guild: The Designer's Reference Book of Artists

Linda Winse

**Penelope's Web
Route 4, Box 930
Flagstaff, AZ 86001
(602) 779-3776**

For 15 years Linda Winse has been weaving primarily tapestries and rugs. Her award-winning work uses vibrant, bold colors to depict abstract or realistic imagery. Using traditional techniques with natural fibers (wool, silk, linen), the tapestries and rugs are virtually maintenance free.

Commissioned pieces require approximately three months to complete. The wholesale price ranges from $125–$175 per sq. ft., depending upon size and complexity. A design fee of $150 includes drawings, yarn samples and a woven swatch.

Left: *Butterfly Imagery*
Right: *Peace*

A conversation with B.J. Adams
(fiber installations)

Q How did you choose the medium of fiber to work in?

A I started with painting and working with sculpture. Then in the '60s I saw a fiber exhibit, and I became interested in all aspects of the medium -- stitching, knotting, basketry. I was attracted to the idea of working with flexible materials. What focused my interest in the area I'm in now is that, frankly, I saw more of a demand for commissioned work for wall-hangings.

Q How do you feel about collaborating on a commissioned piece?

A A while ago, I completed a piece commissioned through Corporate Annual Reports, Inc. Their client had come up with the title "Investing in the Fabric of Society" for their annual report. I was to create a piece to be photographed for the cover, illustrating this theme. This was the first time I had created anything for the purpose of reproduction and I discovered how a graphic artist works. They were very specific about certain images that needed to be included in the piece, ranging from a cellular phone to a hospital building, but there was a lot of back and forth communication during the designing stages. One of the first things they asked me was if I could work with fiber optics. I showed them my first image sample and they said "more realistic," and the next time, "more color," and then, "we would like something to look more three-dimensional." I think it took three attempts in order to come up with something that was right for each image. But I enjoyed the challenge.

Q What do you want out of a commission?

A I don't feel it's necessary that the people I'm working with know the exact terminology or understand my technique; I will develop what they need. That's my role as a commissioned artist. What I do hope they understand about my work and my technique is that there are endless possibilities, and I am capable of doing different things -- different styles, different colors, whatever . . . When I did the commission for the annual report cover, they wanted to photograph the piece with the edges trimmed. I was hesitant, and asked them to photograph it once before I cut off the edges. I realized I liked the trimmed edge and I've since done that to a couple of my other pieces. It's the give and take that I really like in commissions.

B. J. Adams

Art in Fiber
2821 Arizona Terrace, NW
Washington, D.C. 20016
(202) 364-8404 (S)
(202) 686-1042 (H)

B. J. Adams creates wall art of flexible materials for commercial and residential interiors. Collaborating with clients, commissioned works can be illustrative, geometric or flowing abstract designs. Easily installed, single or modular panels can have highly textured or flat surfaces, bright or subdued colors, earthy or elegant materials.

Adams will work with clients, art consultants, interior designers, and art directors to meet their specific design, scheduling, and budget requirements. Timing and price are based on complexity and size of the work commissioned.

Work has been commissioned by individual collectors as well as business, medical, banking, and hotel facilities.

Brochure and commission information is available on written request.

Top Left: Embassy Suites (hotel lobby), Des Moines, IA, pieced and stitched fabrics, 4' x 8½'
Top Right: detail, Embassy Suites commission
Bottom/Inset: commissioned for BELLSOUTH corporate annual report cover

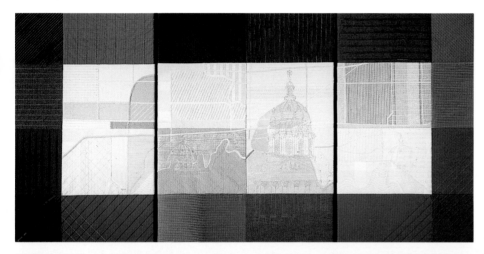
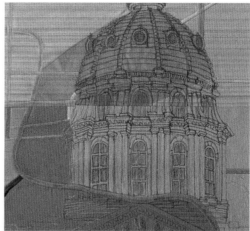

Investing in the Fabric of Society, owned by BELLSOUTH Corporation, machine stitchery on painted canvas, 20" x 32"

Robert W. Alexander

(Bill Alexander)
Industrial Strength Art
P.O. Box 599
Morganton, GA 30560-0599
(706) 374-5792

Bill Alexander's work spans the range from massive fiber installations to exquisite miniatures. In hand-wrapped industrial yarns, as well as premium metals, mylar and silks, his tapestries are the intersection of creative energy and careful design, a distinctive blend of natural and abstract imagery.

Alexander has received major commissions and worked with designers and architects to create works of beauty and durability. Prices begin at $100 per square foot; design fees begin at $250. Average delivery time is 90 days from contract/design approval.

Top: *Practice of the Presence*, detail, 10'10" x 6'8"
Bottom Left: *Virtual Light*, 68' x 8'6" x 1', Tennessee Valley Authority Complex, Chattanooga, TN
Bottom Right: *Bend in the River*, 14' x 3'6"

Lucy G. Feller

Photo Linens
941 Park Avenue
New York, NY 10028
(212) 628-1360

Lucy Feller will create a unique piece of art for your office or home. She calls these Photo Linens. The intent is to preserve important moments in time or chronicle a series of events. By manipulating photographs, these images are then transferred onto fabric. Stitching, embroidering and found objects add artistic accents.

There is no limit to the creative possibilities, once a client's wishes are known. It can be as political as one client's dinner at the White House or as personal as a child's youth recaptured on her old favorite bath robe.

Feller's work is seriously humorous, detailed and precise. Prices range from $2,000 to $10,000 depending on size and intricacy and are encased in lucite boxes easily installed.

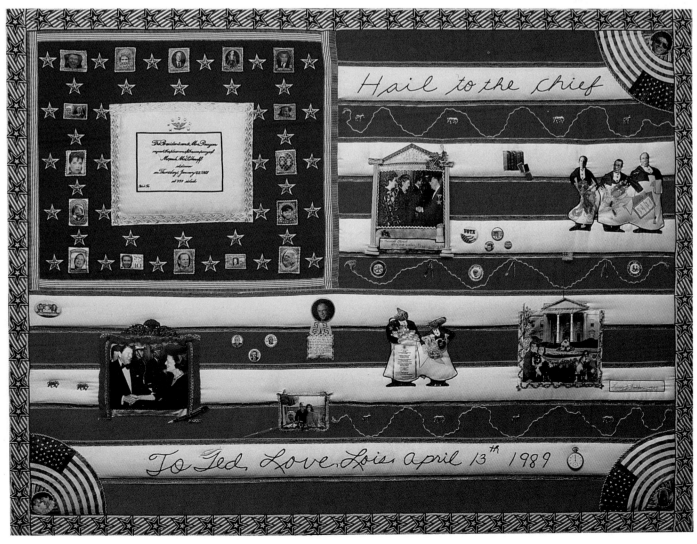

Barbara Grenell

1132 Hall's Chapel Road
Burnsville, NC 28714
(704) 675-4073

Architecturally scaled tapestry constructions relating to the landscape, Barbara Grenell's works in fiber are internationally collected. Awarded a National Endowment for the Arts Fellowship, her diverse landscapes are included in installations for corporations in communications and technology, in hospitals and health care facilities, and in conference centers, hotels and in the residences of collectors throughout the United States. Unrestricted in size, wall mounted or free-standing. Completed works are also available.

Casino, Jackpot, NV, 32" x 84"

Earthforms, 36" x 98" x 6"

Printed in Japan ©1992 Kraus Sikes Inc. The Guild: The Designer's Reference Book of Artists

Janis Kanter

1923 W. Dickens
Chicago, IL 60614
(312) 252-2119

From the "high tech" to the "subtle and serene" Kanter will create fiber artworks for your environment. Works are designed to have a dialogue with their setting while still maintaining a strong voice of their own.

As can be seen in the photo below, this open office setting allowed Kanter to design a piece which related to the Chicago location. Incorporated into the tapestry weaving is neon tubing which allows elements from the piece to bounce on and off of the glass wall dividers.

In the top photo, Kanter created a piece to hang within this interior garden space. Her vision was to envelop something from "outside" and take it "inside." By creating an outdoor lily pond, with a giant dragon fly, one has the sense upon walking into this entrance way that perhaps one is still in the open air.

Collaborative projects with architects, designers and individuals are welcomed. Finished works are also available.

Marie-Laure Ilie

M-Laure Studio/Cocoon
1241 Kolle Avenue
South Pasadena, CA 91030
(213) 254-8073

Ilie's hand-painted silk wall hangings recreate the masterpieces of the ancient world, using the styles of Medieval Europe, the Middle East, the Orient, and American Colonial. A delicate crackling pattern gives an antique appearance to these designs.

The same antique effect also graces the floral compositions.

Commissioned works can adapt to the client's required decorative theme, historical period, cultural region, specified colors, and sizes.

Available either for framing or for hanging with a rod. Colors are fade proof. Commissions require one month after approval of sketches.

Prices from $500. Additional photos, slides, or samples available on request.

Marie-Laure Ilie

M-Laure Studio/Cocoon
1241 Kolle Avenue
South Pasadena, CA 91030
(213) 254-8073

Ilie creates large abstract tapestries by layering transparent organza on top of a large hand-painted silk background. Her appliqué technique combines rich colors and distinctive texture with the inherent sophistication of silk. These paintings come ready to hang like tapestries. They can also be framed. Colors are fade proof.

For the past 20 years, Ilie has exhibited extensively in the United States and Europe. Patrons include private collectors, as well as corporations like Bank of America, Bank of New Zealand, Neiman-Marcus, Marshall Field, Gale Research Company, and major hotels.

Prices from $600 to $6000. Commissions welcome. Additional photos, slides, or samples on request.

Top: *Odyssey*, 72" x 120"
Bottom: *Mauna Loa*, 51" x 50"
Below: *Blue Sailing*, detail

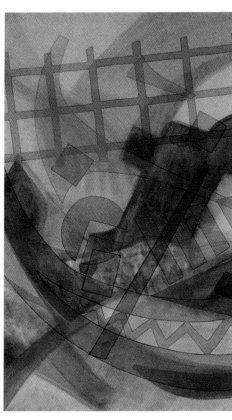

Candace Kreitlow

5655 Skara Brae Lane
P.O. Box 113
Mazomanie, WI 53560
(608) 795-4680
FAX (608) 795-2822

Candace Kreitlow creates dynamic, sparkling works for the wall by weaving rich, colorful yarns with reflective, metalized polyesters. Her sculpted, gemlike works interact with even commonplace lighting to add elegance and warmth to any interior. Her work is exhibited nationally with clients, including public art programs, corporations and collectors.

Candace works with architects, designers and clients in proposing and developing designs. She enjoys site-specific challenges in which she can produce classic works that are compatible with the full spectrum of architectural styles. Her easily hung pieces range in size from 8 to 200 square feet. All require minimal maintenance. Modular construction of her larger works allows for versatility in display. Pieces can connect in various ways to form a unit or they can be hung separately. The "which way is up" question becomes an advantage as Candace encourages clients to realize the multi-directional potential of her works.

For commissioned work Candace prepares a visual presentation using sketches, color studies and samples. Commissioned works are typically completed within 6–12 weeks of design approval. Prices range from $120–$170 per square foot. Resume, slides, and prices are available.

Top: *Meetings,* modular diptych,
  44" x 58" x 6" (x 2)
Bottom: *Turbulence/Fluid Dynamics,*
  modular diptych, 58" x 44" x 3.5" (x 2)
Below: *Turbulence/Fluid Dynamics,*
  Public Library, Black Earth, WI

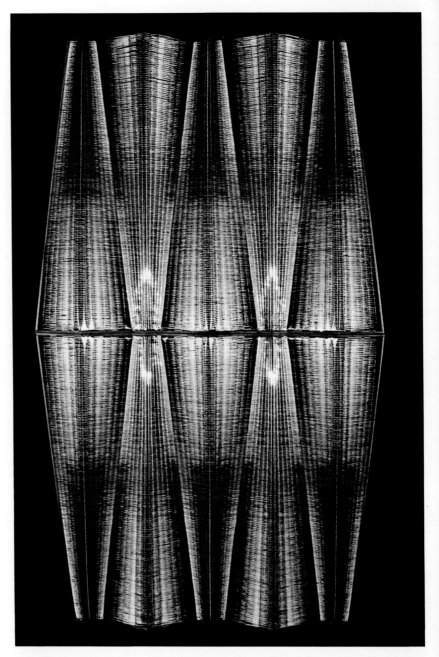

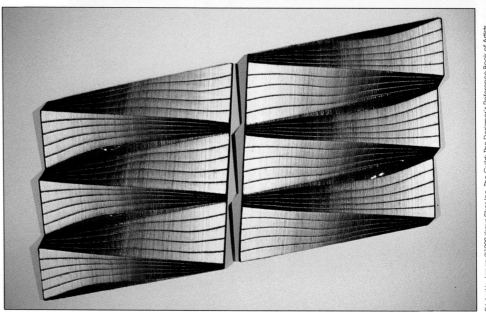

Bonny Lhotka

5658 Cascade Place
Boulder, CO 80303
(303) 494-5631
FAX (303) 494-3472

Bonny Lhotka has created a new process called MonoGraphic Transfer. It enables her to create a wide range of imagery from abstract to realistic. Transferring the work from a plate to linen using a one-step process, she creates unique painted tapestries of nearly unlimited size. Her ability to work with the client's concepts and color schemes makes her one of the most sought after artists in the nation.

A professional for two decades, her work has been commissioned by Charles Schwab, The Johnson Space Center, United Airlines, Marriott Hotels, AT&T, McDonnell Douglas, National Conference of State Legislatures and many others.

The average 4' x 8' work retails for $4,500 FOB.

Color brochure, $10 deposit. See page 272 *THE GUILD 5* and page 205, *THE GUILD 6* for additional media.

Night of the Moon, MonoGraphic Transfer, 36" x 36"

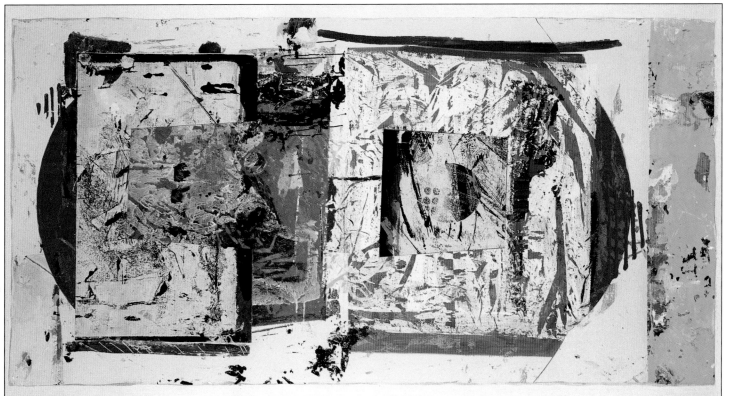

Uncoupled, acrylic MonoGraphic Transfer, 52" x 100"

Junco Sato Pollack

103 Reservoir Avenue
Rochester, NY 14620
(716) 461-5915
FAX (716) 461-5915

Junco Sato Pollack produces sculpture and wall panels that combine weaving with surface design figured by silk-screening, embroidery, and gold and silver leaf. Her art fabrics, which interpret the aesthetics of Japanese screen paintings, are included in the collections of Renwick Gallery of the Smithsonian Institution and the Wallace Library of the Rochester Institute of Techology, and she exhibits internationally in museums and galleries. Commissions accepted. Price ranges from $2000 to $4000 per panel (3' x 4'). A brochure is available upon request.

Spring/Summer from *Triptych: Spring/Summer/Fall/Winter*, 30"H x 36"W (overall size of the three framed panels is 4'H x 10'W)

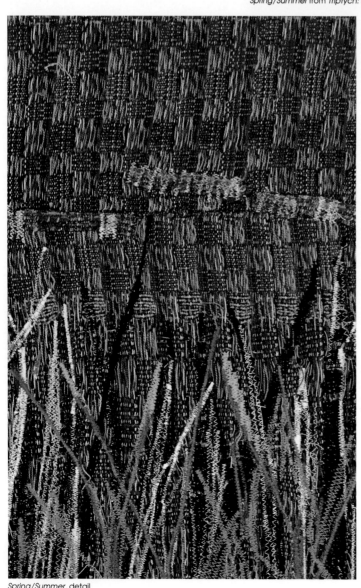

Spring/Summer, detail

Fall, detail

Bernie Rowell

Bernie Rowell Studio
1525 Branson Avenue
Knoxville, TN 37917
(615) 523-5244

Combining skillful stitchery with painted fabrics, Rowell cuts, weaves, tears, pleats and layers canvas to achieve texture. Metallic fabrics and thread add jewel-like detail.

Stretched and padded over wood 2" x 2"s the artworks are crisp, contemporary, and require no additional framing. Modular formats fill large space requirements.

Varnished with acrylic these canvases combine the look of fiber with the durability of a painted surface.

Commissions/custom colors
$90 a square foot.

Top: *Pinwheels*, Dallas Rehabilitation Institute, 48" x 72" x 3"
Bottom: *Aerial View Diptych*, 52" x 92" x 3"

Amanda Richardson

Richardson Kirby
P.O. Box 361
Underwood, WA 98651
(509) 493-3928

The rich, light-reflective tapestries of Amanda Richardson respond to their environment, the image varying with the angle and intensity of light allowing the viewer to become actively involved in the artistic experience.

The artist developed the technique of Richardson-tapestry in which fabrics are hand-dyed, cut into intricate forms, and bonded together, layer on layer, to build up a rich and complex final image. These images give the impression of great spatial depth, with a visual impact few art mediums can equal.

A graduate of Goldsmiths' College, London University, and a professional artist for fourteen years, Richardson has had numerous shows both in America and Europe. The majority of the artist's work is commissioned, including large tapestries for public places. Recent clients include Embassy Suites Hotels, Marriott Hotels, Hilton Hotels, The Rouse Co., The Oliver Carr Co. and the University of Alaska.

Pricing, scheduling, and commission details are available upon request.

Late Summer Garden, oil painting, 36" x 48"

Crescent Sand, Richardson Tapestry, South Lake Tahoe Embassy Suites, CA, 5' x 16'

Island Garden, Richardson Tapestry, 5'6" x 7'3"

Amanda Richardson, Richardson Kirby, P.O. Box 361, Underwood, WA 98651, (509) 493-3928

Ava R. Tevvs

134 Lincoln Street
Bath, ME 04530
(207) 443-5165

Multimedia artist Ava Tevvs, inspired by a deep understanding of nature, weaves wallhangings and fiber sculptures capturing the essence of the natural world. Panels of Irish linen are woven, stitched and painted with acrylic paint. Easy to maintain, they are suitable for private, corporate and public installations.

Prices begin at $600 depending on size and complexity of design.

Commissions and collaborations are welcome.

Delivery is six to eight weeks following design approval and price contract.

Slides are available upon request.

Top: *Red Flight*
Bottom: *Wings of Spirits*

Ava R. Tevvs

134 Lincoln Street
Bath, ME 04530
(207) 443-5165

Ava Tevvs weaves elegant wallhangings designed to both evoke and enhance visual awareness of timeless inner landscapes. Constructed of the finest yarns, frequently dyed and handspun to achieve specific color and texture, they are light of weight and simple to install. Maintenance is minimal and therefore suitable for meditative, residential and corporate space.

The artist welcomes collaborations and commissions. Completed works are available. Allow up to twelve weeks for delivery of custom work following design approval and price contract. Prices range from $125–250 pr. sq. ft., depending on size and complexity of design.

Brochure and slides are available upon request.

Top: *Moon Streams,* 36" x 53"
Bottom Left: *Silence,* 33" x 43"
Bottom Right: *Harmony,* 36" x 51"

A conversation with Ray Tomasso
(paper installations)

Q How do you make your paper?

A I start by soaking the rags, which I buy in 500 pound bails, and then I beat the fiber. This makes the hair on the fiber stand up, which is what controls how the paper bonds together. It takes anywhere from two to eight hours to prepare about six pounds of paper, depending on the thickness. It takes a couple of hours to form the sheets, and then anywhere from two to seven days for the drying process to be complete. Most paper makers use vacuum tables to remove water during the drying process, but I prefer gravity. Letting the paper air-dry after it's been cast gives it a higher relief and a different result. Then I go back and treat the surfaces. At the end of the process, I end up with paper that is bendable yet durable.

Q Are you limited because paper is the material you work with?

A Most people think my work looks like concrete or metal, anything but paper. I can get almost any effect, depending on the materials I use. I can color the paper with pigment, pencil, or paint, or any combination of those. I feel there are almost no limitations.

Q What is your procedure when dealing with clients?

A I talk with them by phone or meet with them and get an idea of what they want in terms of the colors and dimensions, and any other pertinent information. Maybe there is a certain aspect of some of my other work that they like and want me to incorporate in their piece. Then I will go back and, following the guidelines that were discussed, I'll make three pieces for them to choose from, so there is bound to be something they like!

Karen Adachi

702 Monarch Way
Santa Cruz, CA 95060
(408) 429-6192

Karen Adachi creates her three-dimensional handmade paper pieces by using layers of irregularly shaped vacuum-cast paper. She makes free-standing, two-sided sculptures and wall-pieces for corporate, private and residential interiors. Her works is shown nationally through major galleries and representatives.

The pieces are richly-textured and embellished with dyes, acrylics, metallics and pearlescents. Painted bamboo and sticks are used to create a dramatic statement of pattern and line. Three-dimensional sculptures are mounted on painted metal bases for stability and strength.

Prices range from $250–5,000 depending on size. Custom work in any size, shape and color is available.

Contact artist for further information and slides.

Lucinda Carlstrom

1075 Standard Drive
Atlanta, GA 30319-3357
(404) 231-0227

Texture and design play an important role in Lucinda Carlstrom's mixed-media constructions and quilts. She incorporates handmade papers, new and antique silk and 23K gold leaf and metal leaf in these piecework tapestries. Lucinda currently explores the play of color and reflection from mixing various shades of metals to an intensely rich surface design. Another series of work involves architectural themes. Traditional American quilt patterns were the foundation for this work and are still available.

Lucinda welcomes commissions from architects and designers for corporate or personal spaces. Prices begin at $100 per square foot and are determined by the complexity of the piecework and materials used. This work is framed under glass for permanent installation.

Top: *The Power of Gold—Gold,* 19" x 57"
Bottom: *Architectural,* 28 x 58"

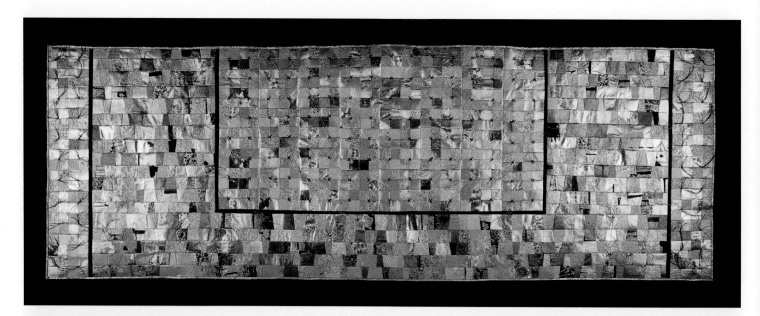

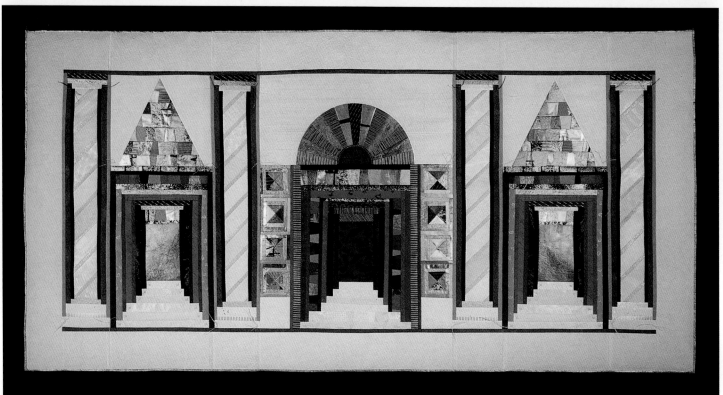

Printed in Japan ©1992 Kraus Sikes Inc. The Guild: The Designer's Reference Book of Artists

Martha Chatelain

Artfocus, Ltd.
833 "G" Street
P.O. Box 127238
San Diego, CA 92112
(619) 234-0749

Martha Chatelain creates richly textured three-dimensional handmade paper and mixed-media wall sculptures enhanced with fiber dyes and iridescent powders.

Call to discuss design specifications, client environment, and/or site-specific commissions. Allow 4–6 weeks following design approval.

Prices, from $800–$5000, depend on size and complexity.

Selected Collections: Bank of America, Champion Paper, Hilton Hotels, IBM, International Paper, Nordstrom, Potlatch Corporation, Sheraton Hotels, Upjohn Corporation, Xerox Corporation.

Top: *Acuarela,* 25" x 45" x 3"
Bottom: *Rhythmic Sea,* 40" x 56" x 3"

Beth Cunningham

32 Sweetcake Mountain Road
New Fairfield, CT 06812
(203) 746-5160

Beth Cunningham produces collaged
paintings by airbrushing acrylic paint onto a
rough, unprimed canvas background, and
overlaying it with a smooth strip or grid
surface of muslin, paint and silk tissue paper.
Her one-of-a-kind wallpieces are sealed with
an acrylic polymer that enables it to be
exhibited without additional protection.

Ms. Cunningham is experienced in following
the client's colors and architectural
concepts, and can produce both large and
small scale work. Imagery can vary from
abstract patterning to reflections of sky,
water and land.

Involved in commission work for 15 years,
her paintings are in the collections of Heinz
Corporation, NYC; St. Luke's Methodist
Hospital, Computer Craft, Inc., PruCare,
Sagestone, Inc., Houston, TX; and many
private collections.

A 4' x 3' unframed work retails for
$1500–1800 FOB CT.

Top: detail, *Marshland*
Bottom: *Marshland*, 48" x 36"

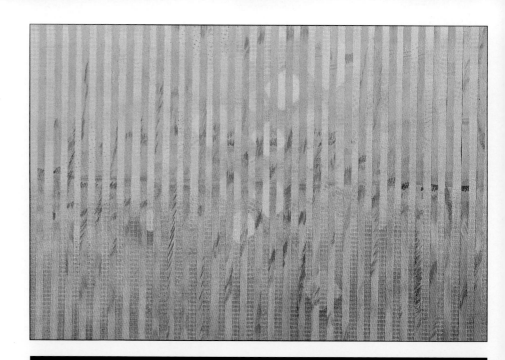

Jean Deemer

1537 Briarwood Circle
Cuyahoga Falls, OH 44221
(216) 929-1995

Jean's innovative torn paper paintings suggest geological transformations, uniting man with nature. Layering, tearing, peeling the paper's surface, using transparent and opaque acrylic glazes result in richly textured three-dimensional works that pull the viewer in to discover color nuances and intricate line work. Critics have referred to her as "pushing watercolor to the edge."

This nationally recognized artist is a frequent award winner and her work is represented in many corporate, public and private collections.

Pieces may be framed in shadow or plexiglass boxes. Information regarding commissions, prices and slides is available on request.

Top: *Fault Line: Earth Forms Series No. 18,*
  40" x 32" x 2½"D
Bottom: *Breakup: Earth Forms Series No. 19,*
  32" x 40" x 3"D

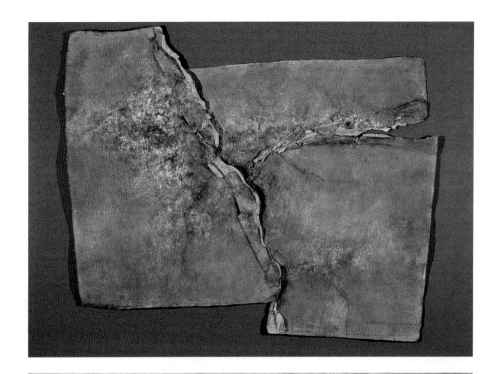

John D. Hubbard

53 Stonegate Heights
Marquette, MI 49855
(906) 249-1188

Bold designs and richness of color and texture are trademarks of the wall-hung paper constructions of John Hubbard. Ranging in size from twenty inches to six feet, he makes his own handmade paper, highlighted with painted patterns and found objects.

Installations of Hubbard's works are found in such corporate collections as Kemper Group and Michigan Bell Telephone as well as numerous museum and university collections.

Prices range from $500 to $4000, each work being presented in plexiglass cases. The artist is eager to collaborate and completes most works in four to eight weeks. Contact the artist for further information and slides of available work.

Top: *Spinal Flight*, 41" x 41" x 5"
Bottom Left: detail, *Flight Forms IV*,
    40" x 48" x 6"
Bottom Right: detail, *Spinal Flight*

Jeanne Hughes

Hughes-Hunter
3542 Veteran Avenue
Los Angeles, CA 90034
(310) 839-8601
FAX (310) 839-8601

Jeanne Hughes is an energetic and flexible artist who excels at working in a wide variety of mediums and materials. Collaborating regularly with designers, art consultants and architects, she enjoys developing new compositions based upon a client's needs. Also available is her line of original artwork which can be custom colored to match any decor. Call for a catalog.

From paintings on canvas and paper to dimensional artwork, Jeanne has the talent and resources to make your project a success. Turnaround times average 2–6 weeks, depending upon complexity. Retail prices range from $300–4,500.

Top: *Majestic Kimono*, handpainted fabric, woven, braided and airbrushed in a handpainted frame, 48" x 60"
Bottom: *Medallions*, faux finished gator board with gold accents.

Margie Hughto

**6970 Henderson Road
Jamesville, NY 13078
(315) 469-8775**

Margie Hughto, nationally recognized for her ceramic wall pieces, also maintains her own handmade-paper studio and creates two and three dimensional paper works. These paper works often reflect her involvement with landscape imagery and incorporate collage, handmade lithograph imagery, and rich, lush, color.

The works range in size from small intimate framed pieces to large scale site-specific installations. Commissions are welcome and existing works are available. Prices, slides and further information are furnished upon request.

Works are represented in numerous museum, corporate and private collections including: Albright-Knox Art Gallery, IBM, Blue Cross-Blue Shield.

Top: *Flora's Passage, Summer Sunset,* handmade lithograph on collaged handmade paper, $700 unframed (retail price), 23" x 33"
Bottom: *Dark Summer Waves,* handmade paper wall-relief sealed with acrylic medium to be displayed unframed, $2100 (retail price), 36" x 42"

Printed in Japan ©1992 Kraus Sikes Inc. The Guild: The Designer's Reference Book of Artists

Anna Karesh

Art Studio West
P.O. Box 900528
San Diego, CA 92190
(619) 258-0766

Anna Karesh creates three-dimensional wall sculptures. The artist transforms her handmade paper into flowing forms and utilizes cast paper elements to produce unusual textures and designs. As easy to install as a painting, each sculpture is structurally reinforced, lightweight and sealed with an acrylic medium which insures durability. These works do not require framing, although plexiglass boxing adds sophistication. The artist has worked with designers and art consultants for 20 years and is willing to collaborate on architectural format to meet design specifics, budget and time frame for special projects. Call for consultation.

Commissioned wall sculptures have been made for corporations, medical facilities, public spaces, libraries, and private residences. Recent clients include Home Federal Savings and Loan, Mercy Hospital, Capital South Corporation, CPW Corporate Headquarters, Gold Medical Center and Anderson Financial Planning.

Commissions may specify color, size and type of design. Retail prices range from $800 to $4000.

Bronzed Luna Forms, 32"H x 44"W x 4"D

Chasma, 38"H x 82"W x 4"D

Joan Kopchik

1335 Stephen Way
Southampton, PA 18966-4349
(215) 322-1862

Joan Kopchik integrates woven strips of handmade paper sheets with basketry reed and cast forms to create her distinctive style. She holds a BFA from Carnegie Mellon and has been creating handmade paper constructions for fifteen years.

Her elegant sense of design combined with archival quality materials and processes are a hallmark of her work. The completed works are tastefully framed to protect them. She has successfully worked with clients for site-specific pieces and welcomes inquiries from architects, design professionals, corporate and private collectors.

Selected commissions/collections: Hercules Incorporated, Johnson & Higgins, DuPont, Chemical Bank, Fidelity Bank, Wilmington Trust, McNeil Consumer Products.

Retail prices: $850–$3500. Resume and slides available upon request.

Top: *Medicine Wheels*, 36"H x 48"W x 2½"D
Bottom: *Gaea's Cloak*, 48"H x 34"W x 2½"D

Beverly Plummer

2720 White Oak, Left
Burnsville, NC 28714
(704) 675-5208

Beverly Plummer designs colorful images suitable for either home or public spaces. The images appear in and on heavily textured handmade paper that has been formed from cotton fibers and light-fast pigments. Many pieces also glisten from the addition of luster pigments. After framing, the work requires no further care.

Pieces vary in size, beginning at 24" x 24", and can be designed to fit any space requirements. Custom designs require four to eight weeks after design approval and deposit. They are priced according to size and complexity.

Available work begins at $250.

Beverly Plummer's work is represented in galleries and collections internationally.

Top: *Lady in Blue Hat*
Bottom: *Second House on the Left*

Raymond D. Tomasso

Inter-Ocean Curiosity Studio
2998 South Bannock
Englewood, CO 80110
(303) 789-0282

A definitive statement in corporate, hospitality or private collections, the three-dimensional cast handmade rag paper wall sculptures of Raymond D. Tomasso integrate dynamic, sharp edged elements with a palette of subdued, natural hues to create timeless archaeological images. For 17 years Tomasso has focused his talents on developing a distinctive technique based on his in-depth understanding of the age-old craft of papermaking through history and from around the world. Each piece of the artist's work is composed of hand-formed sheets of 100% cotton rag paper for a durability that ensures a 100-year life expectancy. Tomasso's subtle color range is derived from a combination of pure pigment, colored pencil and latex paint, which is protected by a finish of clear flat lacquer. The artist will design his work to fit custom architectural specifications. Selected corporate collections: AT&T, Century 21, Coca Cola Co., Drexel Burnham Lambert, Hyatt Regency, IBM, Knoxville Museum of Art, MCI, MKI Securities, Mountain Bell, Munich Marriott Hotel, Museum of Art, U. of Az., Prudential-Bache Securities, Sheraton Hotel.

In an Ancient Cumbrian Dream, The Epic Journey Continued, 1991, 47" x 46"

Views from the Epic Dream of the Waste Land, 1991, 40" x 62"

Marjorie Tomchuk

44 Horton Lane
New Canaan, CT 06840
(203) 972-0137

As a professional artist for 28 years, Marjorie Tomchuk has art placed in more than 50 major corporations, including IBM, Xerox, Citicorp, AT&T, GE, and also in museums including the Library of Congress. She specializes in limited edition embossings on artist-made paper, the style is semi-abstract.

The embossings are editions of 100, retail for $700, and are available immediately. A 16-page color brochure packet can be obtained for reference, price: $5 ppd. Commissioned art: sizes up to 4' x 6', retail $2,000–5,000 per panel. Maquette fee $150, delivery: 4–6 weeks. Also available: a hard cover book *M. Tomchuk Graphic Work 1962–1989,* 143 pages, $32 ppd.

Edan Flow, embossed, hand-colored, edition 50, $2800 retail, approx. framed size 5' x 7'

Blue Ridge, embossed, hand-colored, edition 100, $700 retail, 25" x 36"

Michele Tuegel

Michele Tuegel Paperworks
433 Monte Cristo Boulevard
Tierra Verde, FL 33715
(813) 867-5771
(813) 822-4294

Combining cotton and linen fibers, light-fast pigments and gels, Michele Tuegel has developed a distinctive style of imagery with her wall sculptures and bowls. Both decorative and whimsical, these handmade paper pieces are vibrant in color, richly-textured, and coated for durability and easy cleaning.

Prices range from $200–$3000 depending on size and complexity. Commission time: 1–2 months. Existing works are available, suitable for both interior corporate and residential spaces. Slides and price list available upon request.

Corporate collections include: Oxmoor House, Hercules Paper, Southwest Bell, Southern Progress. Tuegel's work has been featured in national publications and she received a Florida Fellowship in 1986.

Top: *Tribal Pattern*, African-inspired paper bowl, 36" x 36" x 10", hung with plexi stand
Bottom: paper bowls and wall sculpture, installation

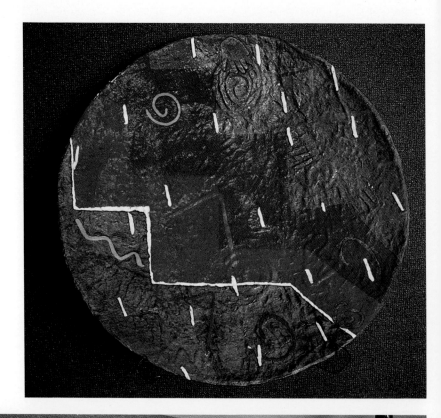

Printed in Japan ©1991 Kraus Sikes Inc. The Guild: The Designer's Reference Book of Artists

The Care and Maintenance of Fiber Art

Hand-crafted works in fiber have enriched the lives of both royalty and peasantry since the beginning of humankind. Persian brocades, Indian chilkats, Indonesian ship cloths, Asian ikats, Turkish rugs -- the artistry and craftsmanship of textiles from centuries past are kept alive in countless museums around the world. And, it's a marvel that they exist at all for us to enjoy today. Homage is paid first to the artists who toiled over these works and second to the conservators who have preserved them for safe passage into this century.

Likewise, today's fiber art deserves our thoughtful attention to care and maintenance. Regarding contemporary textiles as the heirlooms of tomorrow is the best way to ensure their preservation for future generations to enjoy.

You don't have to be a museum curator to purchase and display contemporary textiles, but you do have to remember that they are perishable works of art. While a designer's most important function is to choose the right art or artist for a client's taste, project and budget, in this medium there is also an important role to be played in several pragmatic areas. The most exquisite art in the world will be diminished by inappropriate positioning, lighting and overall maintenance. Aesthetics and conservation should get equal consideration.

Successful presentation begins with selecting the right environment -- a space, position and illumination that shows off the ultimate quality of a piece. On an artistic level, attention must be given to spatial considerations, proportions, focal points. On a practical level, solutions must be found for safely showcasing fiber art.

If the art is commissioned as part of the overall design process and the installation plan thought through in the conception stage, this task is easier. But if a work has been commissioned or purchased for an existing space, solutions need to be found for lighting that will neither diminish the piece aesthetically nor destroy it physically. Because fiber is somewhat fragile, these questions of endurance and care are important. Fiber art that has become shabby, or soiled, with its color faded is an all too familiar and disheartening sight.

Jean West, former director of the Center for Tapestry Arts in New York City, brings home the point with a reminder of the short-lived craze of the 1960s and 70s. Jute and sisal, many clients learned the hard way, are extremely fragile -- if unprotected, they deteriorate rapidly. Because there was little history in this field, and scarce information on protection was available, a large body of this work has been lost to the elements. Harsh light and moisture took their toll.

Fiber art has long been recognized as a springboard for explorations in a variety of media; this is a field that continues to evolve through the use of new materials. Peruse the pages of THE GUILD, and you'll find works in metallic yarns, new lustrous cottons, silk, wools, handmade papers, synthetics, bamboo and wire. Often you'll read in the artists' descriptions of their works, assurances that they are "custom-dyed, lightfast, mothproof, treated with fabric protectant, fireproofing available." Our contemporary fiber artists have become

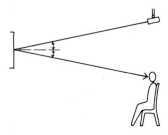
knowledgeable in areas of
durability and maintenance.
Conservation gets a good start
with their expertise, but ensuring
textiles a long-term existence
takes an ongoing effort, one in
which designers and art
consultants play an important
role. In addition to the advice
offered here, there are a number
of other resources available
regarding the care and
conservation of textiles.
(See sidebar, Textile
Conservation Resources.)

POSITIONING. Safe positioning of a piece of fiber art is
very important. In the area of
illumination, ultraviolet rays
(sunshine) are the most harmful.
But incandescent light can also
break down natural fibers.
Works in fiber should not only
be placed out of direct sunlight,
but at a safe distance from
artificial light where heat can
destroy the material. Likewise,
heat vents, radiators, and hot
wires need to be kept at a
distance.

Too-close or too-intense
lighting presents not only
physical harm to fiber art, but
will diminish these works
aesthetically as well. Intense
bright light destroys the colors

of textiles, which have, quite
naturally, been painstakingly
and masterfully chosen for the
ultimate effect. Work lit too
brightly can be totally distorted;
the colors washed out in the
beam. Work with subtle
transitions in color and those
in which light plays on fibers,
and in which spatial depth are
critical, must also be lit very
carefully.

Laurence Korwin, in his book
Textiles As Art, provides an
extensive guide to optimum
lighting combinations, including
suggestions on positioning of
lights. (See sidebar, Overcoming
Glare.) Korwin presents many
lighting solutions for the
problems facing the installation
of a fiber piece: adding lenses to
a fixture to soften potential
bright spots; using up-lights from
a floor canister; lighting from
across the room; choosing
between incandescent and
halogen bulbs. He also suggests
talking to major lighting
distributors in your area. Many
of them have showrooms where
lighting solutions can be tested.

Korwin details the color
spectrum enhancement
properties of different sources
of light. The choice of halogen,
incandescent or daylight is
critical in preserving the color
quality intended by the artist.
Cool colors are enhanced by
daylight; incandescent lighting
is high on the red, or warm, end
of the spectrum; halogen light is
visually less blue than daylight,
less red than incandescent

and has a crisp, almost icy whiteness. The lighting should be compatible with the mood of the work. Is it dramatic, moody, romantic, cheery? Choosing the right light source will enhance the aesthetics, not contradict it.

FRAMING. There are many considerations in framing textiles as well. While glass protects against humidity, dust, insects, and touching, it is important, advises West, to allow an air space for the work. It is essential to back with adhesives that won't discolor the fibers. Spacers that keep the glass from coming in direct contact with the material is also critical, since the acidic quality of glass can adversely alter the fibers. While there are plastics on the market today which offer protection from ultraviolet rays, these, as well as glass, may present glare problems.

INSTALLATION. Hanging presents another set of challenges. West says the Center for Tapestry Arts has used the solution of hand-stitching a four-inch wide twill tape (used in upholstering) onto the backs of tapestries. A strip of velcro is attached to the tape and another stapled to a board (shellacked so no acids can leach out) which is covered in muslin. Screw eyes secure the board to the wall, giving the piece adjustability.

While many artists block their work before installation, in some instances gravity can take its toll. The Center solves problems by reshaping works in a squaring up frame. They tack the work down, iron with the use of damp towels, and then let the piece dry overnight. Heavily textured pieces that can not endure the press of an iron are simply wetted down in blocks, squared out, and left to dry.

CLEANING. While the new fabric protectors solve many of the problems associated with soiling, insect infestations and humidity, periodic cleaning may still be needed. Some pieces can be carefully vacuumed, with a mesh screening placed over the work to avoid fibers being either disturbed or extricated from the piece. Dry cleaning though, by anyone other than a well-versed conservator, can be dangerous business.

There are textile conservators around the country who specialize in cleaning. The new fabric protectors are much better, but it's helpful to be aware of these resources should the need arise.

When it is appropriately cared for, contemporary fiber art will endure long after its original purpose. Good care from the beginning will guarantee that the best of our textile treasures will be passed on within the family or to museum archives for future generations to enjoy.

TEXTILE CONSERVATION RESOURCES

Caring for Textiles, Karen Finch, O.B.E., & Greta Putnam, Barrie & Jenkins, Ltd., 1977. A guide for the maintenance of textiles.

Considerations for the Care of Textiles and Costumes, Harold F. Mailand, Indianapolis Museum of Art, 1978. General handbooks on textile and fiber care.

Textiles as Art, Laurence Korwin, a layman's book with easy to understand, basic instructions, includes diagrams such as ideal lighting angles. Available through the author, Laurence Korwin, 333 N. Michigan Ave., Chicago, IL 60601.

The Fabric and Fiber Sourcebook, Bobbi McRae, The Taunton Press, 1989. A mail-order guide, includes companies that specialize in varieties of textiles, threads, and fibers, in addition to listing textile collections nationwide, magazines, educational opportunities, and preservation services.

The Textiles Conservation Laboratory of Cathedral Heights is a working textile laboratory that advises on specific questions. 212-316-7523

The Conservation Analytical Laboratory, Smithsonian Institute provides workshops on the preservation and care of textiles and fiber art. 301-328-3700

Bruce Breckenridge

1715 Regent Street
Madison, WI 53705
(608) 238-8681

Although trained as a painter, Breckenridge has been working with ceramic processes for the past twenty-five years. He has exhibited widely in this country and abroad, and is represented in numerous private and public collections.

He adapts the ancient Majolica technique to a contemporary style of geometric painting in the creation of his ceramic tile murals. The use of the opaque technique is one of the many unique qualities of his work.

Because of the effects specific to the ceramic process, the rich, intense color is impervious to the effects of sunlight. This, coupled with the medium's durability, makes these murals especially well-suited for installation in public places.

Prices range from $185–$300 per square foot and do not include shipping or installation.

Top: *Boyle Heights Series #1*, 88" x 110"
Middle/Bottom: *Boyle Heights Series #2*, 88" x 220"

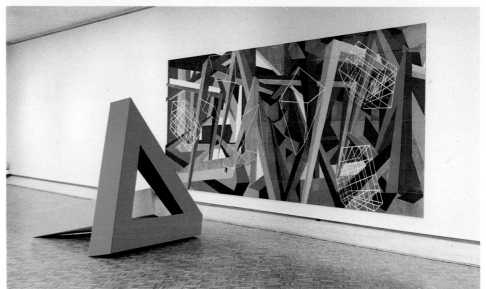

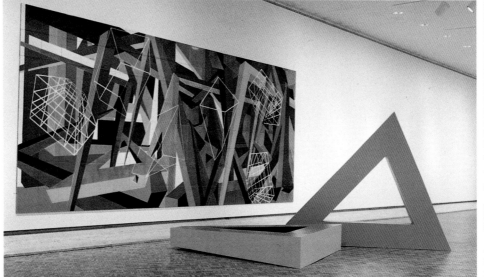

Printed in Japan ©1992 Kraus Sikes Inc. The Guild: The Designer's Reference Book of Artists

Ceramic Murals & Mosaics

George F. Fishman and Ellie Stein
103 N.E. 99 Street
Miami Shores, FL 33138
(305) 758-1141
FAX (305) 751-1770

Ellie Stein creates custom and site-specific glazed ceramic tile murals and bas-reliefs. Her work is enjoyed in cruise ships, hotels, residences, corporate offices and public art settings.

George Fishman's mosaic murals combine glass, porcelain and glazed tiles to create pictorial images. Sculptural formats, as well as flat panels can be commissioned. Pictured (Right) is a ten-foot-high column of portraits from a series installed in a Maryland park.

Both artists encourage collaboration with designers on concept and theme development. Meticulous attention is given to details of expediting any scale project through installation. Works are packaged and coded for easy on-site mounting. Durable, easily-maintained materials are suited for exterior and high-traffic settings.

Please send project description for price quotation.

Nancy Weeks Dudchenko

Dudchenko Studios
M.C. Weeks Bldg.
3815 Ridge Pike
Collegeville, PA 19426
(215) 489-7231
FAX (215) 489-7233

Nancy Dudchenko has been a full-time producing artist since 1968. Her works are one-of-a-kind glazed and painted ceramic sculptures for the wall.

She has shown her work nationally in one person exhibitions, invitationals and juried competitions throughout the United States. Her sculptures hang in over 200 corporate collections and numerous museums and private collections.

These multi-sectional unique works are high-fired stoneware using oil paint and stains over parts of glazed surfaces.

Prices begin at $250 per sq. ft. (retail). Most commissions can be completed within several months. Many finished works are available and are wired for easy hanging. Unlimited size restriction. Please write or phone for prices and further information.

Top: *Where Eagles Soar*, 100" x 48"
Bottom: *Gateway to Heaven*, 55" x 73"

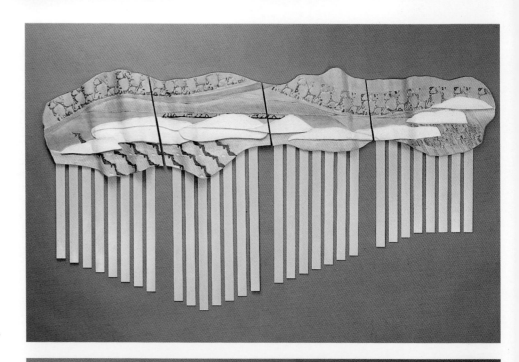

Printed in Japan ©1992 Kraus Sikes Inc. The Guild: The Designer's Reference Book of Artists

Penelope Fleming

**7740 Washington Lane
Elkins Park, PA 19117
(215) 576-6830**

Penelope Fleming designs wall pieces for public spaces, corporate collections and residential environments. The primary material is modulated black and white clay with some additions of slate, bronze and collective other materials. Color and scale are unlimited. These pieces are lightweight, easily shipped and installed.

Fleming has worked with many designers, art consultants and galleries for the last sixteen years to meet the criteria of design integrity, budget and completion deadlines. Commissioned wall pieces have been hung for many corporations such as Smithe Kline Beckman, Reichhold Chemical Incorporated and Ragu Food Inc. as well as private individuals across the USA.

Call or write for a catalog, prices and the availability of already completed pieces.

Left: *Stiacciato*, Private collection, Elkins Park, PA, 60" x 28" x 4"
Right: *Singular Reflection*, Artist's Collection, 72" x 30" x 7"

Deborah Hecht

Custom Design on Tile
6285 Thurber Road
Bloomfield Hills, MI 48301
(313) 855-2475

Deborah Hecht's intricately patterned ceramic art is suitable for public as well as private spaces. The tiles are painted with overglaze, then are re-fired. This creates a lustrous, rich and durable surface. Pieces can be permanently installed or hung as paintings.

Hecht's subject matter is limitless, ranging from landscapes to architectural motifs. Her award winning art has been featured in *Better Homes and Gardens, Contemporary Crafts for the Home,* and *Detroit Monthly.*

All work is custom, done in conjunction with architects, designers, and/or individual clients. Prices start at $150 per square foot.

Top Left: *Page,* 48" x 32"
Top Right: *Triptych,* 28" x 47"
Bottom: *Backyard* (tiles hung separately),
    34" x 60"

Georgina Holt

Handbuilt Porcelain
3737 Cove Court
Jacksonville, FL 32211
(904) 744-4985

Georgina Holt creates unique wall installations for private and corporate collectors in Florida and throughout the southeastern states, having maintained an independent studio since 1979, in Florida.

Each artwork is individually designed for the particular client, using hand-built, high-fired porcelain slabs. The tiles are light-weight, fade-proof, and extremely durable in contrast to their fragile looking quality. The installation shown here, designed for a residence, features twelve 12" x 12" tiles that have been formed by thinly rolled porcelain slabs with underglaze painting. The result is a visual impression of fabric with vibrant to subtle color tones.

Easy to install directly or as a unit mounted on a finished wood panel as in this installation. Production time: 2 to 4 months.

Below: detail;. *Reflections—Summer Sky*, 3' x 4" x 4", Porcelain tiles with under glaze painting
Right: installation: great room, Ortega residence, Jacksonville, FL

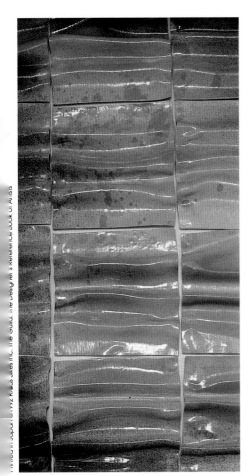

Tom Latka
Jean Latka

Latka Studios
229 Midway
Pueblo, CO 81004-1912
(719) 543-0720

Latka Studios creates 3-dimensional ceramic wall reliefs and large vases for architects, designers and galleries who seek to accentuate living and work spaces with a distinctive, innovative flair.

Pit-fired for a natural finish or painted with acrylic, these sculptural wall pieces, signed and dated, are produced in modular units that can be arranged in a myriad of combinations to cover large wall areas yet are singularly elegant when hung independently.

Professional artists for over 20 years, Latka Studios' wall pieces are represented in the collections of major corporations such as Digital, Hewlett-Packard and McDonnell Douglas.

The ability to work fluently with clients within their color and size specifications has secured Latka Studios' reputation as a leading manufacturer in customized decor.

Estimated time for design and production: 4 weeks

Top left: 3' x 18", $400
Top Right: 6'H x 30", $3,000
Bottom left: 3'Dia., $600
Bottom right: 6' x 18", $600 (all prices retail)

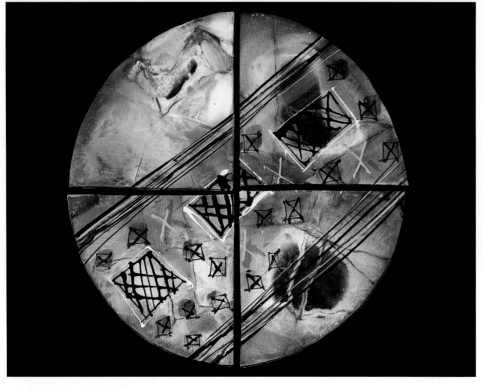

Linda Brendler Studios

P.O. Box 4615
Modesto, CA 95354
(209) 522-3534

Linda Brendler is nationally known for her work in the area of crystalline glazed porcelain. During the last 20 years she has developed unusual colors and special effects. Her vessels can be viewed in previous editions of *THE GUILD* and are exhibited and sold in selected galleries and museums. Her works appear also in many private and public collections.

Large and small scale wall pieces can be designed to meet certain specifications and architectural requirements. Linda has been commissioned to work in contemporary as well as classical formats.

Linda Brendler received an MFA degree in ceramics having studied with Carlton Ball and Dr. Herbert Sanders. Slides and resume are available upon request.

Top: crystalline glazed porcelain vase, 12"H
Bottom: "Whirlwind," 27½" x 38½"W

Thomas Lollar

50 West 106th Street, Suite 2A
New York, NY 10025
(212) 864-7973
(914) 964-0812

Tom Lollar builds clay murals by hand which depict architectural and geographical themes. Subjects depict landmarks in both frontal bas-relief and aerial views. The unique surface color results from applying copper, bronze and platinum metallic paints and glazes. Each rectangular clay construction is approximately 20" x 15" x 4" and may be placed in combinations of unlimited numbers suitable to wall size. Each one-of-a-kind section costs $400–600 wholesale, depending on the intricacy of the surface.

Lollar has a Master's Degree in ceramic sculpture from Western Michigan University and has been creating clay murals professionally for 10 years.

His murals are in the collections of Hyatt Hotels, Revlon and Steelcase. His work has also been featured in the store windows of Tiffany, Fifth Avenue, New York City.

Top Left: *Manhattan I,* (aerial view),
   48" x 48" x 6"
Top Center: *Manhattan II,* (Central Park),
   48" x 48" x 6"
Top Right: *Manhattan III,* (Midtown),
   48" x 48" x 6"
Bottom Left: *Albany,* 12' x 8'
Bottom Right: *Albany,* detail

M.E. Tile Co., Inc.

Pat & Jim Evanko
400 E. Sibley Boulevard, Tech Center
Harvey, IL 60426
(708) 210-3229
FAX (708) 210-3654

M.E. Tile Studio designs and produces approximately 200 hand-crafted, low-relief sculptured tiles that embody graceful elegance with simplicity. These tiles are suitable for individual designs for kitchens, bathrooms, foyers, garden rooms, fireplaces, door frames, and interior commercial spaces. The 6" standard size matches most American field tile.

Current designs include: fruits, vegetables, sealife, birds, flowers, bouquets of various sizes in stylized vessels, fruit and vegetable baskets, columns, moldings, liners, trim and geometrics.

The tile is custom produced for each job in one to four weeks in a variety of colors, including some commercial color matches.

Special edge, cutting, bullnosing, and glazing are available, as is custom tile designing. Prices range from $3.80 to $36 per piece.

Catalogs are available for $3 each.

E. Joseph McCarthy

Custom Tile Studio
39 Eleventh Street
Turners Falls, MA 01376
(413) 863-3121
FAX (413) 863-9413

E. Joseph McCarthy and his staff have been designing and executing fine ceramic tile environments for over a decade. Specializing in large-scale murals, each piece is custom designed to fit into the decor and configurations of each location.

Ranging from representational to abstract, his work encompasses a variety of styles and imagery.

Prices range from $50 to $200 per sq. ft.

Photography by Michael Brown

Top Left: *Oriental*, 18"W x 30"H (6" x 6" tiles)
Top Right: *Abstract*, 16"W x 32"H (8" x 8" tiles)
Bottom: *Fish and Coral*, 6'W x 4'H (8" x 8" tiles)

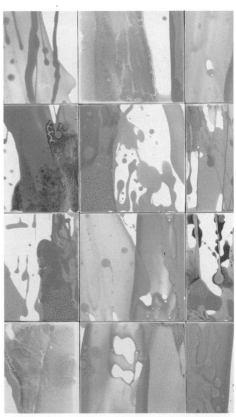

Printed in Japan ©1992 Kraus Sikes Inc. The Guild: The Designer's Reference Book of Artists

William C. Richards

Clay Canvas Designs
756 Garfield
Seattle, WA 98109
(206) 286-9171

Will Richards' work hangs in private and corporate collections as well as residential environments. His ceramic plates and panels are unique creations combining textural surfaces and dimensional materials. The surfaces are colored with multiple layers of acrylic stain and sealed for longevity. Each piece is wired for wall mount.

He welcomes commissions and custom orders. Plates are sized 11" to 45" in diameter and up to 34" x 71" overall for panels. Professional profile and detailed information available. Price range $130–$1950.

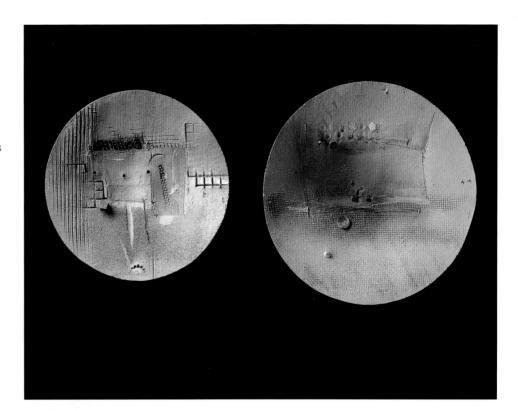

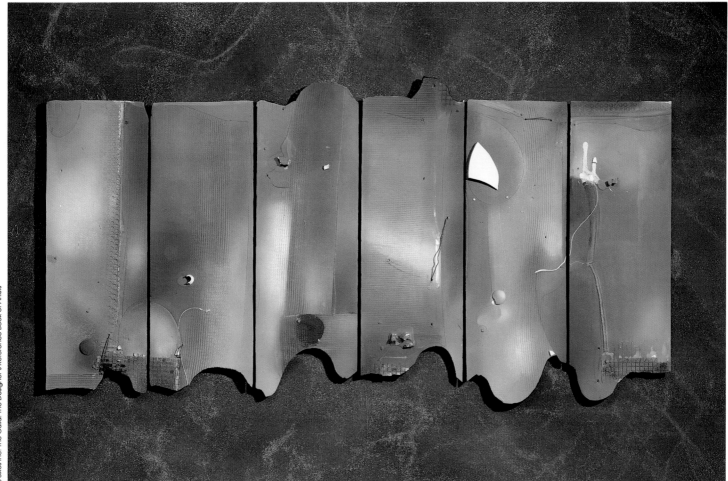

Six panel set, 34" x 71"

Barbara Sebastian

1777 Yosemite Avenue, Suite 4B
San Francisco, CA 94124
(415) 822-3243

A professional for 15 years, Barbara
Sebastian's work is in many corporate
and private collections.

Collaborating with architects, designers, and
private individuals, she creates murals which
are painted, fired ceramics and stretched
canvas creating a layering and balancng
of surface and design. The modular
construction allows for simple installation
regardless of scale.

Murals from $75–$150 per square foot. Allow
6–8 weeks for completion.

Right: ceramic/canvas mural, ClubSport
   lobby, Fremont, CA, 20' x 16' x 3"
Bottom: detail, ClubSport lobby commission

Printed in Japan ©1992 Kraus Sikes Inc. The Guild: The Designer's Reference Book of Artists

A conversation with Victor Jacoby
(tapestries)

Q Are time requirements ever a problem for you?

A People can be surprised at the time required to make a tapestry. Sometimes the deadlines are not realistic. I had a potential client call me in early June, and wanted three 4' x 20' tapestries by September. That's about the time it takes me to do one piece that size. It would have been a great commission, but I had to turn it down. Actually, I think I have a reputation for being fairly fast, which has been both a blessing and a curse. There are pleasant and unpleasant working conditions, and I try not to push the physical demand of leaning over the loom for more than eight or ten hours a day.

Q How do you set up your loom?

A Weaving is very structural -- I think it's almost more similar to architecture than art. When an architect designs a structure, if the foundation isn't laid correctly, then the whole building will be off. It's the same thing with setting up the loom. I use cotton to set my warp, because it's more forgiving than linen and stronger than most wools. And I draw my main lines of the design right on to the warp, as opposed to putting a cartoon behind it. Without the cartoon, I'm able to experiment with the little details based on how the piece looks as I'm working on the loom, instead of what I may have sketched on the cartoon, and it also saves me the step of having to enlarge my designs. I choose to work in tapestry because I like the structure, and I like the intensity and the saturation of color I can get.

Q What's involved in your design process?

A I begin with establishing the budget, the size of the piece and the client's color needs. Then I take that information and start sketching in black and white. I like to stress values -- when I'm designing, the darks and lights are more important to me than color. The next step is to transfer the design into color, with yarns, not paint. I start pulling out colors, twisting different colored threads together. It usually takes me about two days to narrow the colors down. Then I will sit down at the loom and check the colors. When that's right, then I will go back and color the sketch and send that off with yarn samples to the client.

Dawn Adams
Dale Steffey

338 S. Madison Street
Bloomington, IN 47403
(812) 333-2903

Dawn Adams' and Dale Steffey's fused glass wall pieces are exclusively one-of-a-kind works that combine modern sensibilities with timeless influences. The works consist of originally designed fused glass tiles mounted in hand painted found frames.

Glass professionals for twelve years, Adams and Steffey will accept commissions. Prices range from $500 to $4000.

Slides of currently available work on request.

Top: *The Wall,* 40" x 48" x 3", $2400
Bottom: *Devotion,* 36" x 54" x 8", $2700

Printed in Japan ©1992 Kraus-Sikes Inc. The Guild: The Designer's Reference Book of Artists

Shawn Athari

Shawn Athari's, Inc.
13450 Cantara Street
Van Nuys, CA 91402
(818) 988-3105
FAX (818) 787-MASK

Always looking for the next challenge, Shawn Athari has started producing abstract glass wall hangings utilizing white glass as her palette and then fusing hundreds of pieces of hand-formed glass into the surface. These exceptional pieces capture the viewer's interest through their playful and unique qualities.

Each piece is original and an accumulation of various glass techniques acquired throughout the last 17 years.

Galleries:
Elaine Horwitch, Santa Fe, NM
Symmetry, Saratoga Springs, NY
Eileen Kreman, Fullerton, CA
Madeline Posner Gallery, Farmington HIlls, MI
Glass Growers, Erie, PA

Top: *Confusion Abounds, Family Matters,*
 29" x 31" x 2"
Bottom: *Three's a Crowd,* 24" x 42" x 2"

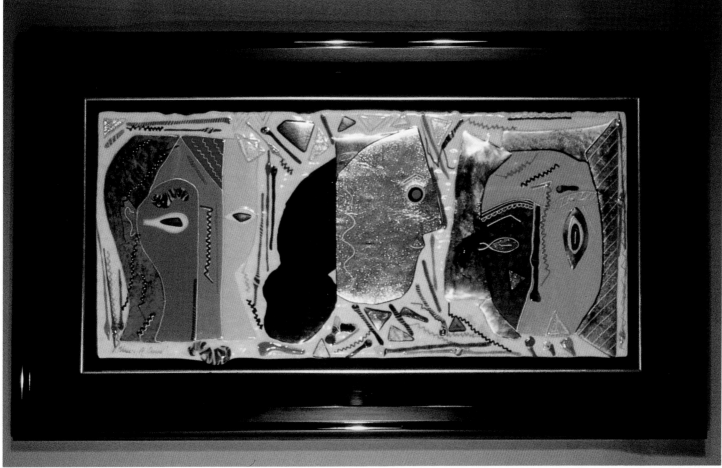

Photo: Robert Baumbach

Martha Desposito

75 Solether Lane
Chagrin Falls, OH 44022
(216) 247-2925

Martha Desposito's mixed media pieces incorporate acrylic, fabric, pastel, and oil stick on 100% rag paper or canvas. Colors are bold and bright; style is impressionistic. Subject matter ranges from architectural to animal to figurative. Works are sprayed and can be hung without framing.

Desposito's award-winning works are in private and corporate collections throughout the United States. She received her BFA from the University of Louisville in fiber design and her MFA from the University of Kentucky in painting. Her work has been published in FiberArts Design Book Four.

All work is original. Prices and slide portfolio available upon request. Commissions and collaborations invited.

Style: Queen Anne, 1890—Portland, OR (porch), mixed media on paper, 19.5" x 61"

St. Colman's Lion, mixed media on paper, 37.5" x 52.5"

Glenn Elvig Studios

Glenn S. Elvig
7716 Lakeview Lane N.E.
Minneapolis, MN 55432
(612) 780-2028

Glenn Elvig personally selects the 1–3 ton burls used in creating these unique wall pieces. Once selected, the burls are chainsaw-cut, cured up to 4 years, and then thin sliced and stacked for further drying.

The burled wood panels are sequentially cut and displayed in the spoke framework, creating a dramatic sweeping effect.

Panels are available in maple, myrtle, boxelder, and walnut burl. Spokes are natural walnut or finished in black lacquer.

Sizes from 36"–12' wide.

Prices from $1500–$20,000.

Left: burled and spalted myrtle wood, 96"W
Right: burled and spalted myrtle wood, 36"W

Yoshi Hayashi

351 Ninth Street, 3rd Floor
San Francisco, CA 94103
(415) 552-0755

Yoshi Hayashi's designs range from very
traditional 17th Century Japanese lacquer
art themes that are delicate with intricate
detail, to those that are boldly geometric
and contemporary. By skillfully applying
metallic leaf and bronzing powders he adds
illumination and contrast to the network of
color, pattern and texture. His original
designs include screens, wall panels,
furniture and decorative objects.

Hayashi's pieces have been commissioned
for private collections, hotels, restaurants
and offices in the United States and Japan.
Prices upon request.

Arthur Higgins

Oak Run Studios
P.O. Box 509
Mosier, OR 97040
(503) 478-3451

Arthur Higgins is seeking site-specific wall sculpture commissions using combinations of metals and wood. Of his 30 years as a professional artist, 15 have been focused on public art commissions from 2' x 2' to 17' x 50', from $2,000 to $40,000, or starting at $100/sq. ft. He designs artwork that is maintenance free and vandal resistant, and he delivers on time and within budget. He handles all aspects of design, fabrication, shipping and installation himself and welcomes collaboration with architects and interior designers.

Top Right: Columbia Bank, mixed wood and metal, 10" x 14"
Top Left: DNR 1%, State of Alaska installation
Bottom: DNR 1%, State of Alaska, aluminum, copper, wood

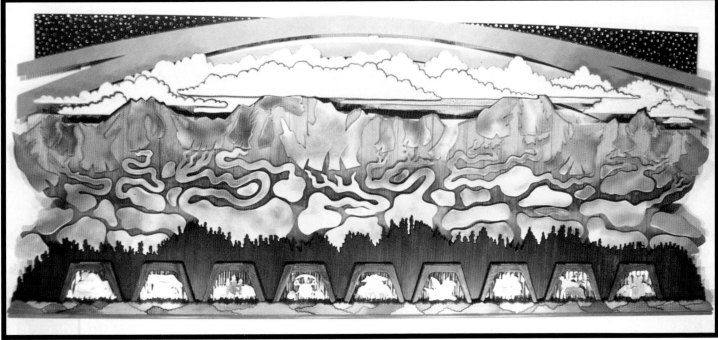

J.E. Jasen

36 East 10th Street
New York City, NY 10003-6219
(212) 674-6113
FAX (212) 777-6375

Unique Lead-free Vitrified Enamel Art!

Investment Quality Art!

Dynamic Designs!

Commissioned Murals and Accessories!
The non-institutional look can be achieved through the individualized design with an emphasis on the aesthetic, as well as the functional aspect of each specific job to meet the needs of the client.
May be used in interior or exterior public spaces, such as: lobbies, executive suites, dining rooms, kitchens, reception areas, elevator interiors or exterior, recreational centers, malls, schools, children and adult facilities, hospitals, health facilities, spas, etc. . . .

Permanent Colors!
Excellent retention of colors and gloss, that will not peel, blister, and will resist oxidation so that it will not fade due to excessive lights, heat, cold, chemicals or pollution.

Resistant to Weather and Public Elements!
Can be used in the interior or on the exterior of buildings. Recommended for high traffic areas because it has scratch, corrosion and abrasion resistant qualities. Graffiti resistant.

Durable with Low Maintenance!
If maintenance is necessary it can be cleaned with water or mild soap and disinfectant without damaging the permanent lifetime finish.
Sturdy enough to lean against.

ENAMEL-ART IS A PERFECT SURFACE FOR ALL ENVIRONMENTS!

More information available upon request.

Printed in Japan ©1992 Kraus Sikes Inc. The Guild: The Designer's Reference Book of Artists

Viviana Lombrozo

7777 Starlight Drive
La Jolla, CA 92037
(619) 452-0477

Viviana Lombrozo designs and creates wall reliefs, free-standing pieces and suspended sculptures for public, commercial and residential settings.

Materials, colors, themes, and designs are carefully selected to fit each specific site and to suit the clients' practical and aesthetic considerations. All pieces are durable, easily installed and can be designed for interior or exterior locations. Sizes range from small pieces to installations of architectural scale.

Collaborations and commissions are welcome and existing pieces are available.

Fabrication time varies with the complexity and size of each project. Portfolio and price list available on request.

Top: detail, enameled metal,
    48"W x 96"H x 6"D
Bottom Left: detail, mixed media,
    174"W x 24"H x 5"D
Bottom Right: installation of above detail

Joyce P. Lopez

Joyce Lopez Studio
1147 W. Ohio Street
Chicago, IL 60622
(312) 243-5033

When it comes to the selection of Fine Art, Lopez's work and her professional manner make her a favorite choice of the design community as well as with private collectors.

Her unique sculptures come highly recommended for their dramatic design concepts, as well as for their innovative solutions to site-specific situations and budgetary limitations that can arise in selecting art work.

Attention to detail as evidenced by her craftsmanship continues throughout the installation. This work is easily maintained; commissions and collaborations of any size are welcome.

Clients include: Burroughs Corp., Sony Corp., Michael Reese Hosp., State of Illinois, Bank of America, Jim Beam Brands, etc. and private collectors.

Prices start at $4500 for a mid-sized sculpture. Call or write for additional information.

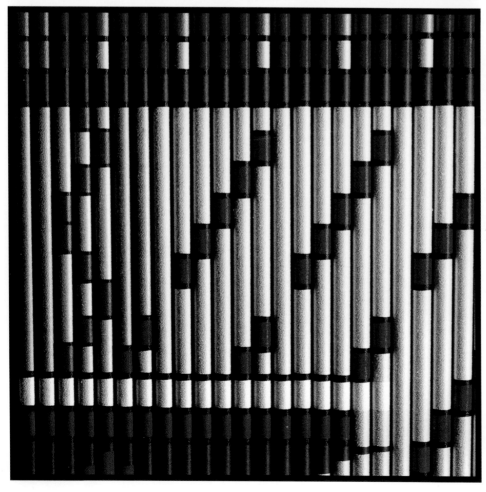

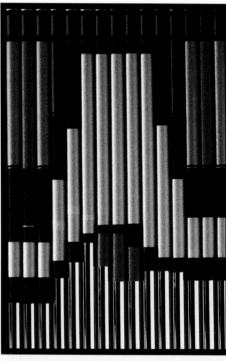

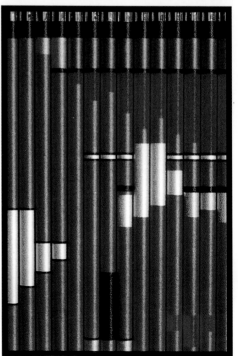

Printed in Japan ©1992 Kraus Sikes Inc. The Guild: The Designer's Reference Book of Artists

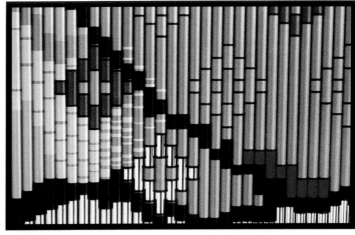

North Pier Apt. Tower lobby, Chicago, each sculpture: 10' x 52" x 2"

Dan McCann

Dan McCann Enamels
1440 East Broad Street
Columbus, OH 43205
(614) 253-5834
FAX (614) 794-1145

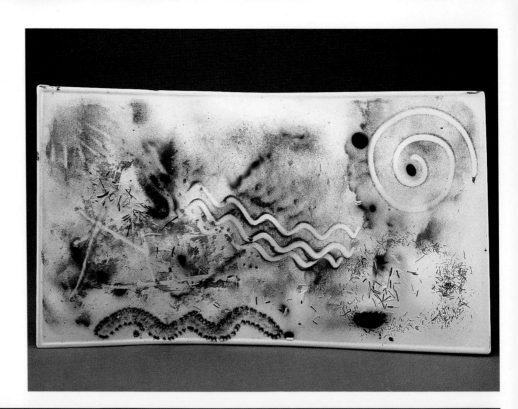

McCann's work coordinates issues of concept, color, perception and process. His enamels are included in many public and private collections.

Each piece is hand fired on industrial grade steel tiles. From framed wall pieces to large scale permanent installations, the options are endless. Quality and durability are built into every aspect of production. Prices begin at $300. Portfolio available.

Dan meets deadlines with architects and designers who demand uniqueness for commercial and residential space.

Top: *Belize*, 17" x 30"
Bottom: *Harmony*, 15" x 21"

Printed in Japan ©1992 Kraus Sikes Inc. The Guild: The Designer's Reference Book of Artists

Maya Radoczy

Contemporary Art Glass
P.O. Box 31422
Seattle, WA 98103
(206) 527-5022
FAX (206) 524-9226

Maya Radoczy creates work for site-specific corporate, public and residential projects. She employs unique techniques for creating blown and fused glass which allow original treatments for each site, including new concepts in fused glass wall pieces which integrate blended colors and textural form.

She exhibits internationally and is featured in numerous publications and books including, *The New York Times* and *Interior Design.*

Selected installations include: Trump Plaza, N.Y., Linpro Co., DE, Intrex Inc., N.Y.

A brochure is available upon request.

Photos: Dick Springgate

Top: wall sculpture, fused glass, private
  residence, Seattle, WA, 3' x 4'
Bottom: wall sculpture, fused glass, U.S. Bank,
  Seattle, WA, 3½' x 6½'
Below: detail

Sofya Smith

723 Solano Drive
Prescott, AZ 86301
(602) 445-0949

An odd facet of Sofya Smith's work is the lack of visual relationship between the thousands of art pieces that she's developed for public spaces in a fifteen-year period. Each installation is a singular response to a specific context. Dimensionality and texture are constants because of their ability to make artwork accessible and tangible. The materials used in the commissions pictured here include bamboo, aspen poles, copper, stucco, raw silk, hand-tinted photography, aluminum wire, air-brushed canvas and glazed tile. Pricing for custom pieces ranges from $25 to $200 per sq. ft.

A line of framed pieces is also available to galleries and for guest rooms within hotels and hospitals. It includes dimensionality, hand-tinted photographs and a variety of collaged textures. The pieces range in size from 11" x 14" to 24" x 36" and have been designed to be consistent with a number of regional and interior design parameters. They are available at popular prices.

Top Left: The Nicco Hotel, Chicago, 8' x 8'
Top Right: The Westcourt in the Buttes Hotel, Phoenix, 17' x 8'
Bottom Left: The Sheraton Grand Hotel, Los Angeles, 25' x 25'
Bottom Right: The Maui Grand Hotel, dimensional guest room artwork, 30" x 20"

Susan Starr & Co.

1580 Jones Road
Roswell, GA 30075
(404) 993-3980
(404) 992-1697
FAX (404) 642-8960

Tapestry, wall and free-hanging constructions by Susan Starr are rich in color and texture. A wide variety of materials are used, including hand-dyed wools, silk, cotton, rayon, plexiglass, wooden rods and hand-made papers. Starr's work has been featured in publications such as *USA Today, Interior Design* and *Contract*. AT&T, Bank of America and Marriott and Hyatt Hotels are among her many corporate clients.

Works are available in a range of sizes; the largest to date measures 50' x 27". Designed for specific sites in consultation with architects, interior designers, galleries and individuals, her wall pieces hang in hospitals, office lobbies, hotels, residences and restaurants.

Types of work available include: flat and dimensional tapestries, stick constructions, kite forms, and handmade paper constructions.

Spectrum Contemporary Fine Art

73-655 El Paseo
Palm Desert, CA 92260
(619) 773-9281
FAX (619) 779-1347

Spectrum Contemporary Fine Art represents over 100 multi-dimensional artists. All mediums are available in a broad variety of styles. Services include site-specific commissions, custom framing, shipping and installations. Art leasing is an attractive sales feature for corporate and client acquisitions.

Northern Californian, Phyllis Pacin (Top), works ceramic into elegant wall pieces, their geometric patterns and coppery glazes enhancing the smooth texture of the clay. These raku-fired clay works can be commissioned for site-specific needs, the size and glazes defined to meet individual taste.

Robert Stimmel (Middle), creates wall constructions made of lacquered wood, natural wood and aluminum. Bright colors mixed with pastels enhance the dynamic forms of the collaged wood. Created as either free standing sculpture or as wall pieces they bring a jazzy and energetic ebb to all environments.

Using an ancient Indian method of tapestry, Evan Riter (Bottom), weaves titanium burnished wire into large woven structures. Different chemicals are used to achieve a variety of colors. Wire can be thin, wavy and loosely woven or thick, straight and tightly woven as seen here.

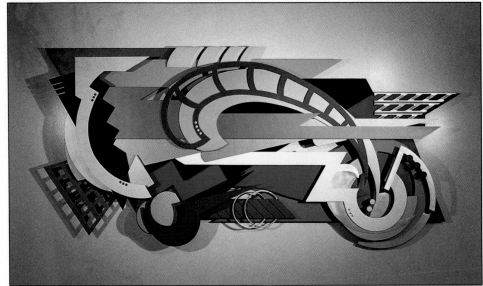

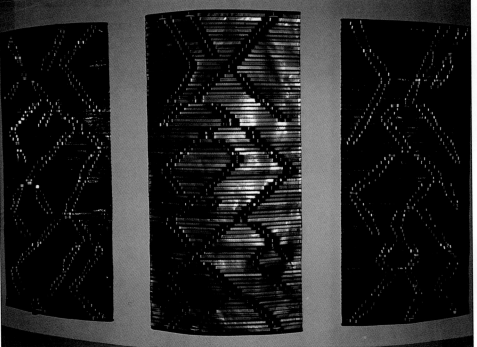

Printed in Japan ©1989 Kraus Sikes Inc. The Guild: The Designer's Reference Book of Artists

Vincent Tolpo
Carolyn Lee Tolpo

55918 U.S. Hwy. 285, P.O. Box 134
Shawnee, CO 80475
(303) 670-1733

Since 1981, Vincent and Carolyn Lee Tolpo have created site-specific wrapped fibers, metal, and stoneware tile art works for public, corporate, and residential spaces. They are collaborative artists who are sensitive to color, concept, space, and budget as it pertains to each project. Pieces may be commissioned directly. Artists will provide pre-approved color drawings and material samples.

Commissions or available work can be delivered within one to ten weeks. Budgets range from $80–250 per square foot. Delivery and installation are available.

The wrapped fibers, metal, or stoneware tile are extremely durable and very easy to maintain.

Further information, prices, slides/photos are available.

Top Left: *The Explaination*
Bottom Left: *Garden of the Gods*
Right: *Anasazi*

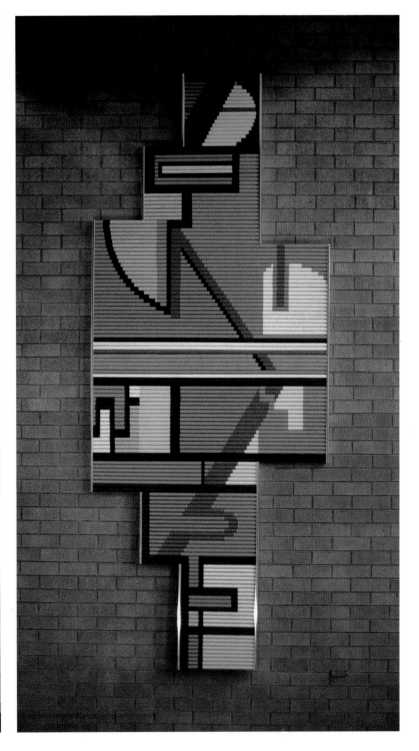

Bill Wheeler

Studio 1617
1617 Silverlake Boulevard
Los Angeles, CA 90026
(213) 660-7991

Bill Wheeler has been creating limited edition original prints and paintings for public and private commissions since 1970. He also has over 10 years experience working in collaboration with designers and architects doing site-specific installations. His wall constructions are made of masonite and/or archival plastics incorporating iridescent and metallic surfaces, designed to be security mounted.

He is a versatile artist able to accept and incorporate into his artwork suggestions and modifications supplied by the client. Such teamwork creates an installation that becomes an integral part of the interior space.

Mixed media on masonite and plastic

Monotype on masonite with acrylic and wax crayons

Printed in Japan ©1992 Kraus Sikes Inc. The Guild: The Designer's Reference Book of Artists

Furniture

Furniture

Furniture

Screens

Furniture

The artists represented in this section of THE GUILD exemplify the world of choices in today's hand-crafted furniture market. In the realms of both beauty and function, there has never been more diversity, more possibilities for satisfying personal tastes.

With limitless imagination, extraordinary talent and skill, these furniture artists contribute lasting monuments to the American studio movement. Here, you'll discover chairs masquerading as sculpture, dressing tables that invoke the reverence of a shrine, a bed that looks like a vessel waiting to take its occupant to sea, cabinets and chests and screens that tilt toward the exotic.

This is furniture that transcends function. Individuals and small teams of artists are working out of their studios to create furniture that heightens the experiences of home and workplace.

Here are contemporary artists who have returned to traditional values. They believe in quality, permanence, and the importance of singularity. They pay exquisite attention to detail -- to joinery, to finishes, to embellishments. They employ interesting textures and materials. They take great pride in their craft -- both structural and artistic, setting their own high standards for workmanship and aesthetics.

Professional in all aspects of their craft, and experienced in commissioned work, these furniture makers ensure integrity of design and materials. They are equally professional in matters of budget and deadlines. They may be contemporary by design, but they still provide old-fashioned, traditional guarantees of quality and performance.

These standards serve them well as more and more people today search for quality, custom-made furniture. In private homes, there is a desire to have furnishings that express personal values, whims, eccentricities. Businesses are eager to convey their corporate image, to establish a relationship with their public even before business is transacted, to project a mood compatible with the organization's mission.

Only artists who "encourage active participation of clients in the design process," "welcome collaboration with design teams," and "invite innovative commissions" are included here. Custom-designed, custom-made furniture brings limitless choices in style, materials, technique, scale, color, form and ornamentation.

This is furniture with spirit. You won't find furniture from these pages of THE GUILD in a mainstream furniture showroom or home furnishings store. These furniture makers are creating one-of-a-kind heirlooms of tomorrow. Their clients will be people who care about quality, ingenuity, design singularity and craftsmanship.

John Blazy

John Blazy Designs
P.O. Box 364
11729 Peckham Avenue
Hiram, OH 44234
(216) 569-7134

Using a vast array of visual references and design influences, from cooling fins on engines to Oriental architecture, John Blazy creates limited production furniture using wood, glass, and man-made materials to exactly fulfill the vision of the client/designer.

John will be glad to collaborate with design professionals on work normally installed within one to two months.

Prices start at $990 for oriental tables, $2900 for neon tables.

Top: *The Orient Goes Modern,* ebonized oak, 60" x 19" x 17"
Right: *Crimson Tunnel Syndrome,* neon, walnut veneers, ABS pipe, mirrors and melamine, 43" Dia. x 18"
Inset: *Crimson Tunnel Syndrome,* overhead view shows inter-reflective effect of neon and mirror

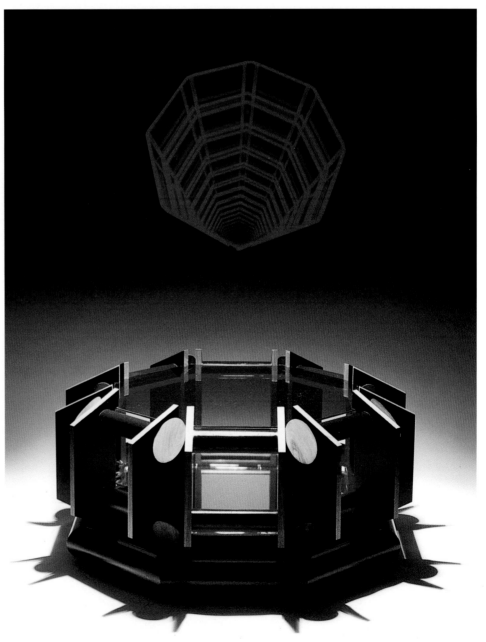

Tomas Braverman

TOMAS
1135 N. Topanga Canyon Boulevard
Topanga, CA 90290
(310) 455-1184
FAX (310) 455-1184

Tomas designs and builds furniture, and bas-relief sculpture for designers, architects, and individual clients. His training in Kyoto, Japan; Seville, Spain; Florence, Italy and Mexico provides the broad base of design and technical skill which he applies to each commission. He himself cuts many of the woods used. Each is carefully selected for color, texture and grain, and finished to achieve an antique-quality patina.

Prices range from $500 to $28,000. Allow from two to six months for delivery, following design approval and price contract.

Collectors of TOMAS furniture include Sidney Sheldon, Larry Hagman, Louis L'Amour, Robert Wagner, Harry Reinsch (Bechtel Corp.) and Robert DeNiro.

Each commission is executed with the specific needs of the client in mind.

Andalusian sofa table, top from a single slab of oak, hand-forged hardware, 28"H x 20"W x 86"L

Florentine breakfront (built-in), 9'H x 16'L

Headboard, carved from a single slab of walnut, 2 1/4" x 42"H x 6'6"L

Printed in Japan ©1992 Kraus Sikes Inc. The Guild: The Designer's Reference Book of Artists

Robert Caldwell

Designer/Craftsman
Rt. 1, Box 40-A
Brownsboro, TX 75756
(903) 852-6400

Robert operates a one-man woodworking studio located in the peaceful woods of rural east Texas. He is devoted to the creation of fine, contemporary furniture and decorative accessories, available both in limited editions and one-of-a-kind. A carefully selected array of pieces can be produced in larger quantities and are available to the wholesale market.

Robert is open to collaboration with client and professional alike. Custom work is encouraged.

Robert's work can best be characterized as contemporary in design yet traditional in technique. He strives to create work which reflects a blending of straightforward architectural elements with a reverence for the beauty of the wood itself. He values gracefulness, delicacy, and harmony.

Paul Caron

Furniture Magician
328 Stone Mountain Road
Black Mountain, NC 28711
(704) 669-4625

Mainly a custom furniture designer/builder for 20 years, Paul Caron is a craftsman of broad experience, including architectural woodworking, aircraft interiors, and antique restoration. Spiral stairs are a specialty. Any classic style can be reproduced or Paul is happy to create new designs or collaborate with other designers. Quotations will be promptly submitted on receipt of drawings.

Tiara, shown, a limited edition series in maple includes: bed ($3,100), night stand ($450–$700). Also designed are: 4 drawer chest, highboy, lowboy, mirror, armoire. Other pieces can be designed to match. All are available plain, with the rose-lattice carving in padouk (inset) or a custom designed medallion (extra cost). Crating and shipping or personal delivery extra.

Printed in Japan ©1992 Kraus Sikes Inc. The Guild: The Designer's Reference Book of Artists

Tony Clarke

Clarke Fine Furniture
One Cottage Street, 5th Floor
Easthampton, MA 01027
(413) 527-2127

Tony Clarke offers a wide range of design and fabrication possibilities; marquetry, parquetry, custom veneering, inlay, relief and sculptural carving, decorative joinery, turning and stained glass. Clarke's work is often characterized by strong geometric shapes, bold inlays, and graceful curves.

Clarke's architectural work has included kitchens, wet bars, offices, staircases, a wide range of built-in cabinetry, custom moldings, and furniture.

A high standard of quality and respect for budgetary and scheduling requirements is brought to every project. Prices for furniture range from $500 to $20,000.

Photos: Steve LaKatos

Top: end tables, walnut, curly koa, ebony
Bottom: dining table, mahogany, ebony, marble

Culin Colella

Ray Culin, Janis Colella
632 Center Avenue
Mamaroneck, NY 10543
(914) 698-7727
FAX (914) 698-6457

Ray Culin and Janis Colella bring together a special marriage of backgrounds in architecture, furniture design, sculpture, and woodworking.

Their distinctive blend of artistic flair and attention to detail has raised the combination of the fanciful and the practical to an artform. This is profoundly evident in their design and production of unique furniture, cabinetry, sculpture, architectural woodworking, and specialty finishing. Wide-ranging services, from design to fabrication, include one-of-a-kind and limited edition pieces, as well as contract furniture.

Works by Culin/Colella, which incorporate over thirty years of experience, are on display at Burlington House, Phillip Brothers, and Citicorp, and may be found in many fine homes and galleries in the tri-state area.

Details are available upon request.

Photos: Rick Albert

Top Left: *Purple Heart Coffee Table*, purple heart, black dyed veneer, inlays and gloss lacquer, 36" x 15" x 52", designed by Ray Culin
Bottom Left: *Mahogany Poster Chest*, mahogany, curly maple, fiddleback mahogany, satin rub lacquer, 48" x 64" x 32", designed by Janis Colella
Right: *Curly Maple Print Chest*, curly maple, semi-gloss lacquer, 26" x 30" x 53", designed by Janis Colella
Opposite Page: *Giagni Dining Table*, myrtle & anegré veneer, curly maple legs, 78"D x 29"H, designed by Janis Colella

Printed in Japan ©1992 Kraus Sikes Inc. The Guild: The Designer's Reference Book of Artists

Culin Colella; Ray Culin, Janis Colella, 632 Center Avenue, Mamaroneck, NY 10543, (914) 698-7727, FAX (914) 698-6457

Photos: Rick Albert

Jeffrey Cooper

Designer of Sculptural Furnishings in Wood
135 McDonough Street
Portsmouth, NH 03801
(603) 436-7945

Animal Chairs are special pets!
They are child sized chairs for:
 your living room,
 your child's bedroom,
 the nursery or playroom,
 the day care center or preschool,
 a Children's Museum,
 a Children's Hospital,
 a public library children's room,
 a dental, pediatric or therapists office,
 a grandparent's house.

Animal Chairs brighten the lives of children
and adults. They have received the Stewart
Nelson Award from the League of New
Hampshire Craftsmen, a scholarship from
the American Crafts Council, and the major
commission for the Texas Children's Hospital
pictured at right.

Please call or write for "More About Animal
Chairs by Jeffrey Cooper," for prices, and to
learn how to purchase or commission Animal
Chairs for your setting.

Ask about Animal Chair Kits.

112 Furniture

Marc D'Estout

1040 N. Branciforte Avenue
Santa Cruz, CA 95062
(408) 458-1752

Working from an aesthetic foundation in fine arts (MFA in sculpture from San Jose State University), award winning designer Marc D'Estout produces furnishings and lighting that combine an elegance of form with the visual and tactile drama of diverse materials.

Residential and commercial commissions are created with the utmost concern for structural integrity and utility.

Photographs and prices are available upon request.

Top: *Shield*, sconces, steel with patina, 34"H x 4"W x 4"D
Bottom: *Josephine*, table, copper, steel, etched glass, 31"H x 35"W x 19"D

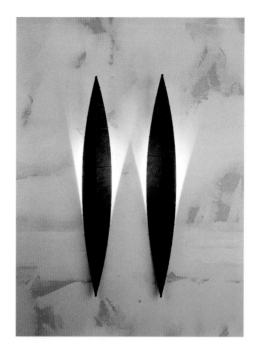

Jeremiah de Rham

de Rham Custom Furniture
43 Bradford Street
Concord, MA 01742
(508) 371-0353

Building commissioned furniture since 1981, de Rham designs pieces in response to customers functional and aesthetic requirements, as well as his own artistic vision. de Rham emphasizes the sculptural and spatial qualities inherent in furniture without neglecting function. Every piece is meticulously crafted.

See de Rham's work in *THE GUILD 5 & 6.*

Collaboration with architects and gallery inquiries welcome.
Slides, prices and scheduling available upon request.

Recent price range: $2,000–$14,000.

Top Left: bench, curly cherry
  55"W x 18"D x 23"H
Top Right: detail, desk
Bottom: desk, cherry crotch slab,
  rosewood, 66"W x 40"D x 29"H

Printed in Japan. ©1992 Kraus Sikes Inc. The Guild: The Designer's Reference Book of Artists

Glenn R. Dilts

Glenwood Crafts
18436 Knox Lake Road
Fredericktown, OH 43019
(614) 694-4373

Heirloom quality rocking horses in cherry and walnut are the specialty of woodcrafter Glenn Dilts. Introduced to woodcarving at the age of five by his father, who needed shear pins for a corn cultivator, Dilts has been carving ever since. He has displayed his work in Ohio, Michigan, Indiana, the Carolinas, Tennessee, Pennsylvania, West Virginia, and Washington, D.C.

Horses for rocking are approximately 20 inches at the shoulder on 4-foot rockers. A smaller version (@ 15 inches at the shoulder) is available on 3-foot rockers. Each horse is numbered and dated.

Bridles and saddles, for decorative purposes only, are available. Horses begin at $500. Average completion time: 1–2 months.

Top: walnut rocking horse, 4'L
Bottom: cherry rocking horse, 4'L, walnut rocking horse, 3'L

Kevin Earley

1231 E. Wilson Street
Madison, WI 53703
(608) 256-5171

Kevin's recent designs explore the decorative possibilities of dyed veneer used as inlay and textured paint complementing wood.

Collaborations with the client are encouraged.

Delivery time is two to six months and prices are available on request.

Top: dining/console table, 1991, maple, paint, 29" x 36" x 86"
Bottom: detail, chifforobe, 1991, English sycamore, beech, dyed inlay
Inset: wardrobe, 1991, English sycamore, beech, dyed inlay, 92" x 83" x 27"

Joseph I. Galvan

Joseph Galvan Studio
3533 Kelton Avenue
West Los Angeles, CA 90034
(310) 390-7940
FAX (310) 391-0961

Joseph has created sculpture and functional art in acrylic for fifteen years. He has developed original techniques for carving and harmonizing acrylic with media such as glass, metal, and lighting. Projects include commissioned one-of-a-kind creations, made-to-specification architectural installations, and limited editions.

Brochure and price list available.

Top: lighting: art glass and copper foil shade, acrylic column, halogen lighting. Left: 67"H; center: 40"H; right: 71"H
Bottom: console table, acrylic base with handcarved design, neon lighted, glass top, 60"W x 34"H

Johanna Okovic Goodman

Okovic/Goodman Studio
718 S. 22nd Street
Philadelphia, PA 19146
(215) 546-1448

Johanna Okovic Goodman uses "found chairs" to create functional sculpture. These wood chairs are built up directly with acrylic medium or stuffed and painted to create a unique object.

The colors are protected with multiple coats of polyurethane. Goodman's color and execution are of the highest quality. Only natural wood chairs are used. The Santa Fe and Folk Art styles featured employ mixed media: ribbon, fabric, beads, hemp, oil cloth, and hand-made paper. All add to the three-dimensional qualities without sacrificing functionality.

Clients can use their own chairs or the artist will supply them. Prices range from $250 to $800. Two week delivery.

Goodman's work is featured in galleries and stores across the country.

Photos by Robert Goodman.

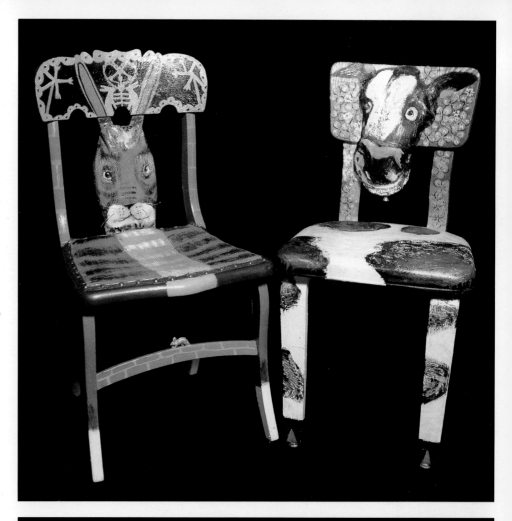

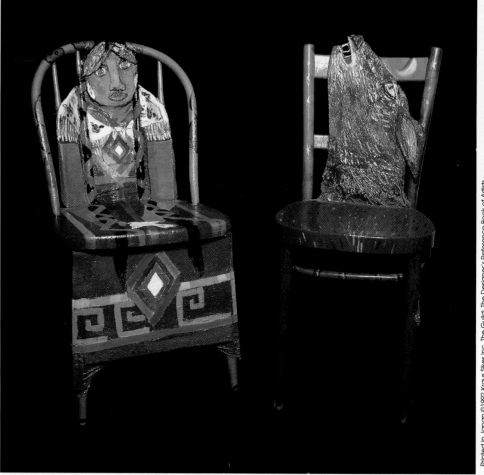

Printed in Japan ©1992 Kraus Sikes Inc. The Guild: The Designer's Reference Book of Artists

Greg Sheres Studio

Gregory D. Sheres
9902 NW 52 Terrace
Miami, FL 33178
(305) 477-4200

Greg Sheres brings fine art to furniture. Experienced as a painter and sculptor, the artist designs and creates innovative furniture in a variety of quality mediums including: marble, stainless steel, brass, wood, and glass. Mr. Sheres is internationally reknowned for his hand-painted granite and marble tables. All of these tables are done to the clients custom specifications. In addition to these original art tables, the artist is now designing and producing a striking line of stainless steel table bases, accented with gold plated brass. These sculptural pieces take glass tops, and are available in any size or height from end tables to conference tables.

List prices range from $1,800 to $20,000. Lead time is 2–3 months.

Call or write for catalog.

Top Left: *Milano,* dining table base, polished stainless steel with gold-plated brass
Top Right: end table, hand-painted marble, 36" x 36" x 19"H
Bottom: cocktail table, hand-painted granite, 68" x 38" x 17"

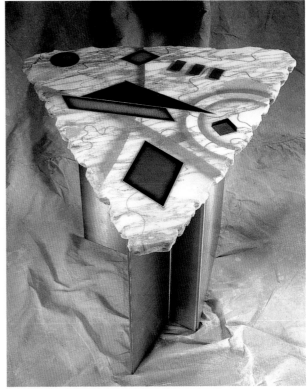

Jeanine Guncheon
John Jandy Anderson

128 Chicago Avenue
Oak Park, IL 60302
(708) 386-8208

Guncheon and Anderson design, construct and paint art furniture. The well-built pieces are hand-painted with water colors. The paintings draw on symbolic, mythical, whimsical and folk elements while defying stylistic classification.

All surfaces are hand finished with six coats of lacquer for permanence and beauty.

Guncheon and Anderson will create original designs or collaborate with designers, architects and clients.

Prices range from $450–$3,500.
Slides available upon request.

Right: lingerie chest, 70"H x 19"W x 19"D
Below: *Circus Woman*, 48"H x 16"W x 12"D

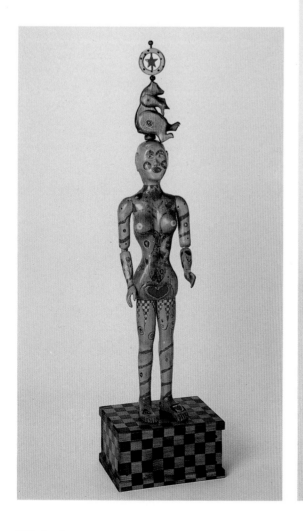

Printed in Japan © 1992 Kraus Sikes Inc. The Guild: The Designer's Reference Book of Artists

Bernard Henderson

Bernard Henderson, custom cabinetmakers
230 West Queen Lane-Rear
P.O. Box 44153
Philadelphia, PA 19144
(215) 843-1811
FAX (215) 438-7844

Bernard Henderson has designed and built furniture for individuals, architects, designers and corporate clients. He is comfortable working in a wide range of styles, woods, veneers and custom finishes.

He is pleased to provide prompt quotations for individual commissions and professional projects.

Top Left: detail, entertainment center
Top Right: curved-door entertainment center, mappa burl, ebony, 36"W x 75"H x 26"D
Bottom: breakfront, african mahogany, 84"W x 72"H x 20"D

Trent Hickmon

7217 Eckstrom Avenue
San Diego, CA 92111
(619) 560-0490

Trent Hickmon accepts commissions to design and build furniture for private, commercial and public spaces. Trent's designs utilize the images and objects of our daily lives to awaken the traditional and create the new. Each piece is designed with the needs and proportions of the individual and their environment in mind to assure maximum comfort.

Prices begin at $1,000 with delivery time from two to six months.

Below: *Let's Rock,* first in a series of musical chairs, rosewood, spalted beech, mahogany and acrylic

Craig Houx

Branch Water Trading Co.
P.O. Box 568
Big Sur, CA 93920
(408) 667-2474

The organic, wild feel of Craig Houx's sculptural willow furniture adds vitality and aliveness to all interior settings. These rustic and contemporary, Zen-like designs blend well with all decors giving one a sense of happiness and well-being.

Houx especially enjoys creating custom pieces for designers and architects. His work gives distinction to homes, bed and breakfast inns, wineries, ski lodges, and spa/retreats throughout the country. Heartfelt designs go into creating works of beauty, comfort, and durability. Like the craftsmen of previous ages, Houx creates his willow furniture to last beyond a lifetime.

Award Of Merit received at Mill Valley Fall Arts Festival.

Lead time for orders is four to twelve weeks. Studio appointments are accepted, and brochures provided upon request.

Wild Equinox Chair, $350

Santa Lucia Settee, $575; High Mesa Table, $200; Ottoman, $150; Nacimiento Chair, $350

Keralas

Bill Flusche
Rt. 1, Box 315
Moatsville, WV 26405
(304) 457-2078

Whether integrating his vision into existing environments or creating a single piece, Bill Flusche translates the intense dialogue between clients and wood.

Personalizing the instruments of clients' daily lives is his special interest.

The cradle is an example of Bill fusing his vision with the clients'. This is an aesthetic solution to practical problems of height, balance, safety, and soft lines.

The china cabinet with its concave sides and faceted front is a result of close collaboration with the clients.

As a result of working closely with his clients, Bill's work "looks like it's always been here."

Dimitrios Klitsas

705 Union Street
West Springfield, MA 01089
(413) 732-2661

The challenge of surpassing the client's woodcarving expectations is Dimitrios Klitsas' main goal. Mr. Klitsas works in close collaboration with professionals and individuals while adding his considerable experience in the fine art of wood carving.

You are cordially invited to discover custom-designed, meticulously hand-carved architectural elements or interior furnishings. Examples include capitals, columns, brackets, entrances, tables, chairs, beds, mantles, etc. These lavish creations can be used in exterior or interior applications, as dictated by the client's needs.

Custom designed hand-made carvings have been destined for, among others, Allan Greenberg, Architect; John Blatteau, Architect; Robert A.M. Stern, Architect; Kohn Pedersen Fox Associates; The Heritage Trust of Rhode Island and world-renowned celebrities.

Photo: Ilias D. Kanaveros ©1991

Photo: Ilias D. Kanaveros ©1991

Bill Klug

Art Glass Environments, Inc.
174 Glades Road
Boca Raton, FL 33432
(407) 391-7310
FAX (407) 391-8447

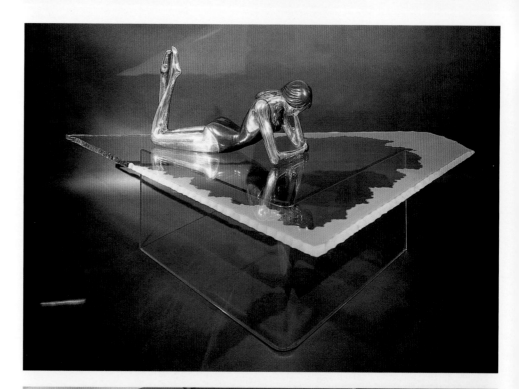

"Highly" carved "heavy" glass is a specialty of Bill Klug and his company, Art Glass Environments, Inc. which produces a comprehensive line of custom tables, table bases, and screens.

Using state of the art techniques, Klug may choose to laminate colored glass to the clear glass and/or bend the glass to suit his design, creating striking special effects.

A.G.E., Inc. employs several experienced artists/craftsmen dedicated to excellence in their skills.

Commissions include furniture, screens, and sculpture, as well as leaded, stained and beveled glass architectural projects. See page 48 in *The GUILD 7: The Architect's Source of Artists and Artisans,* for more information about his company.

Brochures and quotations upon request.

Photos by Photographers II, Miami, FL.

Top: carved glass cocktail table with bent glass base, 60" x 60" x ¾"
Bottom: carved bronze glass partition/screen, 80" x 80" x ½"
Below: bent glass "bench table" with carved southwestern design, 20" x 60" x ¾"

Ray Lewis

Fauna Collection
P.O. Box 370
Depoe Bay, OR 97341
(503) 765-2620

Ray Lewis creates chairs of fantasy and function. They are equally impressive in a corporate collection or residential setting.

The chairs are made of sand-cast aluminum alloy, hand-polished to a fine silver tone. Seats are black leather. Each limited edition chair is numbered and signed by the artist.

They are at once collectible art and fine handcrafted furniture.

The Eagle Chair was the recipient of the 1990 Niche Award for Metal Sculpture. Fauna Collection was featured at the Atlantic International Museum of Art and Design.

The Fauna Chairs are shown in numerous galleries and in corporate and private collections throughout the U.S.

Each chair is $2,800. Please allow 4 to 6 weeks for delivery. A brochure is available on request.

Top Left: *Rabbit*
Top Center: *Table*
Top Right: *Horse*
Bottom: *Dolphin, Impala, Eagle*

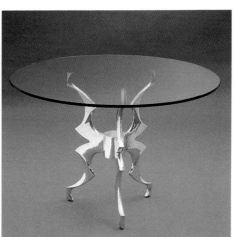

Malakoff & Jones

Peter Malakoff and Norman Jones
Schoonmaker Building
10 Liberty Ship Way #4139
Sausalito, CA 94965
(415) 332-7471
FAX (415) 332-2481

Peter Malakoff and Norman Jones have designed and built art cabinetry and furniture in the San Francisco area for the past eight years. With their knowledge and appreciation of both ancient and foreign cultures, they demonstrate in their work a distinctive interplay between craft and fine art, with a sensitive attention to detail.

They welcome innovative commissions from the architectural, corporate and private worlds.

All photos: *Egypto-Deco Pharaoh Cabinet*, inspired by objects found in Tutankhamun's tomb. Privately commissioned. Completed 1/8/89. 120"W (180"W open) x 90"H x 28"D. Materials: sycamore, satinwood, ebony, ivory, gold, lacquer

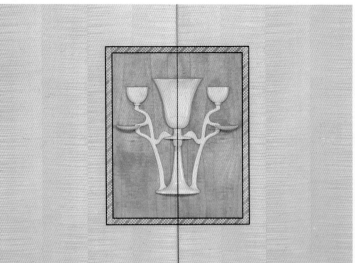

David J. Marks

David J. Marks Designer Craftsman
2128 Marsh Road
Santa Rosa, CA 95403
(707) 526-2763

David Marks, a self-taught furniture maker with a background in art, enjoys making sculptural pieces that are finely detailed. Adhering to high standards of quality, he draws on skills of bent wood lamination, carving, inlay, veneering, and fine finishes.

A faculty member of the Baulines Crafts Guild in Sausalito, CA, since 1989, Marks has maintained his studio in Santa Rosa, CA for the past twelve years, designing and building one-of-a-kind pieces for commissions and galleries. He has also created marquetry dining tables, marquetry floors, and limited editions of chairs. Marks' work is currently in collections on the east and west coasts. He has received numerous awards including Best of Show 1988, 1991, from the Sonoma County Museum, CA.

Top Left: glass top dining table, 1988, Burmese padauk, Brazilian rosewood, 74" x 46" x 30"

Top Right: *Scarab Chair*, 1991, wenge, maple, ebony, 24" x 24" x 37½"

Bottom: table, inspired by ancient Egypt, 1991, mahogany, quilted mahogany, gold leaf, lapis lazuli, ivory, ebony, 71" x 18" x 16"

George F. Martell

Martell's Metal Works
76 Dewey Avenue, P.O. Box 1054
Attleboro, MA 02703
(508) 761-9130

Award-winning designer metalsmith George F. Martell creates functional art for designers, architects, individuals, and corporations. He enjoys collaborating to create one-of-a-kind or limited edition pieces. His work, appreciated for its fine lines and durable materials, also includes baker's racks, brass and copper weathervanes, gates, 23K goldleafed items, and historic commissions, Martell is a part-time faculty member at the Rhode Island School of Design.

His *Newportia* table (Below) displays classic lines in black laquered steel graced by a blue pearl granite top.

Dragon Master (Top) is made of steel with a verde wash and features a hand-forged dragon's head and tail with bearded faces on the armrests.

Milton David McClaskey

Point Reyes Cabinet & Furniture Co.
11101 State Route One
P.O. Box 441
Point Reyes Station, CA 94956
(415) 663-1482
FAX (415) 663-1856

Milton McClaskey designs and builds furniture in the San Francisco Bay Area. For the past nine years he has worked together with clients to create unique pieces that fit the homes and serve the needs of the clients. His use of unusual native California hardwoods produces furniture that is singular and beautiful; exotic woods are also used, as in the pictured bed of bubinga and wenge with white lacquered armoires and headboard surround.

He will provide prices and delivery times from your drawings. References and other information upon request.

Motorré

Mark T. Bolesky
154 N. Diamond Street
Mansfield, OH 44902
(419) 526-9663
FAX (419) 526-0075

Motorré creates furniture and furnishings for the home and the professional office suite where space calls for distinctive pieces that speak elegance and class.

Our studio, stocked with rare woods from South America, Africa, Asia and the forests of North America, brings together the requirements of the client with our creative design and craftsmanship.

Tables, credenzas, divider screens, desks, book cases and cabinetry can be created for the home, the professional office, or the private apartment.

Your vision can be hand-crafted in any material and shape to provide unique pieces to define your home, office or apartment.

Motorré offers consultant services for the interior designer, the production shop, as well as the private client.

Quatre Yeux Collection

Motorré, Mark T. Bolesky, 154 N. Diamond Street, Mansfield, OH 44902, (419) 526-9663, FAX (419) 526-0075

John A. Morrison

Cornerstone Glassworks
2530 Joe Field Road #11
Dallas, TX 75229
(214) 247-8188

John Morrison has been producing fine carved and etched glass for architects, interior designers, and private collectors for the past nine years.

After opening Cornerstone Glassworks, his Dallas area studio, John has produced award-winning art pieces displayed in galleries and shows from Seattle to New York, and California to Norway.

In addition to fine art, John designs and carves glass for tabletops, lamps, entry ways, enclosures, mirrors, firescreens, wall clocks, and divider walls.

John's company, Cornerstone Glassworks, offers the broadest application of carved glass techniques available anywhere.

Below: *Rock Edge Table,* 48" x 96"

Peter Handler Studio

2400 W. Westmoreland Street
Philadelphia, PA 19129
(215) 225-5555
FAX (215) 225-3964

Peter Handler designs and produces custom and limited production anodized aluminum, glass, granite, leather, and fabric furniture for the home and office. Using high-strength clear adhesives to join metal and glass or stone, he creates furniture which is eminently functional, yet esthetically and structurally minimal.

Working with an excellent commercial anodizer, Handler produces a broad range of colors, frequently developing new hues to meet his client's needs. Anodized aluminum, with its luminous color spectrum, has a hard, permanent surface that is highly resistant to scratches and stains, retaining its beauty with a minimum of care.

Retail prices range from $1300 for an occasional table to $9,000 for a conference table. Delivery time ranges from two to four months. Catalog and aluminum samples are available upon request.

Top Left: *Elemental,* coffee table, 40" x 54" x 15"
Top Right: *Metronome,* table, glass design by Joan Irving, 20"H x 22"D
Bottom: *Gabrielle,* loveseat, designed by Peter Handler and Paul Murray, 30" x 70" x 40"

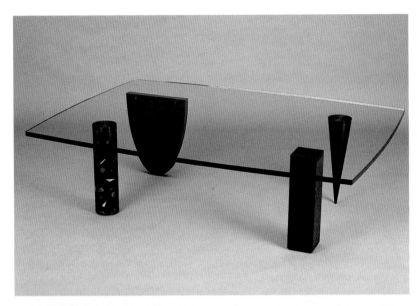

David A. Ponsler

Wonderland Products, Inc.
5772 Lenox Avenue
P.O. Box 6074
Jacksonville, FL 32236
(904) 786-0144
FAX (904) 786-0145

David A. Ponsler has been producing furniture and architectural metalwork for 16 years. He enjoys collaboration and designing creative solutions to specific and vague design criteria.

The coffee table (Top), of forged steel and copper was created in response to a request for a table with organic ornamentation within a geometric framework.

The twin size *African Bed* (Below), with its stylized horns and setting sun was an integral part of a designer's vignette of an African theme.

Design time is generally one to two weeks, with production averaging three to seven weeks.

Photography by Daryl Bunn.

William Rosenberger

(George Rosenberger)
13611 Beskeen Road
Herald, CA 95638
(209) 748-2679

George creates functional and aesthetically pleasing works of art which are shown in many galleries and museums. His tables and abstract female sculptures have also been featured in previous issues of THE GUILD.

In his latest series, George is creating one-of-a-kind chairs by heating, bending and welding 1/4" stainless steel rods into delightful patterns. The crazy quilt cushions for these chairs are created in collaboration with California artist, Lizabeth Ruden. Lizabeth uses vintage fabric, lace, buttons and beadwork which she has collected for years. Her wonderful sense of color and pattern add a finishing statement to each unique, artistically free-form chair.

Brochure and prices available upon request.

R. Walsh Forge & Foundry

Rt. 1, Box 83, Studio G
Stockholm, WI 54769
(715) 442-3102
FAX (715) 442-3102

Detail of table leg

Tables, lighting, candle holders, curtain hardware, fireplace tools, and clocks are a few of the items available through R. Walsh's line of fine furnishings. The R. Walsh Forge & Foundry also offers custom work which can be based on the client's concept, or they will design and forge custom metalwork ranging from coffee tables to large architectural projects, gates, fencing, railings, etc.

The R. Walsh Forge & Foundry is accustomed to working long distance and can design large architectural projects working from a blueprint, sketch or snapshot. All ironwork is available in a full pallet of colors, patinas, and textures. The R. Walsh Forge & Foundry has been serving the design industry for 18 years.

Call or FAX for brochure.

Hand forged table with leaves

Brian F. Russell

Brian Russell Designs
2537 Broad Avenue
Memphis, TN 38112
(901) 327-1210
FAX (901) 452-1281

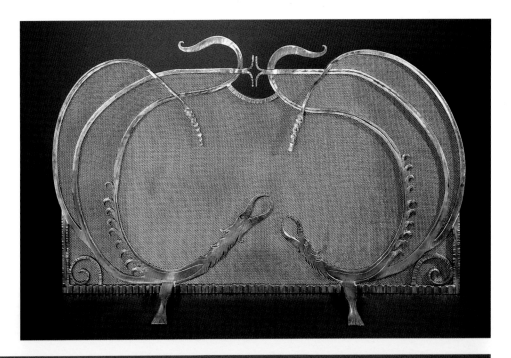

Brian Russell specializes in creating original functional designs using forged and fabricated metals as his primary medium. Influenced by Art Nouveau and Deco, he is developing his own language through the articulated forms and sensuous surfaces of the furniture, gates, railings, lighting, firescreens and accessories highlighted in his brochure. Firescreen prices range from $525 to $4000. Forged steel table bases start at $900. Gates and railings are priced on a per job basis

Top: *Phoenix*, firescreen, $1200
Bottom: *Communique*, coffee table, $4200

Jeffrey Sass

Jeffrey Sass: Metal Work
231 Quechee-W. Hartford Road
White River Jct., VT 05001
(802) 295-6689

Jeffrey Sass integrates industrial scrapmetal, antique castings and sentimental bric-a-brac into heirloom-quality art furnishings. Each one-of-a-kind creation reflects something of the client or setting, be it playful whimsy, city chic, stately Adirondack repose or the southern grace inspired by Sass's collection of Savannah castings.

This "Home Welcome" twin bed was inspired by a tiny antique parlor stove with ceramic insert. It's recessed headboard provides a private cove for personal essentials.

The Nursery Rhyme Mirror is a harmony of one client's cherished rhymes and memorabilia, and Sass's interplay of machined steel gunparts. The gunpart sculptures of Jeffrey Sass are delightfully provocative, appreciated by some as whimsy and others as profound moral statements.

Innovative solutions in metal. Inquiries welcomed. Brochure upon request.

Martha Sears

264 West 77th Street
New York, NY 10024
P.O. Box 1153
Washington Green, CT 06793
(212) 877-7873
FAX (212) 877-7873

Martha Sears designs and builds provocative table sculptures using mixed media: ceramics, glass, wood, metals and plastics. They are visually intriguing and challenge one's sense of furniture as sculpture and sculpture as furniture. Tactile qualities of the clay predominate. Pieces range from game tables to coffee tables to conference tables.

Commissions and collaborations are accepted.

Low to no maintenance is required. Typical turnaround time is 4–16 weeks.

A portfolio and price list is available upon request.

Top Left: *Dance Table Series I,* mixed media, 22" x 30" x 30"
Top Right: *Dance Table Series VI,* mixed media, 20" x 24"
Bottom: *Dance Table Series V,* mixed media, 20" x 26" x 28"

Anne Shutan

RR1, Box 991
Newfane, VT 05345
(802) 365-7118

Anne Shutan creates one-of-a-kind pieces of furniture and sculpture, affirming the sensuous nature of wood. Through her work, she has discovered that art has as much to do with finesse and taking chances as with intelligence and craft. Anne travels all over the country to discuss projects with her clients. She then returns to her studio to design and create the piece. The process from conception to delivery can take anywhere from one to six months. Please contact the artist for information regarding commissions.

A portfolio is available upon request.
Prices: $2,000–$10,000

Top: bench, walnut, 16" x 60" x 60"h
Bottom: dining table, walnut, 30" x 40" x 30"h

Steve Smith

Smithwork Studio
13691 State, Route 249
Ney, OH 43549
(419) 658-2812

Unyielding materials like stone and steel
become functional sculpture in the studio of
Steve Smith. His enthusiasm and awareness
of symbolism are evident in his work. Smith
designs tables of steel and stone (from
quarry slate to Baroque marble). Custom
designs are available, made to a client's
order.

Trained as a sculptor, Smith has been
working with clay, stone, and steel to
produce decorative, functional, and
architectural work for more than 16 years.

His current works include adding wood
to some of his tables and wallpieces.

Prices for stone and steel tables begin
at $550.

Top: sandwich table, slate, forged and
   fabricated steel, 25" high, $800
Bottom: dolmen table, slate and forged
   steel, 26" high, $500

Bill Stankus

611 Bradford Parkway
DeWitt, NY 13224
(315) 446-6761

Bill Stankus designs and builds custom furniture for the home and office. His work helps create spaces that are inviting, functional and warm.

Available items include:
   Tables and chairs
   Writing desks
   Cabinets
   End tables
   Beds

All items are made in the customer's personal choice of wood, finishes and sizes. Each piece features the true comfort of handmade furniture with soft edges and handcrafted patina.

Prices for typical pieces begin under $2000. Most orders can be met eight weeks after approved design.

To create a one-of-a-kind environment, contact Bill Stankus at his workshop.

Top: silver chest, koa, bubinga and ebony
Bottom: cabinet, walnut, white oak and
   canarywood

Marcia Stuermer

Fossil Faux Furniture
619 Sanchez
San Francisco, CA 94114
(415) 861-1933

Marcia Stuermer merges the primitive with witty glimpses of the future in the one-of-a-kind sculptural works which appear to be made of stone but are actually made of hand-carved wood, with whimsical fossil carvings and miscellaneous inlaid electronic circuitry and components. These unique "Fossil Faux" works have been commissioned for both private and commercial use in the States and Europe, as well as seen in major publications worldwide.

Any color/tonal range is possible. All of the pieces are finished with a protective acrylic coat which makes them moisture-resistant and extremely durable. Average completion time is 2–3 weeks.

Custom and commercial commissions as well as collaborative installations are welcome. A complete price list and portfolio is available upon request.

Left: *There's No Hiding,* folding screen, 54"W x 72"H
Top Right: *Bedrock Dreams,* double bed, 66"W x 83"D x 52"H
Bottom Right: *Executive Power,* desk, 30"D x 48"W x 31"H

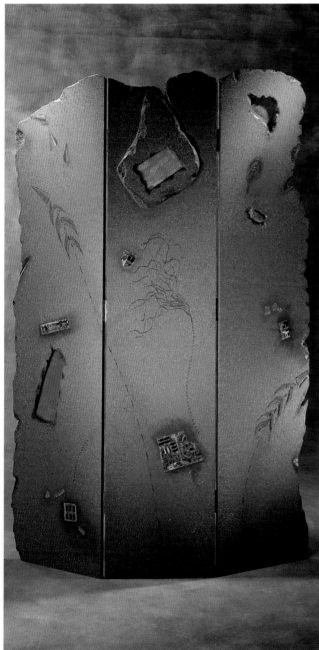

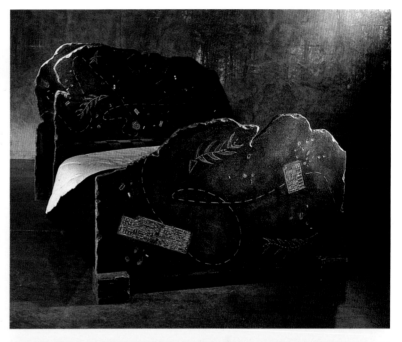

Brian Swanson

727 16th Avenue West
Kirkland, WA 98033
(206) 827-0398

Represented by:
MIA Gallery
536 First Avenue South
Seattle, WA 98104
(206) 467-8283

Brian Swanson's vision is inspired by the cast off machine parts, tools, and appliances that he collects. His designs highlight the function and beauty of parts made during an earlier time, proving durable for indoors or out. Surprise, innovation, humor, and elegance can be found in his pieces. A strong sense of design is evident along with a straightforward handling of materials.

Collaboration with design teams are welcome. Timelines negotiable.

Prices range from $800–$4,000.

Top: writing chair
Bottom: counsel chair

Photos by Eduardo Calderon ©1990

Tom McFadden Furniture

Tom McFadden
1901 Guntly Road
Philo, CA 95466
(707) 895-3606

Tom McFadden has been making fine furniture since 1963. He produces pieces of his own design for consignment to galleries as well as working closely with design professionals on custom pieces. He also enjoys collaborating with other artists.

He works in beautifully grained North American hardwoods, using time-honored construction techniques such as mortise and tenon, through dovetails, and frame and panel. All pieces are finished inside and out with polyurethane varnish and rubbed out with steel wool.

Prices begin around $1500. Production time is usually 90 days or less. A resume and portfolio are available on request.

Top: oval table, grafted walnut and ash, 48" x 72" x 30", $6500
Bottom: executive desk, california walnut, cherry and curly maple, 42" x 82" x 30", $5800

Paul Tuller

Ishiyama Company
Pierce Road, Box 64
Dublin, NH 03444
(603) 563-8884

Paul Tuller designs and builds Japanese style furniture, doors, architectural details and structures. Shoji, fusuma and wood panel doors, ranma, tokonoma, tatami rooms and post and beam structures are all executed with subtle design and precise joinery. Integrating traditionally constructed pieces into contemporary settings is a specialty.

Top: display Tansu, cherry, sitka spruce and Washi, 12" x 36" x 36"
Bottom: Shoji doors, fir, cypress and Washi, 80" x 88"; transom Ranma, white pine and fir, 13" x 88"; table, elm and granite, 12" x 27" x 31"

Printed in Japan © 1992 Kraus Sikes Inc. The Guild: The Designer's Reference Book of Artists

Gary Upton

Gary Upton Woodworking, Inc.
12856 Loma Rica Drive
Grass Valley, CA 95945
(916) 273-1449
FAX (916) 273-0619

Gary Upton has been creating collectible furniture since 1976. His work with contrasting elements is uniquely balanced through the refinement of form. A distinct impact is created through fine joinery, sculptural detail, and the sensitive use of materials.

Gary's work has been shown internationally and featured on the cover of Creative Designs in Furniture.

Custom commission / limited edition / one-of-a-kind.

Brochure and price list are available.

Top: *Chenpo Table,* black lace slate, wenge, ash, 84" x 45" x 29"H
Bottom: *Chenpo Table,* detail
Below: *Chenpo Chair,* wenge and ash, formed upholstered seat, 27" x 24" x 43"H

Wm. B. Sayre, Inc.

One Cottage Street
Easthampton, MA 01027
(413) 527-0202
FAX (413) 527-0502

Fine commissioned furniture executed to
the designs of specifying architect, interior
designer, or residential customer.

Working in the finest hardwoods available,
collaborating in a wide range of other
media to produce heirlooms of distinction
and innovation.

Full design services available. Complete
production facilities.

Brochure available upon request.

Bookcase designed by William Sayre.   ©1991 Wm. B. Sayre, Inc.

Printed in Japan ©1992 Kraus Sikes Inc. The Guild: The Designer's Reference Book of Artists

150   Furniture

Woodfellows

Jean Wagner
Middleton Business Park
8512 Fairway Place
Middleton, WI 53562
(608) 831-9337
FAX (608) 836-6514

Woodfellows welcomes extraordinary design challenges in commissioned furniture, architectural millwork and custom cabinetry. We work with specifying architects and designers for commercial, corporate and residential customers, and take pride in our uncompromising dedication to all aspects of our craft, from exquisite design to detailed construction, and from excellent response time to absolutely reliable delivery.

Woodfellows provides full service design (architectural AUTOCAD), state-of-the-art production equipment, an extensive inventory of hardwoods and veneers as well as the superb skills of a staff of 10 master artisans.

Prices, work samples on request.

Scott Wynn

1785 Egbert Avenue
San Francisco, CA 94124
(415) 467-0638

Scott Wynn has been designing and fabricating fine furniture and interior woodwork for individuals, architects, and designers for over fourteen years. He works in a wide range of styles and periods, both European and Asian, utilizing the finest of traditional and modern techniques. He can provide decorative and figurative carving as well as veneered, turned and curved work. As a licensed architect and builder, he brings a broad range of experience to his work and can collaborate with a designer on construction and stylistic detailing, as well as provide presentation, construction, or shop drawings.

All inquiries are invited.

Top Left: side chair, stained ash, aluminum
Top Center: valet chair, stained ash, birdseye maple
Top Right: arm chair, Honduras mahogany, spalted maple, redwood burl
Bottom: Inglenook, Honduras mahogany

Printed in Japan ©1992 Kraus Sikes Inc. The Guild: The Designer's Reference Book of Artists

A conversation with Bill Sayre
(furniture)

Q How do you choose and obtain your materials?

A Learning what wood to use with what piece of furniture comes with time, experience, my years of teaching and a lot of exposure to different kinds of wood. The basic woods, such as cherry, maple, and oak, I can obtain here in eastern Massachusetts. If I choose a species that is more difficult to find, I have to go to certain dealers. Sometimes I purchase wood from unexpected sources. I have a complete walnut tree in my shop that came from a church in Portland, Maine which wanted it removed from the front lawn. More recently, I've been involved in a project to import wood from Mexico. Several artists will utilize this wood and plan a show of their work. This wood is harvested in a sustainable manner, using practices that will not be harmful to the indigenous people and the forest.

Q Why do people choose custom-made furniture?

A I think by the time a client has sought me out, they've already come to the realization that what they are looking for will be an heirloom, and the piece will be worth the time, effort and money. No manufactured piece will have that same feel to it when you slide the drawer, or close the door. And just as important, the design of the piece must be as successful as the performance. When I design, I have to know what technique I will use to execute the design, or else the piece may not be structurally sound. In order to build my designs, I am constantly making new jigs and tools, and the trick is to make these things quickly yet sturdily, so I'm not spending more time making tools than I am on the piece.

Q How do you explain the process of designing a piece to clients?

A When I meet with a client, I like to take them through the process of past projects I have done. I tell them how it came to be, how long it took, why it looks the way it does. That way the client can get an overview of the process; it also gets them excited and gives them ideas of their own. Then I will produce some renderings using a basic idea with some variations. After the design is narrowed down, I make a full working drawing, and then choose the specific types of materials. My experience is that with every step, the client becomes more and more excited. People become interested in the process, and like to come to the studio. In the process they gain a greater appreciation of the time involved and the quality of a unique handmade piece.

Andrea M. Biggs
Timothy G. Biggs

279 Sterling Place
Brooklyn, NY 11238
(718) 857-9034

Andrea and Timothy Biggs are producing unique, yet classic decorative screens, utilizing specialized painting techniques from architectural trompe l'oeil to landscape and figurative work. Also shown is a faux tapestry; these, like the screens, can be commissioned in a wide variety of period and stylistic modes. Each piece involves a collaborative process between the artists and client, and includes scale drawings and maquettes.

The Biggses also produce mural paintings and specialized painted finishes for walls, ceilings, and floors. Inquiries are welcome.

Amanda Degener

1334 6th Street NE
Minneapolis, MN 55413
(612) 788-9440

Amanda Degener combines sculpture, painting, and crafts in her one-of-a-kind room dividers. Degener processes and colors all her own kozo fiber in order to guarantee archival quality handmade paper with lightfast color.

The paper panels are backed with plexiglass and are then mounted in a hardwood frame. The only maintenance required is an occasional vacuuming of dust off the paper surface.

A professional artist for over 14 years, Degener's commissions can be found at Herman Miller Inc., MI; Claremont Development Assoc., MA; CASA Midtown Center, MO; Cowles Media Co., MN; and in many private collections.

Degener works with clients from concept to installation. Snapshots and color samples may be requested for this custom-made product. Allow 4–6 weeks for delivery. Prices start at $5,000.

Top Left: *Sky on Lake*, oak, plexiglass, kozo paper, 8' x 14'
Top Right: *Sky on Lake*, oak, plexiglass, kozo paper, and sunlight, 8' x 14'
Bottom: *Quilt Beginnings* and *Mountain Echoes*, hardwood, plexiglass, and kozo handmade paper

Christina Forte

Forte® In Glass
7632 Campbell Road #308
Dallas, TX 75248
(214) 380-0011

Christina has designed and fabricated stained glass creations for public and private concerns since 1980. She has an outstanding talent for working with designers and clients to capture their imagination in glass.

Christina's own imagination seems to have no boundaries. Her works are meticulously executed in both leaded glass and the Tiffany copper foil method.

She continuously wins accolades: in the Glass Directions Show held annually by the Dallas Society of Glass Artists and most recently was applauded at the 1991 International Glass Craft Expo in Dallas. As seen in the screen below, Christina often uses Dichroic glass for a special effect in the design. At the 1990 Glass Directions Show she placed second for her originally designed lamp, *Reminiscent Rose*, that used Dichroic glass in the entire background.

Production time varies from one to two months depending on the complexity of the commission. Forte® In Glass has an extensive glass inventory to ensure the client an excellent selection for custom-designed pieces on a timely basis.

Michalene Groshek

W313 N8558 Kilbourne Road
Hartland, WI 53029
(414) 966-1074

Michalene Groshek's folding screens are distinctively shaped and rich with dense and colorful surfaces. Lush imagery and color are revealed through a merging of surface design techniques on fabric. This custom-designed fabric is laminated to contoured wood panels and integrated with painted finishes and textures. All screens are easily assembled and sealed with acrylic and polyurethane finish.

Sizes and shapes of screens vary. Heights range from three to eight feet. Color preferences and complexity of subject matter are considered in pricing. Professional designs, color models and fabric swatches are included. Commissions are welcomed. Screen prices start at $1,500.

Groshek exhibits nationally and internationally with her sculptures, screens and installations. Her work is featured in *Fiberarts Design Book Four.*

Top: *Surroundings #2,* detail, fabric on wood, mixed media
Bottom Left: *Surroundings #2,* front view, fabric on wood, mixed media, 7' x 6'6"
Bottom Right: *Surroundings #2,* back view, screen print on wood, 7' x 6'6"

Cathy Richardson

Nature's Image Studio
1201 Airport Road, Suite D
Ames, IA 50010
(515) 232-4529

Cathy Richardson combines the materials and techniques of modern studio glass art with the traditional craft of stained glass to create dynamic, colorful work. As her sculptures emerge from the heat of the kiln, she carves and etches them by sandblasting to produce vibrant, yet delicate forms. Sculptures and folding screens, made with imported and American glass, are ready to grace the most elegant homes and offices. Wall sculptures, mounted in plexiglass display boxes, are easy to hang and care for.

Production time varies from two to eight weeks, according to the size and complexity of each piece. Richardson is happy to work with clients or collaborate with designers and other craft artists. Prices range from $350 to over $5,000.

Sandblast-carved bowl, 13" Dia., $360

Mahogany and glass screen, 6' x 6 1/2', $5,000

Painted birch and glass screen, 6 1/2' x 6 1/2', $5,000

Printed in Japan ©1992 Kraus Sikes Inc. The Guild: The Designer's Reference Book of Artists

Accessories

Accessories

Accessories

Contemporary artists who create textiles, floor coverings, lighting, sculpture and objects have found the last decade to be an immensely exciting and gratifying period in their professional lives. They have been inspired by the new appreciation for their crafts as art, and by a growing market for art in corporate spaces.

An artist who creates turned wood vessels says that this area is one of many that has gained new status in recent years. Once deemed pure craft, it has in the last five years been elevated to art. Likewise, glass has gained new stature and baskets are in increasing demand in art circles. We are also witnessing a new wave of artists working in neon, metal, wood, stone and textiles. Curators of museums around the country are seeking them out,

and this new exposure continues to enhance their visibility and popularity among the art-buying public.

Many traditional crafts are also getting a new look. One of THE GUILD's rug makers talks about using new tools and materials to revitalize an old craft. She is free in today's design movement to make bold personal statements, because designers, and art lovers in general, are looking for something special.

If you're furnishing an existing space, commissioning custom-made art means finding an uncompromising match for your needs. Clients won't have to alter their colors, space, lighting or materials to fit the work; these artists specialize in making their creations fit the space. Most offer not only a portfolio of their work but will accommodate clients with drawings, color renditions, samples of materials, even models. It's the zenith of custom design.

These are artists who know the art of give and take; artists who choose to work with interior designers and art consultants because they enjoy the synergy generated by the collaborative process.

Designers benefit in extra ways when they bring an artist into the process before all the details of a building project or renovation are settled. It is at this point that spaces can be designed with the art in mind. Accessories can become dynamic focal points, animating a room, and elevating its aesthetic quality.

Designers find that working with these savvy, immensely talented, professional artists is extremely satisfying. They can be counted on not only to present solutions to design problems, but to do it on time and within the budget.

From hand-woven rugs to candlesticks and vases, freestanding sculptures, baskets and ceramic vessels, the work in this section resonates with today's design freedom -- new images, new language and new ideas. Individualization and personalization have become not only acceptable but desirable.

Art Underfoot, Inc.®

Cathy Comins, president
12 Godfrey Road
Upper Montclair, NJ 07043-1310
(201) 744-4171
By appointment

Art Underfoot, Inc.® is the key resource for contemporary American fiber artists who preserve and excel in traditional American rug-making techniques.

The *Custom Collection* features spectacular, commissionable room-size braided ($45–68 per sq. ft.) and woven rag rugs ($21–43 per sq. ft.), enhanced by the durability of newly-made textiles and the option to custom color.

The *Treasury Collection* includes the most extensive selection of one-of-a-kind museum-quality, newly-made traditionally hooked area rugs ($125–265 per sq. ft.) in America. Choose from among hundreds of patterned, adapted, and original rugs in an extraordinary variety of styles, sizes, and colors.

A catalog of either collection is $10 ($18 for both), applicable towards your first purchase.

Halsa, detail, traditionally hooked rug, Theresa Strack, 1982

Charlton Idyll, traditionally hooked rug, © Jule Marie Smith 1986, hand-dyed wool fabric, 44" x 77"

Braided rugs, © Jan Jurta 1988, wool, 7' round, 5' x 3' ovals

Rhyme & Reason, woven rag rug, © Harriet Giles 1987, cotton/cotton-blends, 10' x 14'

Kathy Cooper

Orchard House Floorcloths
Rt. 5, Box 214
King, NC 27021
(919) 994-2612

Kathy Cooper specializes in custom designed floorcloths. Large sizes are available and priced per square foot. Cooper uses a wide range of imagery in her work including abstract, floral and whimsical depictions of animals and vegetables.

Floorcloths are intended for practical use on hard-surface floors, or may be hung on walls. Made of heavy canvas, each floorcloth is hand-painted and receives several coats of varnish for a durable, yet flexible surface.

Colors will not fade. Floorcloths can be cleaned with mild soap and a damp mop. Periodic waxing is recommended to protect the varnish.

Cooper's canvases have been featured in *New York* magazine, *Country Living, House Beautiful, Gourmet, Metropolitan Home, Better Homes and Gardens Decorating, Country Homes, Come Home to Country* and *Contemporary Crafts For The Home.*

A catalogue is available.

Below: *Diagonal Checks with Stripe Border,* ©1991, private residence, Baltimore, MD, 7' x 9'

Gloria E. Crouse

Fiber Art
4325 John Luhr Road NE
Olympia, WA 98506
(206) 491-1980

Gloria Crouse creates highly textured art rugs and wall works, using unique variations of hand hooking, often in asymmetric shapes. Her work is included in many public collections including: Weyerhaeuser, SAFECO Insurance, Sea-Tac International Airport, Western State Hospital, and Waste Management.

Her book, *Hooked Rugs: New Materials, New Techniques* with accompanying video, has just been published by Taunton Press.

Prices average $125 per sq. ft.

Top: *Chivoree*, mixed yarns/yardage on
   linen, 50"H x 57" W
Bottom: *Wild Queendom*, wools,
   100"H x 36"W

Shirley Edidin

Fibers By Edidin
4149 Rogero Road
Jacksonville, FL 32211
(904) 744-0362

Shirley Edidin designs and weaves rugs
which not only serve a functional purpose
when placed on the floor, but are a
handsome addition to any room when used
as wall hangings. All rugs are reversible and
can be custom made in any size up to 42"
wide by any length to suit the needs of the
discerning customer.

Many colors are available since the artist
does her own dyeing. Fibers used are 100%
wool, or a blend of 55% wool and 45%
acrylic. All are hand-washable or dry-
cleanable.

Top: rug, 40" x 66"
Bottom Left/Right: two sides of same rug
   (showing how pattern reverses), 36" x 58"

Printed in Japan ©1992 Kraus Sikes Inc. The Guild: The Designer's Reference Book of Artists

Marilyn Forth

Handpainted Silk by Marilyn Forth
416 David Drive
N. Syracuse, NY 13212
(315) 458-3786

Marilyn Forth produces paintings on silk which possess a great deal of visual depth and color clarity. She uses a high grade of silk and fiber reactive dyes. The flowers in her art work seem to move and grow and come alive. Her wall panels and framed work bring the garden inside. Any combination of flowers may be ordered. Commissions range from $275 to $4,000 and begin with a sketch and color study on silk. Panels are washable and fade resistant. Installation services are available. Delivery in 4 to 6 weeks. Marilyn Forth has also taught courses in Textile Arts at Syracuse University. Call or write for art consultant references, commissions completed and slide sheets.

Left: *Singing Flowers*, 4' x 6'
Top Right: *Garden Memories*, Rochester Memorial Art Gallery, Rochester, NY, 3' x 3'
Bottom Right: *Primrose Abstract*, Jaro Art Gallery, 955 Madison Ave., NYC, 3' x 3'

Sara Hotchkiss

24 Hanson Street
Portland, ME 04103
(207) 775-4918

Sara Hotchkiss, handweaver, custom designs tapestry rugs which are handwoven of cotton warp and fabric in soft-shaded color variations for walls or floors. Design motifs such as borders, squares, diamonds, triangles and stripes are constructed using a traditional tapestry technique. Quality materials and a dense weave structure ensure the rugs will withstand years of use. Large sizes are available. Work is produced by commission as one-of-a-kind pieces or in limited editions. Prices range from $20–30 per sq. ft., depending on design.

Below: Maine Woods Carpet Collection

Nancy Lubin Designs

Nancy I. Lubin
13 Trim Street
Camden, ME 04843
(207) 236-4069
FAX (207) 236-6211

Handwoven throws in luxury fibers for all seasons. Nancy Lubin is a well known resource of uniquely designed throws for interior designers nationwide. Her throws appear frequently in major home design magazines. She exhibits regularly at prestigious national craft fairs and trade shows. In addition to custom designed throws, Nancy keeps an inventory of throws available for immediate purchase.

All throws pictured: 50" x 72" + fringe, brushed mohair, solid colors available.

Top: olive, taupe and oriental red plaid with design board
Left: black and white optik
Right: teal, green, navy and burgundy contemporary plaid

Old Abingdon Weavers

Grace Richey Clarke
Walcot Weavers
1808 Schuyler Avenue
Lafayette, IN 47904
(317) 742-7707
(317) 742-3472
FAX (317) 742-7707

Old Abingdon Weavers weave coverlets in traditional patterns as well as afghans, yardage, pillow covers and shams, table runners and table linens in wool and cotton. Coverlets in regular colors are from $108 to $325 wholesale.

Grace Richey Clarke has been handweaving window blinds and wall hangings in custom colors and sizes, in a wide variety of patterns, using natural fibers, and wood, since 1945. Blinds may be ordered for residential or contract installations. Prices are from $12 sq. ft., wholesale.

Walcot Weavers handweave throws in natural fibers, rich in color and texture. Custom upholstery and drapery fabrics are also woven. Throw prices are from $45 to $70 wholesale.

Delivery is normally in 4 to 6 weeks from receipt of confirmed order.

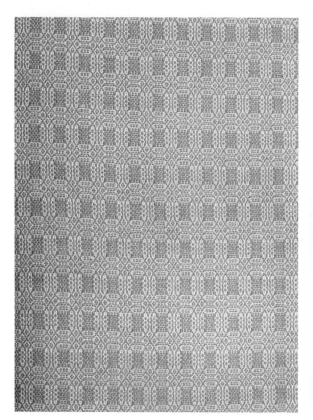

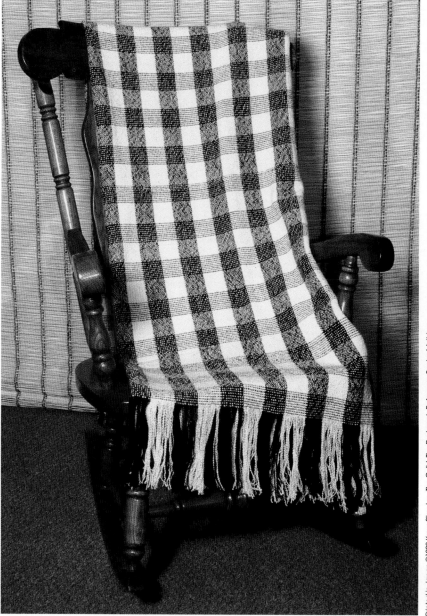

Margaret Story

MHS Designs
27 Paddock Lane
Hampton, VA 23669
(804) 851-7930

Warm and inviting additions to any room, Margaret Story's fiber designs double as hangings or rugs. Plain and textured wools are woven in Navajo designs on heavy linen.

A body of work is always available for review by slides or photos. Commissions are accepted, usually with a 6-week delivery. Durable as rugs or easily hung as hangings, with tops turned and plexiglass rods inserted, prices range $160–$900.

Right: *Desert Shadows,* 25" x 57"
Below: *Desert Blooms,* 25" x 62"

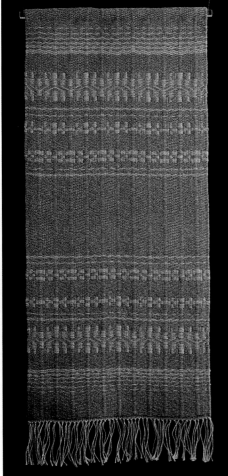

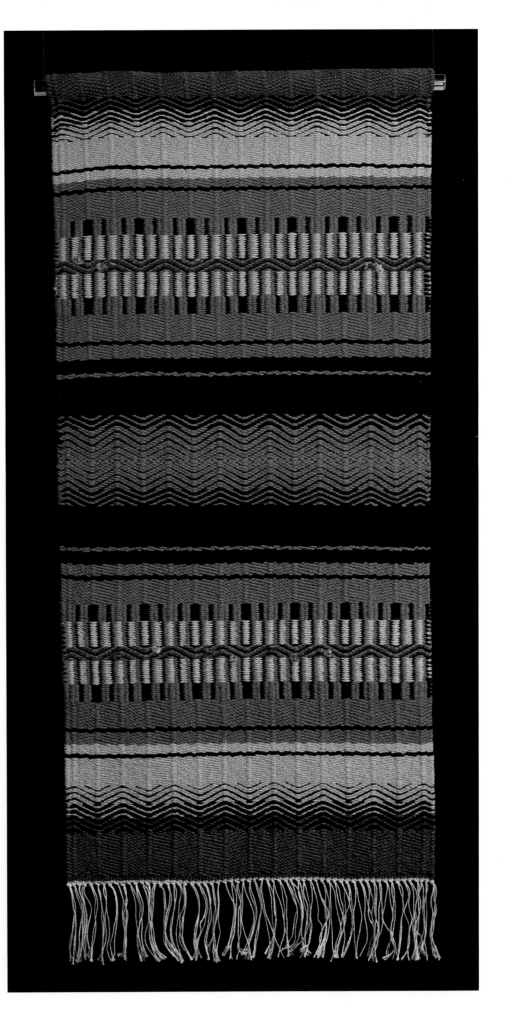

A conversation with Kathy Cooper
(painted floorcloths)

Q How do you price your work?

A In the past, I was using a much more elaborate set of terms to determine discounts, but recently I've moved closer to offering a flat discount rate to both designers and wholesalers (galleries and stores). Because people can buy my work from retail stores as well as through their designers, my main concern is that any price discrepancy between the two sources is not so severe that one outlet is detrimental to the other. I try to offer my work to designers at a discount that is attractive to them, as well as being feasible for me.

Q How did you become interested in floorcloths?

A I made my first floorcloth when I was living in an old farmhouse in Maine in the late 1970's, and was looking for something to put in my own house. My background is in weaving, but I enjoyed the spontaneity the painted medium allowed me; I could execute my ideas more quickly than I could on the loom. I also wanted to make things that were functional as well as beautiful.

Q Why do you think people choose to purchase floorcloths?

A Many of the people who buy my floorcloths are at the age where they are able to buy a nice house and they want to fill their homes with beautiful things, yet they have children at home. With floorcloths, they can have something that's beautiful and special as well as functional. The pieces are not indestructible, but they hold up better and are easier to clean than other kinds of floor coverings. I think designers particularly like to use floorcloths because it's often a more flexible option than other flooring choices; it can be a less expensive option, and the pieces can be customized.

Carol Adams

Dimensional Works of Art
2355 Main Street
Peninsula, OH 44264
(216) 657-2681

Carol's current work incorporates combinations of enamel on steel, fabric, paint, lights, lasers, chrome-plated copper, and mylar. Her "light-sculptures" create fascinating moving patterns on walls and ceilings and usually have remote control switches to change colors, and/or stop movement.

The enamel bases of the "lamps" are expressions of Carol's travel experiences, and may have raised chrome-plated copper elements. The lighting electronics are a newly invented technology by collaborator Dr. Harold Gerdes, which create an optical delight for homes or public buildings.

Carol often collaborates with architects and interior designers to coordinate or contrast these light sculptures with their projects. The sculptures change looks from day to night and add a wonderful glow when emanating from atriums and window spaces.

Brochures, slides, and prices are available upon request.

Top: *Lightscape I: S-Dance*, fabric, paint, mylar, laser, theater lights, 5½' x 5' x 2'
Bottom Left: *Laser Lamp II: Catwalk*, enamel, chrome, fabric, paints, laser, lights, 6' x 2' x 1½'
Bottom Center: *Light-Lamp I: Florida Islands*, enamel, chrome, fabric, paint, lights, mylar, 21" x 8" x 8"
Bottom Right: *Laser Lamp I: Manhattan*, copper, mylar, theater lights, laser, paint, enamel on steel, fabric, 46" x 20" x 28"

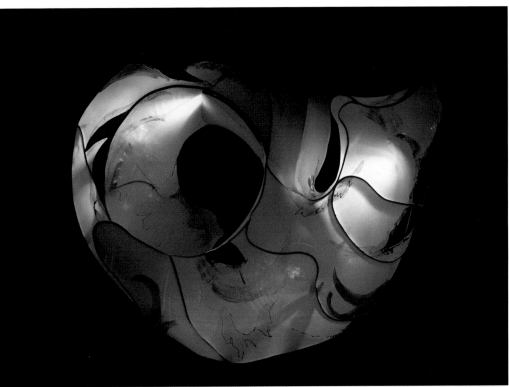

Enhancements

Deborah E. Love Jemmott
269 Solar View Drive
San Marcos, CA 92069
(619) 744-8099

Jemmott designs and builds lighting and other contemporary sculptural accessories for custom installations or limited production needs. A professional artist for over 10 years, her work includes table, wall, and ceiling lamps, candlestands, and vases. Jemmott uses aluminum, brass, copper and glass to create bold contemporary designs in the form of lighting. Her training as a jeweler enables her to produce work with the highest quality of craftsmanship.

Jemmott works with designers, architects and clients on projects for public or private space from conception to installation. Production times average 4 to 6 weeks, but may vary depending on size and complexity of the job.

Retail prices of limited production lamps range from $360 to $1250. Brochure available upon request.

Top Left: *Sealight*, tablelamp, brass, glass, copper, halogen bulb, 15" x 19" x 6", $640
Top Center: *The Beginning of Color*, tablelamp, aluminum, glass, incandescent tube bulb, 26" x 16" x 12", $520
Top Right: *Δπ*, tablelamp, aluminum, glass, brass, 100W globe bulb, 18" x 21" x 18", $550
Bottom: *Angles*, wall sconce, aluminum, glass, brass, incandescent tube, 26" x 32" x 6", $630

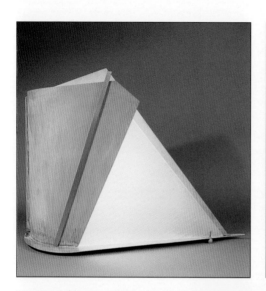
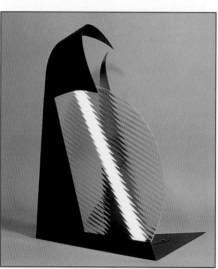
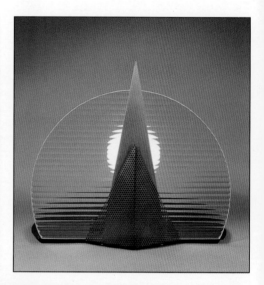

Printed in Japan ©1992 Kraus Sikes Inc. The Guild: The Designer's Reference Book of Artists

Larry Etzen

Larry Etzen Studio
P.O. Box 22384
Kansas City, MO 64113
(816) 363-5980

Larry Etzen has been involved in the fabrication of art glass since 1977. Although versatile, he specializes in the fabrication of light fixtures and leaded glass dome ceilings. Aspects of his work include an innovative use of color and design, quality craftsmanship and durability. His work has been installed throughout the country. Art glass commissions are accepted for public buildings, restaurants, hotels, and private residences. Early planning is recommended. Collaborative efforts are welcome. Inquiries concerning design concepts, cost and installation are encouraged.

Brochure available upon request.

Lamp, glass, lead, copper, 16" x 18"

Liz Galbraith

Galbraith Paper Co.
307 North Third Street
Philadelphia, PA 19106
(215) 923-4632
FAX (215) 923-4632

Designer/Papermaker Liz Galbraith has earned an international reputation with her collection of lighting using handmade paper. Galbraith makes traditional Japanese rice paper using plant fibers imported from Asia.

Galbraith's lighting designs combine the handmade paper from her studio with a variety of contrasting materials—painted and patinated metals, sandblasted glass, turned wood, and terrazzo. Shades and bases are mix and match, and the result is a distinctive line of lighting with subtle shapes, textures, and colors.

Galbraith's handmade paper is lightfast, Ph balanced, and very durable.

She welcomes commissions, including large-scale wall sconces and chandeliers.

A brochure is available upon request.

Girardini Fine Arts

Julie and Ken Girardini
8807 Manahan Drive
Ellicott City, MD 21043
(410) 461-4680

Giardini sculptural steel lighting integrates materials in classic yet contemporary designs which are collected nationwide.

Ken & Julie's designs are constructed of steel and incorporate other materials and glass in striking combinations. Both sculptural and functional, designs range from one-of-a-kind to limited edition pieces.

Lamps are available in incandescent or halogen and have a 'touch' four-level, light intensity control. All finishes are permanent and true to the material. We welcome commission inquiries.

Available mid-1992: Distinctive steel and wood furniture. Call or send for slide portfolio.

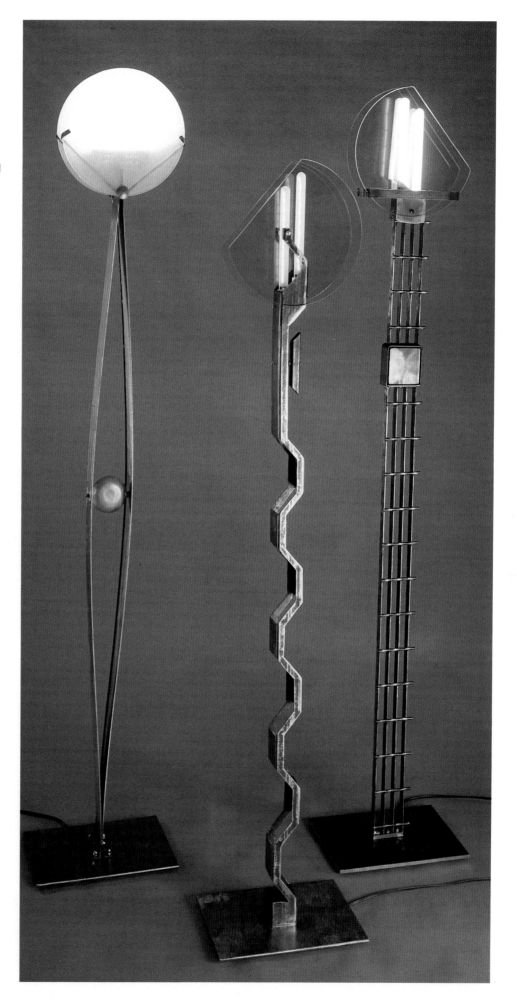

Peter Mangan

634-A Guerrero Street
San Francisco, CA 94110
(415) 431-7060

Peter Mangan creates sculptural lighting. His pieces depart from tradition and explore ideas of asymmetry and chance. His chandeliers, sconces, sculptures, and functional work combine the beauty of glass with the strength of metal.

Peter has worked with glass for fourteen years and exhibits his work nationally. He accepts commissions for residential and commercial applications.

Price range: $800–$5,000
Average completion time: 6–8 weeks

Top: *Scoop Chandelier,* glass, metals,
   40" x 38" x 38"
Bottom: *Oritalia Chandelier,* glass, metals,
   7' x 5' x 5'

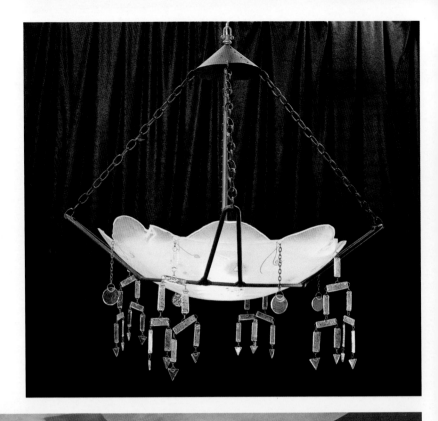

Printed in Japan © 1992 Kraus Sikes Inc. The Guild: The Designer's Reference Book of Artists

Schlitz Studios/ Schlitz Furnaces

James P. Schlitz
245 N. Water Street
Milwaukee, WI 53202
(414) 277-0742
FAX (414) 277-0505

20 years ago, Jim Schlitz discovered the beauty of stained glass. Since then, the quest to convey and combine his love for nature and glass have relied on using glass that can be manipulated in the same way as a painter uses his palette. Jim has spent the last 8 years deeply involved in his own hot glass shop, where he melts his own formulas, creates his own colors, and textures the glass to capture its uniqueness. The studio creates lamps, windows and mosaics that sparkle with a jewel-like splendor or become as impressionistically beautiful as a fine painting. Today, working with his skilled crew, Schlitz strives for perfection by drawing from the past while looking to the future to expand the concepts and ideas which his art is built upon.

Retail prices start at $3,000 for shade and base. Windows range from $370 to $870 per square foot.

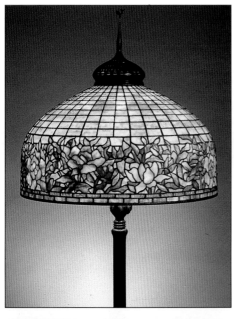

Angelika Traylor

100 Poinciana Drive
Indian Harbour Beach, FL 32937
(407) 773-7640

Specializing in one-of-a-kind lamps, autonomous panels, and architectural designs, Traylor's award-winning work can be recognized by its intricate, jewel-like composition.

These exquisite lamps reflect an original and intensive design process implemented with meticulous craftsmanship and an unusually beautiful selection of glass.

Traylor's attention to detail and vibrant colors have resulted in her work being eagerly sought after by collectors.

Please inquire for more specific information on available work, commissions and pricing.

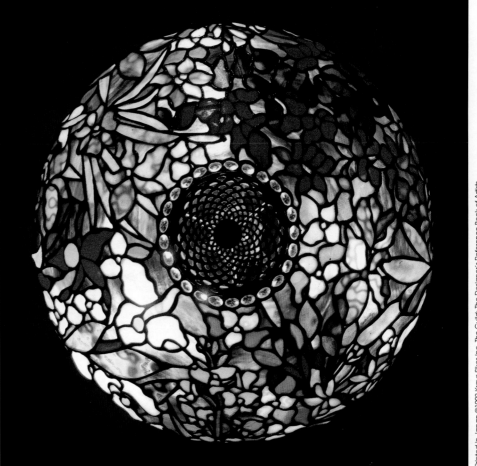

Printed in Japan ©1992 Kraus Sikes Inc. The Guild: The Designer's Reference Book of Artists

A conversation with Charles Pearson
(ceramic vessels)

Q What is involved in the Raku firing process?

A Raku is inspired by a primitive Japanese method of firing pots. It's the process of heating and cooling the vessel during the firing process that gives Raku pots their distinctive color and finish. Traditional ceramic pieces are carefully heated in the kiln to very high temperatures and then cooled down slowly to avoid cracking. In the Raku process, the piece is removed from the kiln while still extremely hot and then buried, in effect, to "suffocate" the piece and stop the burning process.

Because the piece wants to burn and needs oxygen, it "steals" it from the oxides (usually copper, tin and silver nitrate) in the glaze, thereby creating a variety of unusual colors.

My partner, Timothy Roeder, and I have developed a method of burying the red hot piece in a bed of seaweed, and alternately allowing it to breathe and then suffocate until we achieve the desired effect. We also fire our pieces to 1,900 degrees, hotter than usual, for strength and color stability. We like using the seaweed because of the aesthetic print it leaves on the pot. After 20 years of working in this method we are able to "control" the process to a certain degree in order to achieve the effects we want, where we want them -- sometimes, that is! I've also worked in high-fired stoneware and porcelain, but the pure, simple, organic qualities and the element of chance found in Raku have always meant the most to me.

Q What benefits result from collaborating with another artist?

A It gives me the time to study and work within the area of creativity that I do best. When you work with another artist, it teaches you to listen because if it's a good collaboration there are two minds bubbling over with ideas. This listening is also important when talking to a designer or potential client.

Ryan Carey

2430 Ronda Vista Drive
Los Angeles, CA 90027
(213) 668-0888

Constructivist/sculptor, Carey works with mixed media materials to create sophisticated vessel forms that frequently incorporate found/altered objects and contain historic reference.

His highly diversified work with vessels, censers, and sculptural objects has included prehistoric, classical, oriental, southwestern, and contemporary forms.

Materials that have found their way into his work include metal, ceramics, mineral specimens, glass, bone, leather, beads, paint, fossils, textiles, horse hair, rubber and feathers.

Recent directions include slick resin overlays and limited edition bronzes.

Represented in a number of corporate/ private collections internationally. Commissions welcome with a four to eight week delivery. Sizes up to 36" high. Price range: $600–$5,000.

Portfolio available.

Top: *Shimmering Island,* 22"H x 36"W x 18"D
Bottom: *Storied Past,* 9"H x 11"W x 10"D

Frank Colson

Colson School of Art/Colson Studio
1666 Hillview Street
Sarasota, FL 34239
(813) 953-5892
(800) 741-5892
FAX (813) 365-7999

Frank Colson and the Colson Studio offer unique original and limited edition sculptures and reliefs in clay and bronze. Editions of *THE GUILD,* one through six, include visual expressions from this established studio. Since 1963, the artist has placed work in both private and public places of note.

A portfolio and price list are available upon serious intent of commission or acquisition; simply dial 1-800-741-5892, or send a FAX.

The three horses (above) *Armored Horse, Winged Horse, Medieval Armored Horse,* are but a few of a varied breed of horses available; i.e. Tang Horse, Etruscan Horse, Roman Horse, or shown below: *Majestic Circus Horse,* 38" x 33" x 13".

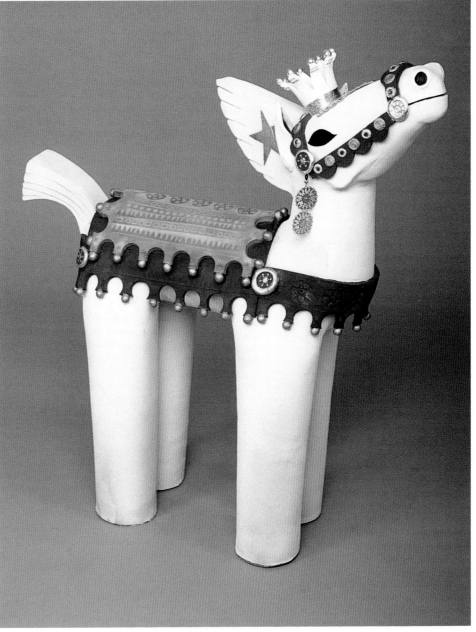

Carolyn Dulin

5660 Livernois Road
Rochester, MI 48306
(313) 651-8715

Dulin has worked with colored porcelain for 18 years, creating sculptural vessels suggesting geological formations and natural forces. These forms led to her Kimonos, a stylized torso, still heavily suggestive of natural processes. These intricately detailed, colorful surfaces and gestural forms have won awards and places in the collections of the Detroit Institute of Art, Shaw Walker Corp. and Monarch Tile Co., as well as many private collections.

The colored clay is layered, stretched, and inlaid. The backs of the Kimonos are often as highly detailed as the fronts. She frequently works with clients in selecting color, form and detailing. Figures approximately 24"H, $750. Delivery up to seven weeks. Slides available upon request.

Left: *Rose Geo*, 24½" x 14½" x 5"
Right: *Blue Green Obi*, 24¼" x 14" x 4½"

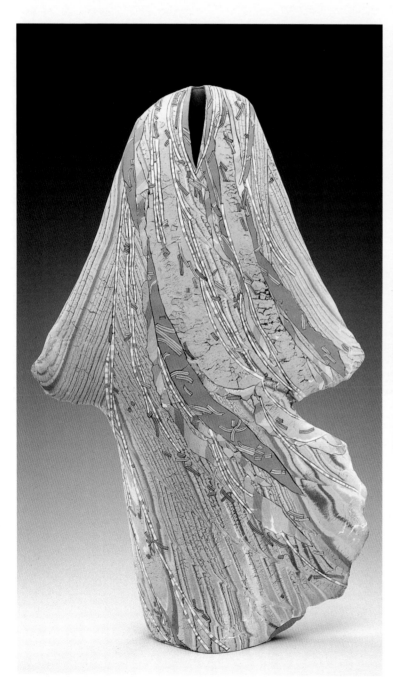

Printed in Japan ©1992 Kraus Sikes Inc. The Guild: The Designer's Reference Book of Artists

Edith A. Ehrlich

Ceramic Artist
1070 Park Avenue
New York, NY 10128
(212) 534-0732

Silver and gold leaf line small decorative
bowls of unglazed porcelain and glazed,
lustered stoneware. Porcelain mixed with
black stain is inlaid with white porcelain
designs, projecting an ancient surface
with a sumptuous interior. The stoneware
pieces (Top) are carved on the outside.
Wholesale prices are $100 to $200 each.
Sizes range from 2½ to 5 inches high.
Although made to specifications,
each piece is unique and several make
a glowing group on a small or large table.

Len Eichler

4178 Griffin Road
Syracuse, NY 13215
(315) 492-0568

Len Eichler's "Time Vessels" are a unique blend of ceramic sculpture and pottery. These hollow vessels are painstakingly constructed in layers, together with imbedded fragments, all made from the same clay. They are fired using the Raku technique which gives the glazes their crackled and archaeological appearance.

The "Time Vessels" have been included in museum, corporate and private collections in the United States, Canada, Japan and Europe.

Ranging in height from 9" to 36", and retailing from $300 to $3,000, these vessels are easily shipped to any location. Slides of available work and a detailed price list will be sent upon request. Commissions are accepted.

Printed in Japan ©1992 Kraus Sikes Inc. The Guild: The Designer's Reference Book of Artists

Ferrin Gallery at Pinch Pottery

179 Main Street
Northampton, MA 01060
(413) 586-4509
1 (800) 732-7091

Ferrin Gallery at Pinch Pottery represents contemporary artists working in clay and selected other media. Recent exhibits include: *A Doll House, Mara Superior, The Chair, Nancy LaPointe,* and *A Tea Party.*

The annual exhibition, *A Tea Party,* has been held since 1979. The work of hundreds of ceramic artists has been shown in this comprehensive survey of teapots, sets and theme pieces. Decorative, sculptural and functional works by artists from throughout the United States present an overview of contemporary styles, techniques and trends.

Video and slide presentations of gallery artists and exhibitions are available. The Ferrin Gallery offers full curatorial and consulting services for private and corporate collections. Referrals and discounts are offered to the design trade.

Below: selections from our collection of teapots by contemporary American artists

Gillberg Design International

Carl Gillberg
1710 Decker Canyon Road
Malibu, California 90265
(310) 457-1768
FAX (310) 457-0124

Artist Carl Gillberg earned his reputation producing large-scale, Raku-fired ceramic vessels, his primary area of focus for over fifteen years. However, his eye for interesting forms has led to his development of new designs in a variety of mediums.

Gillberg Design now boasts a full line of furniture and accessories which include pieces in sculptural-quality cast bronze, slumped glass as well as Raku ceramics.

Gillberg Design has years of experience working with designers and architects and will customize scale, finishes and glazes, even create new designs tailored to the clients needs.

Gillberg Design is represented by leading showrooms in design centers across the nation and has commissioned pieces in numerous collections including, Hyatt Regency Albuquerque, Sheraton Torrey Pines, Grand Tokyo Bay, Grand Hyatt Wailea, and many others.

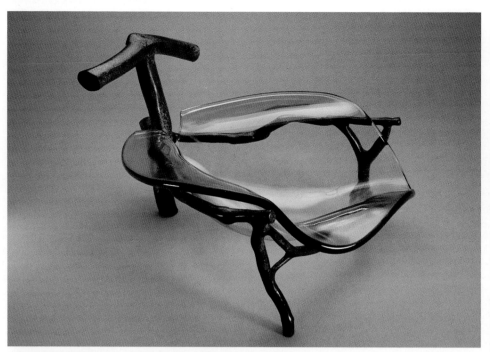

Ikebana Plate, solid cast bronze with slumped plate glass, 15 1/2"W x 11"H

Heroic Jar, raku-fired verde glazes, 32"W x 60"H

Girardini Fine Arts

Julie and Ken Girardini
8807 Manahan Drive
Ellicott City, MD 21043
(410) 461-4680

Girardini's sculptural ceramics integrate materials in classic yet contemporary designs which are collected nationwide.

Individually crafted pieces combine raku-fired pottery with basketry to create one-of-a-kind forms. Weavings of hand-dyed reed and other natural materials are an integral part of each sculpture.

This embellishment is a unique way to meld natural elements, which are often very fluid, with the hard element of the clay. Each piece is a delicate balance between the two.

Sizes range from 6" to 36" and start at $50. Call or send for portfolio of current work.

Melissa Greene

RR1, Box 40
Deer Isle, ME 04627
(207) 348-2601

Melissa Greene's work has been inspired by her natural surroundings, an interest in other cultures, and how those cultures relate to their natural environment.

She has worked with clay since her childhood, studied with Native American potters, and holds a Master's Degree from Wesleyan University. Her limited edition pieces are wheel-thrown and then painted with richly colored terra sigillata, and burnished.

Production time is 4 to 6 weeks, with prices from $1,000 to $2,500.

Additional information is available upon request.

Gatherers, 16"H x 15"W

When the Berries Are Ripe, 16"H x 16"W

Charles Pearson
Tim Roeder

Whitehead Street Pottery
1011 Whitehead Street
Key West, FL 33040
(305) 294-5067

Charles Pearson and Timothy Roeder collaborate to produce large hand thrown and slab built Raku fired vessels.

The forms have a visual strength that demand a response while maintaining the traditional subtleties of color by reducing in a post-firing of seaweed.

Commissions include the Southern Progress Corporation, Rath Manufacturing Co. Inc., Demille Corporation, and various other public sites.

Prices start at $475.

Slides ($3 refundable) and additional information can be obtained by writing directly to their studio.

Represented by:
The Signature Shop and Gallery
    Atlanta, GA
Acropolis Now
    Santa Monica, CA
The Red Lion Gallery
    Vero Beach, FL

Photos: Pete Thosteson

Left: Raku fired, 12" x 12" x 20"
Right: Raku fired, 18" x 12"

Robin Renner

Renner Clay & Beadwork
36 Rd. 5474 NBU 3040
Farmington, NM 87401
(505) 632-0182

Robin Renner's one-of-a-kind vessel and figurative pieces are bisque-fired for durability, then pit-fired, stained, or glazed. Her love of beadwork and ability to combine these diverse disciplines lead to pieces that are unique and enjoyable.

Currently completing a tile mural One-Percent-for-Art grant, Renner has work in galleries throughout the west.

With twenty years experience, she meets deadlines and enjoys commissioned work Please see *GUILD 6* or contact the artist. Prices range from $65–$2000.

Below: *Rainkeeper*

David Rosenbaum

240 West 98th Street, #9C
New York, NY 10025
(212) 222-7180

David Rosenbaum's glazed stoneware fountains are one-of-a-kind pieces incorporating running water and integrated vessels for planting. They range in height from 12" to 24", and are suitable for many spaces previously overlooked or generally deemed too remote for artwork. The flow of water is regulated by a re-circulating pump, and can be easily adjusted to control sound and speed.

The artist often designs for specific environments and welcomes collaborations with architects and designers.

Finished pieces and commissioned work are available. Commissioned work takes approximately 10 weeks to complete.

Prices begin at $1500.

Betsy Ross

1160 Fifth Avenue
New York, NY 10029
(212) 722-5535

Betsy Ross' earthenware vessels are an amalgam of wheel-thrown and hand-thrown components. Her works are hand-painted and embellished with lusters, creating metallic-like qualities. Harmonious for both the home or public display. By virtue of being hand crafted, each piece is assured individuality and is signed by the artist.

Her works are exhibited in prominent galleries and museums nationally, represented in private collections, and showcased in retail concerns.

Ms. Ross enjoys collaborating with architects and designers. Additional information upon request. Prices range from $350 to $950 retail.

Vessels featured on this page range from 13" to 26".

Uli Schempp

10 8th Avenue, Apt. 5
Brooklyn, NY 11217
(718) 783-4825

Uli Schempp's high temperature gas-fired stoneware vessels are individually sculpted using a variety of processes and techniques. The incorporation of steel enhances the architectural quality of the pieces and creates an interesting interplay between lines and solid form as well as positive and negative space.

Pieces may be designed for specific spaces according to specific requests. Recently the artist has been commissioned to design lamps and sconces using his sculptural concepts.

Prices, slides and resume are available upon request.

Top: *Suspended Vessel,* stoneware, oxidized steel, 28"H x 32"D
Bottom: sconce, stoneware, oxidized steel, 16"H x 18"W
Below: *Amphora,* stoneware, 20"H

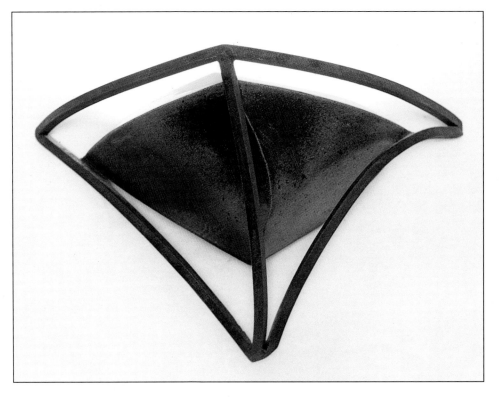

Robert C. Shenfeld

5093 Skyline Drive
Syracuse, NY 13215
(315) 492-0702

Robert Shenfeld's ceramic vessels are wheel-thrown, some with hand-built lids. His recent work incorporates rich, deep tones of slips and underglazes sprayed and brushed onto the surface. Copper fibers melted onto the clay transform into matte black veins imbedded into the high-gloss surface. The pieces possess elegant simplicity in form and expressive decoration; unique in their individuality.

Bowls are available from 8" to 27" in diameter; lidded vessels up to 24" high.

Slides are available upon request; commissions welcome.

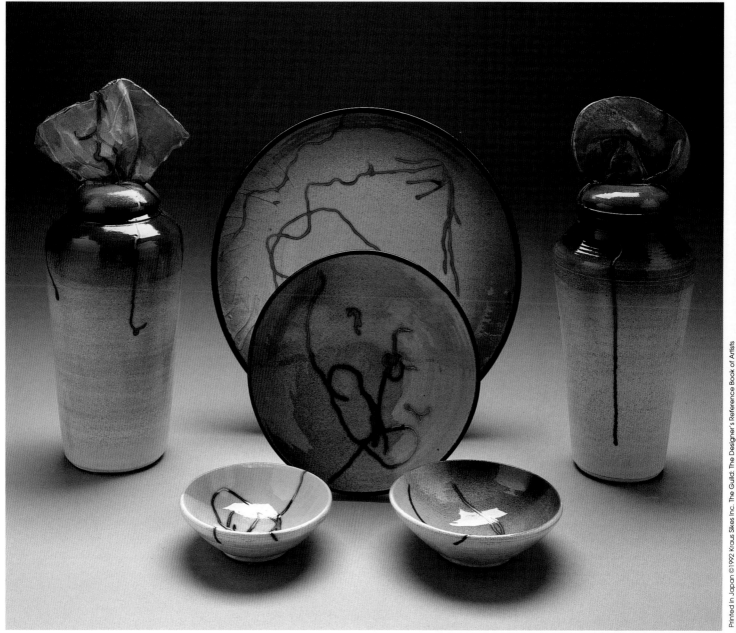

Timothy Weber

Main Avenue Pottery and Gallery
503 Main Avenue
Northport, AL 35476
(205) 758-5002

With an emphasis on the vessel form, Timothy Weber creates functional and sculptural stoneware appropriate for both corporate and residential settings.

Weber has collaborated with clients on varied commissioned works, ranging from fountains and murals to sinks and lamps. All commissioned artwork is completed in a timely fashion and is made to be durable and of outstanding quality.

After being named Alabama Craftsman of the Year in 1990, Weber traveled to Japan and then Denmark. In Denmark he taught in the Danish Folk School system and exhibited his ceramics in three different cities. The ceramic work of Timothy Weber has been exhibited extensively and can be found in the collections of Southern Progress Corporation, South Central Bell, Fine Arts Museum of the South, and the Columbus Museum.

Top: *Crimson Bay covered jar,* 18½"H x 16"
Lower: *White and white footed covered jar,* 28½"H x 17"

Irene Wittig

1619 South Quincy Street
Arlington, VA 22204
(703) 521-8184

Irene Wittig specializes in custom designed, hand-painted ceramics: slipcast and hand-thrown dinnerware, accessories, tiles and murals. She welcomes collaboration with clients, designers and architects to develop original and individualized designs that coordinate with clients' fabric or wallpaper; or incorporate unique personal elements: house portraits, genealogy, favorite places, animals, flowers etc.

The artist's fresh, colorful, European-naif style is especially suited for home and restaurant settings. Unique accessories include tiled tables and letter boxes, lampbases and door plaques.

Price list available upon request.

Irene Wittig is the author of the book *The Clay Canvas: Creative Painting on Functional Ceramics* (Chilton Books, 1990), and placed first in a recent international design competition at SURTEX.

Tom Wolver

2390 Eureka Canyon Road
Watsonville, CA 95076
(408) 724-8436

Influenced by the visual and spiritual nature of the African, American Indian and Ancient Mexican cultures, Tom Wolver's art reflects an attempt to re-unite with the ways of the Shaman, the Sorcerer, the Warrior, and to explore the profound possibilities of the "inner journey" that each initiate travels to become a realized soul.

Each clay sculpture is traditionally kiln-fired, then pit-fired to achieve unique coloring. It is then decorated with such fetish objects as bones, beads, fur and leather. Suitable for outdoors. From $300 to $3500. Portfolio provided upon request.

Necromancer, pit-fired clay, $1500, 17 1/2"H

Possessed, pit-fired clay, $3500, 21"H

Shaman, pit-fired clay, $3500, 26"H

A conversation with Shawn Athari
(glass sculpture)

Q How did you get involved with the medium of glass?

A It started by taking a stained glass class, and I thought it would just be a hobby. I enjoyed it and began to learn more techniques and perfect the skills I had. Then about eight years ago I took a class in fused glass and I really liked that. I started with bowls, and small objects like fish, but I've always been a museum junkie. I love cultural artifacts, and I began doing masks and other cultural artifacts.

Q What is the basic process of making your work?

A My figures are multiple layers of colored glass chips melted, or fused, into each other. When the glass goes in to the kiln it can be up to 3" thick. The glass I use is a combination of blown, lampworked and sheet glass, all of which is made in my studio. After fusing, the glass is considerably thinner and flat. Because glass does not heat evenly, the kiln time depends on the size of the piece. If a large piece heats up too fast, it will cause internal stress and crack, so the kiln must be heated very slowly. For a big piece, it can take two days to bring the temperature up to 1600 degrees. To shape the glass, I create a mold. The fused piece is placed on the mold, returned to the kiln, and fired again at up to 1400 degrees, softening and shaping the glass to the mold. I have also experimented with leaving the pieces flat, and framing them in a traditional manner. A single piece may end up having 100 different components of glass before it is finished.

Q How do you market your work?

A My pieces are in galleries, and I do about 20 shows a year. People who like my work are attracted to it right away, but they don't know why. Then I tell them about the process that's involved in making the piece, and they are usually surprised to find out that it's all glass, and that the colors aren't painted on. All my pieces are researched and I always provide the historic background for each piece. People become more and more excited as they learn the story behind the work.

Shawn Athari

Shawn Athari's, Inc.
13450 Cantara Street
Van Nuys, CA 91402
(818) 988-3105
FAX (818) 787-MASK

Galleries:
Elaine Horwitch, Santa Fe, NM
Symmetry, Saratoga Springs, NY
Eileen Kremen, Fullerton, CA
Posner Gallery, Farmington Hills, MI
Glass Growers, Erie, PA

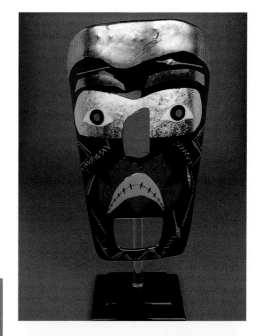

Shawn Athari combines various techniques of glassmaking and occasional metalwork and fuses them together to recreate ancient artifacts in a contemporary form. The resultant pieces are evocative of cultures long since diminished or extinct.

Each sculpture is original and an accumulation of extensive research and glassmaking expertise acquired throughout the last seventeen years.

Left: *Aduma*, from Western Sudan,
  31" x 15" x 5"
Top Right: *Kwakiutl Rattle*, from Fort Rupert,
  23" x 12" x 3"
Center Right: *Puppet Head*, Kwakiutl and
  used by the Shaman people, 16" x 9" x 3"
Bottom Right: *Ceremonial Death Mask* from
  Mexico, 23" x 13" x 3"

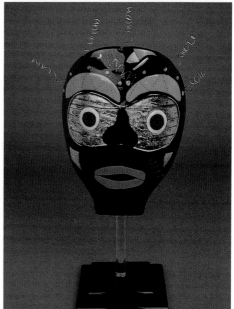

Latchezar Boyadjiev

Glass Studio
950 56th Street, Suite 22
Oakland, CA 94608
(510) 601-0318

Latchezar Boyadjiev graduated in 1985 at the Academy of Applied Arts in Prague, Czechoslovakia. He came to the United States in 1986 and established his studio in 1988.

His one-of-a-kind sculptures are created out of optical glass or cast color glass by cutting, grinding, polishing and laminating.

He exhibits in the USA, Canada, Japan and Europe and works on commissions.

Retail price range $4,500–$9,000.

Photos: Charlie Frizzell

Right: *Facing the Destiny,* optical glass
   sculpture, 19" x 12" x 4.5"
Bottom: *Light in the Space,* cast glass
   sculpture, 13" x 8" x 3"

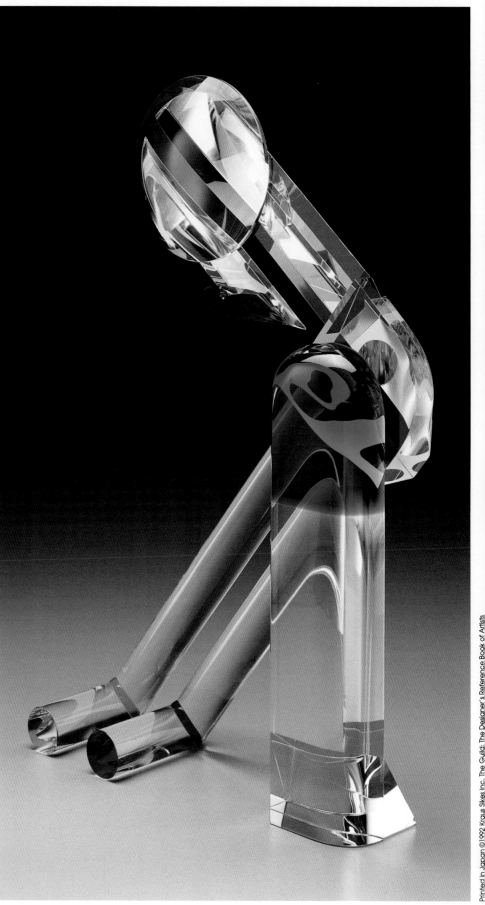

Printed in Japan ©1992 Kraus Sikes Inc. The Guild: The Designer's Reference Book of Artists

Dale R. Eggert

Eggert Glass
1918 E. Beverly Road
Shorewood, WI 53211
(414) 962-0808

Glass and metal combine in dramatic sculptures for residential and business interiors.

By sandblast etching and painting on half-inch or thicker plate glass panels, mounted in simple and elegant wrought iron frameworks, Dale Eggert creates distinctive, contemporary sculpture. His work has been exhibited in galleries and juried exhibitions in both the U.S. and Japan.

These one-of-a-kind pieces are available in floor standing and table top sizes, starting at $2,400. Delivery in thirty to sixty days, site-specific commissions accepted.

Left: glass: 5'H x 14"W (overall height 6')
Top Right: glass: 24" Dia. (overall height 3')
Bottom Right: glass: 24" Dia. (overall height 5')

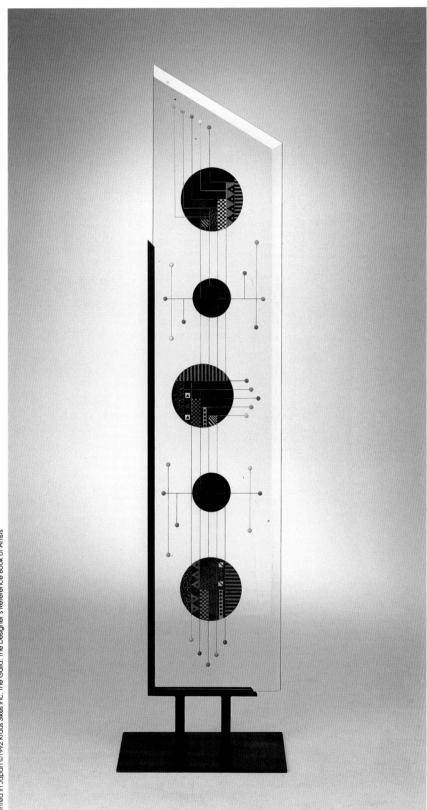

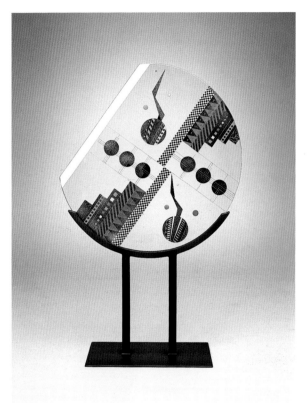

Kevin Fulton

P.O. Box 7033
Bend, OR 97708
(503) 382-8636

Kevin Fulton has been working in all aspects of glass since 1975. He is currently utilizing his furnace blowing skills with a focus on creating sea-life and human forms. He has experience with large-scale commercial installations and is comfortable working with designers and architects. He welcomes special commissions.

He is a recipient of a grant from the Art-in-Public-Places program from the State of Oregon and has a Fine Arts degree from Central Washington University. His work is included in several private collections and is available in numerous galleries across the country.

Left: *Lizard Lady,* 20" x 14" x 6", $2000
Right: *Dolphin Vase,* 12" x 9", $700

Michael K. Hansen
Nina Paladino

California Glass Studio
P.O. Box 215786
Sacramento, CA 95821
(916) 925-9322
FAX (916) 925-9370

Michael and Nina have been working together for 15 years. Their glass is represented internationally in galleries and in private and corporate collections.

Pictured are handblown vessels, lighted glass and metal sculptures.

A complete catalog is available upon request.

Top: *Feathers* Series, one-of-a-kind, diamond shaped vessel and free form bowl
Bottom Left: cobalt lighted glass and metal sculpture
Bottom Right: detail, lighted glass and metal sculpture

David Jaworski

Sunesis
11 Clerbrook Lane
St. Louis, MO 63124
(314) 994-9820

David Jaworski has been producing fine gold jewelry and sculptural works since 1981. His sculptural works are best known for their unique blend of metal and glass in energetic and flowing studies of form, optics and color.

Jaworski is comfortable collaborating with other designers on site-specific installations. Previous projects range from small to medium-scale works for residential, to large-scale, free-standing works as well as wall-hung installations for public spaces.

Corporate clients include AT&T, Monsanto, Max Plank Institute, Carboline, St. Louis Arts & Education Council, Washington University, St. Louis Centre for Holistic Healing, and many others.

Prices for most sculptural works start at $4400.

Slides of portfolio are available.

Right: *Attitudes,* 1991, blown glass, bronze, marble, 18"W x 31"H

Photo: Rudy Enshen

Printed in Japan ©1992 Kraus Sikes Inc. The Guild: The Designer's Reference Book of Artists

Jon Kuhn

Kuhn Glass Studios
705 N. Main
Winston-Salem, NC 27101
(919) 722-2369
FAX (919) 631-8316

Selected Museum Collections:
Metropolitan Museum of Art, New York
Smithsonian Institution, Washington, D.C.
Museum Fur Kunst und Gewerbe, Hamburg,
  Germany
Ebeltoft International Glass Museum,
  Ebeltoft, Denmark
Musee Des Arts Decoratifs, Lausanne,
  Switzerland
Royal Ontario Museum, Toronto, Canada
Huntington Galleries, Huntington, West
  Virginia
Wheaton American Glass Museum, Millville,
  New Jersey
Carnegie Museum, Pittsburgh, Pennsylvania
High Museum, Atlanta, Georgia
Columbus Museum, Columbus, Georgia
Chrysler Museum, Norfolk, Virginia
Mint Museum, Charlotte, North Carolina
Hunter Museum, Chattanooga, Tennessee

Price Range: $10,000–$100,000

Crystal Quadrille, 1991, collection of Hunter Museum, Chattanooga, TN, laminated glass, 11" x 11" x 11"

Blanquilla Bay, 1991, private collection, 24" x 6" x 13"

Steven Maslach

44 Industrial Way
Greenbrae, CA 94904
(415) 924-2310
FAX (415) 924-7397

Steven Maslach has been working in glass since 1969. His portfolio includes functional table top designs, unique vessels and large scale sculpture. *The Dichroic Series* shown is highly kinetic, and changes color depending upon the angle of light. The work is of blown, cast, chiseled and polished glass, laminated with optical color filters.

Maslach's work ranges from nine inches to nine feet. New designs combine glass with marble, granite, aluminum and concrete. *The Dichroic Series* is priced from $3,000 to $8,000. Portfolio upon request.

Museums and Awards:
Corning Museum of Glass
American Craft Museum
Chrysler Museum
High Museum of Art
Kanazawa International, 1990
Baccarat/Taittinger Grand Prize, 1988

Commissions:
Emerald Shapery Center
Portman Barry Architects
Southern California Gas
City of San Francisco

Printed in Japan ©1992 Kraus Sikes Inc. The Guild: The Designer's Reference Book of Artists

Mesolini
Glass Studio

Gregg Mesmer & Diane Bonciolini
13291 Madison NE
Bainbridge Island, WA 98110
(206) 842-7133

Gregg Mesmer and Diane Bonciolini combine extensive backgrounds in art glass production to create award-winning dishware that is both beautiful and practical. Each signed and dated piece in this collection is created from hand-rolled iridescent, transparent, or opalescent glass that is "slumped" into molds during a kiln firing.

Additional examples of their work can be seen in *THE GUILD 5,* page 99 and *THE GUILD 6,* page 248.

Color sample kit available for fifteen dollars, including shipping. Call or write for current catalog.

John A. Morrison

Cornerstone Glassworks
2530 Joe Field Rd. #11
Dallas, TX 75229
(214) 247-8188

John Morrison has been producing fine carved and etched glass for architects, interior designers, and private collectors for the past nine years.

After opening Cornerstone Glassworks, his Dallas area studio, John has produced award-winning art pieces displayed in galleries and shows from Seattle to New York, and California to Norway.

In addition to fine art, John designs and carves glass for tabletops, lamps, entry ways, enclosures, mirrors, firescreens, wall clocks, and divider walls. His company, Cornerstone Glassworks, offers the broadest application of carved glass techniques available anywhere.

Top Left: *Future Antique*, detail
Top Center: *Oriental Collage*, 15" x 25"
Top Right: *Future Antique*, 18" x 21"
Bottom: *Spiramid*, 14" x 12"

Rick Nicholson
Janet Nicholson

Nicholson Blown Glass
5555 Bell Road
Auburn, CA 95603
(916) 823-1631

Rick and Janet Nicholson have worked together for twelve years as Nicholson Blown Glass with an emphasis on creativity and innovation.

Each piece is a free-hand expression of the excitement and risk-taking found only in the small, experimental glassblowing studio.

Other work involves vase and bowl forms which may be attached hot to cast or poured pedestals. Perfume bottles, bud vases, paperweights and ornaments are appropriate for corporate giving.

A portfolio and price list are available upon request. Commissions are accepted.

Top: three cylinders, 18" to 20"H x 5"W,
   $275 to $325 retail
Bottom: folded platter, 24" Dia., $400 retail

Orient & Flume
Art Glass

2161 Park Avenue
Chico, CA 95928
(916) 893-0373
FAX (916) 893-2743
Attn: Douglas Boyd

Internationally acclaimed, the artists of Orient & Flume specialize in one-of-a-kind, handblown vases, perfumes, and paperweights. Using only "off-hand" blowing techniques, each piece is individually designed and created. Motifs range from traditional to contemporary.

Orient & Flume Art Glass can be found in the permanent collections of most major museums, including the Metropolitan Museum, Smithsonian Museum, Chrysler Museum, Steuben Glass Museum, and the Chicago Art Institute.

The following are descriptions and retail prices.

Top: Pilsner Vase/Threaded Rim $310, Octoptus Paperweight $210, Floral Vase–black $670, Floral Vase—tropical green $670, Goriila $77, Flower Form Vase $310, Pilsner Vase—malachite $310

Center: Blue Iridescent Apple $53, Pink Climbing Rose Cased Cabinet Vase $320, Mini Peach $44, Glossy Green Apple $53, Rose Bud Perfume $340, Mini Apricot $44, Blue Orchid Paperweight $330, Phalenopsis Orchid Paperweight $310, Red Laelia Orchid Paperweight $310, White Beauty Orchid Paperweight $310, Red Clown Fish Egg $310, Sea View—Magnum Paperweight $410

Bottom: Rose Paperweight $430, Saguaro Cactus Egg $260, Poinsettia Paperweight $350

Below: Chinese Poppy Cased Cabinet Vase $315, Cypriot Vase $290, Chinese Poppy Paperweight $290

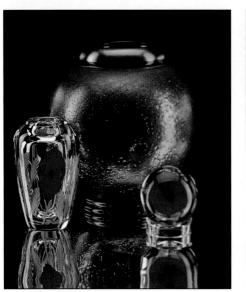

Printed in Japan ©1992 Kraus Sikes Inc. The Guild: The Designer's Reference Book of Artists

Lisa Ridabock
Peter Ridabock

Ridabock Hand Blown Glass
217 Brave Boat Harbor Road
York, ME 03909
(207) 363-4150

Although intentionally abstract, Peter Ridabock's hand-blown glass vessels recall life beneath the ocean. The colorful surface design is a collage of applied canes and shards. Each Ridabock piece is made entirely of glass and is one-of-a-kind.

Peter Ridabock began blowing glass in 1976 and has worked with some of the nation's finest glass artists. Peter was awarded a fellowship to the Creative Glass Center of America and attended Penland, Haystack, and Pilchuck craft schools. Lisa Ridabock brings to the pieces her experience as a painter and professional colorist by creating their brilliant color combinations.

The pieces shown range from 15" high to 18" wide. Large platters and smaller vessels are also available.

Prices range $250–$2000.

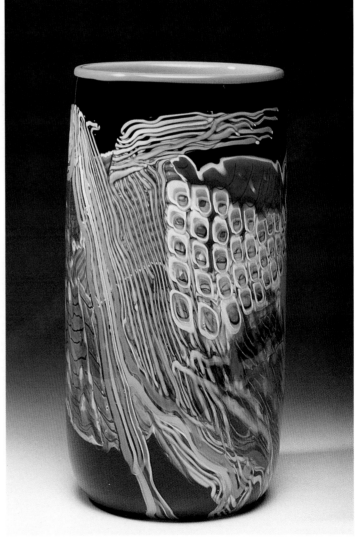

David Van Noppen

Van Noppen Glass Inc.
69 Tingley Street
Providence, RI 02903
(401) 351-6770

David Van Noppen continues to create both functional and decorative art glass. His contemporary designs reflect his versatility with glass. Van Noppen emphasizes the optical qualities of glass, capturing the interplay between color and light. The artist's unique designs reflect his appreciation for the fluidity inherent in the process of glass blowing.

Van Noppen's work is exhibited nationally. His work is also shown in *The Guild 6.*

Silverwrap vases and perfume bottles (Top) are a continuation of work shown in *The Guild 6.*

Both pieces in the bottom photos measure approximately 12" x 12". They are called winged, fluted bowls. They are offered with many variations on a common theme. Smaller ones start at $450. The two shown are $1500 each.

Jonathan Winfisky

Designer/Glass Artist
Potter Road/Legate Hill
Charlemont, MA 01339
(413) 339-8319

Jonathan Winfisky has been designing and producing unique and original blown and cast sculptural glass vessel forms since 1976.

The "Sculptural Design Series" and the "Cast Design Series" are examples of forms which are designed to work collectively or individually when displayed in private residences and public spaces.

Larger pieces are available by commission and all designs can be produced in a wide variety of sizes and colors. Prices range from $70–$2,000. Please call or write for further information.

Top: *Cast Design Series,* ©1991, bowl 15",
    vase 14", vial 6", bud vase 8", ming vessel 8"
Bottom: *Sculptural Design Series,* ©1991,
    bowl 15", vase 12", fluted vase 8", perfume
    vial 5½", tapered vase 10"

A conversation with Ron Fleming
(turned wood vessels)

Q How did you become involved in woodturning?

A I was a commercial illustrator by trade for thirty years, and had done wood carving as a hobby. When I left my design studio, I became more and more interested in wood. I began experimenting with wood turning. After I had made a few pieces on my own and learned all I could from reading books, I wanted to get more information. I became involved in the American Association of Woodturners, which holds annual symposiums that bring together artists, collectors, gallery owners and other art professionals. In five years, the organization has grown to about 2,500 members. The field is changing so fast that it's impossible to keep up. The organization has done an outstanding job in providing information and instruction to the artists, as well as helping to market their work.

Q How has the craft changed?

A In the early days, I think the idea was to remake and copy what potters had done. Now woodturners have learned about form and design, and have started to explore the medium on its own merits. In the past, turned objects had to have a function, usually as a salad bowl! Finally, the work is being seen as an art form. There seems to be a new generation of woodturners, many of whom are entering the craft as artists and then learning the techniques; this is producing a lot of creativity in the movement. There are so many approaches to woodturning -- you can alter the coloring or grain of the wood by putting the piece of wood outside for three months, or turning the piece on a multiple axis, or carving the vessel after it has been turned.

Q Where do you get your ideas?

A I develop my designs based on what I see in the wood, rather than looking for a piece of wood that fits an image I have in my mind. I look at the grain of the wood, and then try and think of ways I can work with or manipulate the grain to achieve a certain look.

Boris Bally and ROY

2D3D Studio
3421 Bigelow Boulevard
Pittsburgh, PA 15213
(412) 682-8118
FAX (412) 682-7244

Both collaboratively and individually, ROY and Boris produce functional tabletop objects, jewelry, lighting, and sculpture. Their pieces reflect a unique contrast of precious and common materials.

One-of-a-kind art pieces and limited editions. Commissionable. Participating in the ACC Baltimore Wholesale Craft Show.

They have been included in Fortunoff Silver Competitions (Rosanne Raab Associates) "Silver: New Forms and Expressions II and III," 2nd Place Award. ROY and Boris have also been featured in *Product Design 3*, Lloyd Herman's *Art That Works*, *Contemporary Crafts for the Home*, and *Jewelry/Metalwork 1991 Survey*, *Vogue*, *Pronto*, and *International Design* magazines.

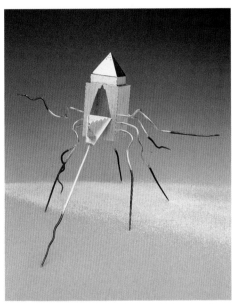

Salt Crustacean, fabricated silver, gold, $1900

Zulu, silver flatware set

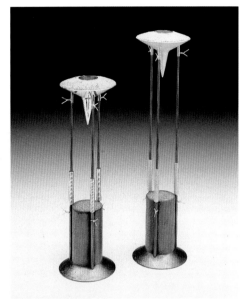

Trirod, candlesticks, from $160

Terminating Triangles, bowl, 35" x 35" x 6", $1800

Frank Barham

3817 Neyrey Drive
Metairie, LA 70002
(504) 454-3210
FAX (504) 836-5506

Frank Barham adapts architectural qualities of cubistic art to personify allegorical matter in producing striking and unencumbered sculptures.

Works range from 8"–24" for table sculptures; 4'–7' for outdoor sculptures. Finishes: patinas, mirror-polished bronze, goldplated and silverplated bronze, polished welded aluminum. Enlargements available; commissions accepted; installations arranged. Architectural and art council collaborations invited. Production time 10–18 weeks. Price range $1,500–$15,000 FOB. Slides available. Professional member: International Sculpture Center.

Top Left: *Planes Man,* bronze,
    14"H x 6"W x 5"D
Top Right: *Person of Confidence,* polished
    bronze, 18"H x 5"W x 4"D
Bottom Left: *Great Planes Man,* aluminum,
    7'H x 3'W x 2.6"D
Bottom Right: *Momenta,* polished bronze,
    18"H x 5"W x 10"D

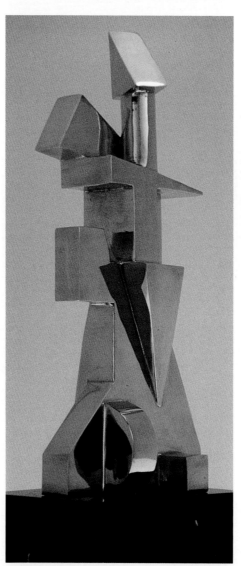
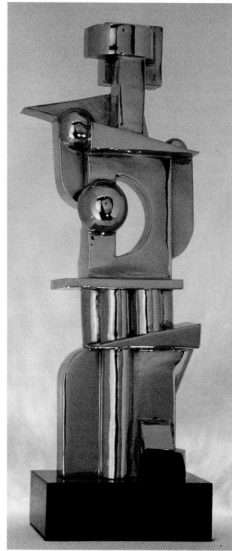

Don Drumm

Don Drumm Studios and Gallery
437 Crouse Street
Akron, OH 44311
(216) 253-6268
FAX (216) 253-4014

Don Drumm, a pioneer in the use of cast aluminum as a sculptural medium, maintains his own foundry where he produces a wide variety of work, including limited edition sculpture, one-of-a-kind sculpture, architectural commissions and craft objects.

During his thirty years of doing commissions, he has produced work ranging from ten-story murals in sandblasted concrete, to monumental free-standing steel structures, wall reliefs in applied cement or cast aluminum for corporations and private homes. In addition, the small sculptures have been used worldwide by executives, government officials, and individuals as gifts, awards and honorariums.

Catalogs and slides of architectural work and/or crafts are available. Please indicate your interest. Call to discuss projects.

Grouping of small totem sculptures, cast aluminum.

Winged Sculpture, cast aluminum, 21"H

Eagle Sculpture, cast aluminum, American Embassy, Tegucigalpa, Honduras, 6'W x 8'H

Craig Lauterbach

The Inquisitive Eye
820 Airport Road
Monterey, CA 93940
(408) 375-3332

Working in hardwoods for twenty years has inspired Craig to venture into the medium of bronze. Like his wood sculptures, there is a combination of function and abstraction, a sweeping motion that flows in all of his creations.

In the Curl (Top) is a collaboration with internationally renowned marine artist, Randy Puckett.

A portfolio and price list is available upon request.

In the Curl, issued 1991 in an edition of 150, 20"H x 16"W x 14"D

Trumpeter, issued 1991 in an edition of 50, 16"H x 20"W x 9"D

Courtship, issued 1990 in an edition of 50, 10"H x 17"W x 9"D

Jeanne L. Stevens-Sollman

Stoneware and Bronze
318 North Fillmore Road
Bellefonte, PA 16823
(814) 355-3332

And now there is bronze. After twenty-five years of handbuilding in clay, Jeanne Stevens-Sollman is now casting her animal forms in limited editions of bronze. Constructed in a material suitable for gardens as well as for interior spaces, these free-standing, natural forms lend harmony and elegance to your chosen area.

Prices vary according to size and complexity of design. Willing to work with clients, Ms. Stevens-Sollman welcomes inquiries and requests. Brochures are available.

Mykiss, bronze, 8 1/2" x 4 1/2" x 3", $400

Mare's Tail, bronze, 27" x 24" x 17 1/2", $6,500

Martin Sturman

M. Sturman Steel Sculptures
20412 Roca Chica Drive
Malibu, CA 90265
(310) 456-5716
FAX (818) 905-7173

Martin Sturman creates original steel sculptures in floral, figurative and abstract designs.

His sculptures range from table top to free standing indoor and outdoor pieces, including sculptured tables and entry gates. These beautiful sculptures are executed in stainless steel, weathered (rusted) steel, powder coated carbon steel and acrylic painted carbon steel.

Martin frequently has sculptures available for immediate delivery, but encourages site-specific and collaborative efforts. Depending upon complexity, most sculptures can be shipped within 10 to 12 weeks of commission.

Sizes: from 12 inches to 10 feet high
Retail Prices: from $350 to $5,000
(FOB Los Angeles)

Top: *Deco Lady,* 43" x 31" x 16", $1,900
Bottom Left: *Flower Stand,* 73" x 42" x 19", $2,200
Bottom Right: *Philodendrons,* 72" x 32" x 17", $2,000

Printed in Japan ©1992 Kraus Sikes Inc. The Guild: The Designer's Reference Book of Artists

Timothy Rose Mobiles

**340 Industrial Center Building
Sausalito, CA 94965
(415) 332-9604**

Timothy Rose has been creating and realizing mobile sculptures for more than 20 years. He has lived and exhibited in Europe and is represented by galleries across the U.S. He presently works out of his studio in the San Francisco Bay area.

The pieces shown here are from his current "Surprise" series of mobiles. They are highly colored, asymmetrically balanced, and evocative of a 'surprise' in the viewer. All are constructed of wire, wood, metal and paint and can be replicated on various scales to suit the location.

Brochure and resume available upon request.

Top: *Caterpillar Mobile,* approx. 36"H
Bottom: *Rocket Mobile,* approx. 42"H

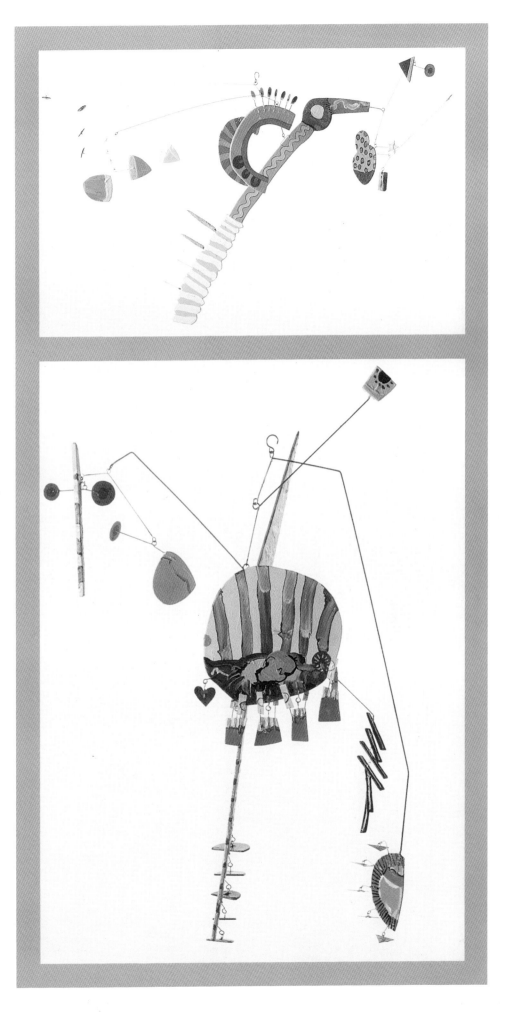

Richard Warrington

W. 3907 Washington Road
Cheney, WA 99004
(509) 448-8713
FAX (509) 448-8544

Richard Warrington creates two and three dimensional sculptures in corten, copper, bronze, stainless and wood. His bold rhythmical designs tend to have an oriental flair and often have an animated life of their own. Use of color and extreme attention to detail make his work stand out.

He specializes in one-of-a-kind site-specific and collaborated work. Sizes: table top to monumental. Production time: 30–40 days. Existing work available.

Prices, resume and slides available by request.

A professional sculptor/designer for 20 years, his work has been exhibited nationally and is represented extensively in private and corporate collections.

Top: *Gismo,* 40" x 48", painted steel
Bottom: *Seahorse,* 5'6" x 6' x 42", painted
   steel, high gloss finish

Photo: Gardens of Art, Bellingham, WA

Photo: Gardens of Art, Bellingham, WA

A conversation with Anne Mayer Meier
(mixed media)

Q How has your work evolved?

A I am a high school English teacher by profession, and in 1977 I took an off-loom weaving course for fun. This progressed to loom weaving, and then basketry. Something about baskets clicked with me, and I progressed quickly from traditional baskets to more complex and original work. This change, away from a less traditional type of work, has been rewarding. One of the pleasant things about being a basketmaker is the sheer simplicity and friendliness of the materials.

The random-weave baskets I create now are very time-consuming. Before I even begin to weave the basket, there's the planning and designing and dyeing of the rattan. To weave a 10" x 14" basket takes about twelve to fifteen hours, and then another eight to ten hours to paint the vessel. As an artist, I want to take time with each piece in order to expand and grow and challenge myself, but that can be frustrating because many wonderful but time-consuming ideas are just not cost-effective.

Q Do you find people hold misconceptions about basketry?

A Yes. Often I think people don't understand how labor-intensive the process is. A lot of times at shows, people say, "Oh, you mean you make these baskets?" They think that I merely embellish an imported basket, or that we're importers or vendors or something, and not artists. When people don't understand the process, then it becomes difficult to justify the price to them. Of course, there are collectors and art professionals who understand and think I price too low.

These same art professionals recognize an artist's need to change and try new materials. This openness is an encouragement to me as I progress into mixed media work. There's a pure joy in working with new materials and moving off into new directions.

Darryl Arawjo
Karen Arawjo

P.O. Box 477
Bushkill, PA 18324
(717) 588-6957

In the past 12 years Darryl and Karen Arawjo have established their work among the most desirable of today's collectables. With a faithfulness to form and function and an uncompromising attitude of excellence, they have designed a line of white oak baskets that are not only functional but uniquely creative and highly prized by collectors throughout the country. Unlike the rough utilitarian baskets of past generations, Arawjo baskets are sleek, highly refined works of art—traditional American basketry for the contemporary home.

Specializing in commissions, executive gifts, custom orders, one-of-a-kind and limited edition work.

Prices range from $200 to $10,000.

Further information and additional photographs available upon request.

D.K. Bell

DB Stone Carving
3752 Catamarca Drive
San Diego, CA 92124
(619) 279-7001

Stone becomes fluid motion in the hands
of D.K. Bell as shown here in recent work.
Marble, sandstone, limestone, and alabaster
are patiently carved and painstakingly
hand-polished to a shimmering finish for
a dramatic, endurable work of art.

Selection of stone types and color can
be chosen to accommodate any setting
according to exposure suitability and clients'
desires.

Commissioned work is completed in 6 to 8
weeks for work 2 to 4 feet high, and 3 to 5
months for large scale outdoor sculptures.

Prices range from $2500 to $15,000
depending on scale, material, and design
intricacy.

A slide portfolio is available upon request.

Top: *Spindle,* Carrara marble, 28"H
Bottom Left: *Seawatch,* Utah alabaster, 37"H
Bottom Right: *Kinetic Ice,* Italian alabaster,
 24"H

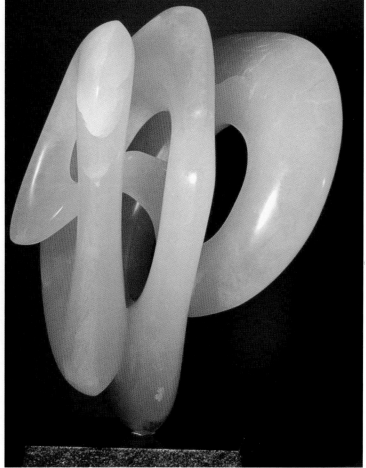

Nancy Moore Bess

5 East 17th Street, 6th FL
New York, NY 10003
(212) 691-2821
Messages (212) 388-0511

Influenced strongly by Japanese folk art and packaging, Nancy Moore Bess relies on the traditional basketry techniques of twining, coiling and plaiting to create her non-functional basket forms and fiber constructions. Some pieces are mounted on lucite for easy installation and maintenance, others rest on Japanese river stones or bamboo. Display elements are included in pricing.

Wholesale prices for these one-of-a-kind and limited edition basket forms start at $125, fiber constructions start at $225.

Bess will collaborate with art consultants and designers on custom work for private collections and corporate installations. Expanded studio allows for prompt attention. Inquiries invited.

Top Left: *Japanese Package,* from series, 4"H
Top Right: *Storage Jar,* from series, 4"H
Bottom: *Fiber Armor* (one of three), 7"H

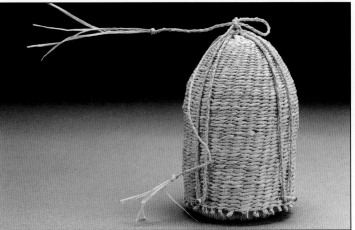

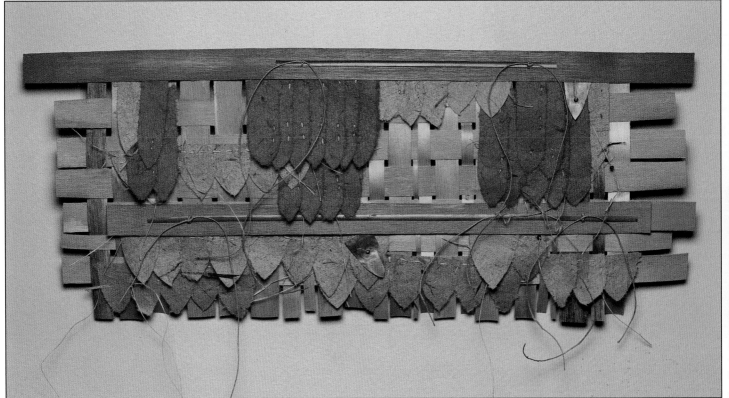

Printed in Japan ©1992 Kraus Sikes Inc. The Guild: The Designer's Reference Book of Artists

Cristina Biaggi

208 Washington Spring Road
Palisades, NY 10964
(914) 359-5450 (S)

1 Ludlow Lane
Palisades, NY 10964
(914) 359-5898 (H)
FAX (914) 359-6941

Cristina Biaggi has been working in wood for 20 years. *Medusa* (Top) is an earlier and more figurative piece. Her recent work, such as *Ziggurat* (Bottom), focuses on the presentation of various parts of the female body, enlarged four to eight times. By presenting enlargements of various parts of the body out of context with the rest of the body, the artist asks the viewer to look at these pieces as architectonic structures, mysterious sculptural fragments that contain a new macrocosmic dimension.

Biaggi has exhibited widely in the U.S. and in Europe and her work is in numerous collections.

Prices range from $1000 to $10,000 depending on size and intricacy of work. Inquiry on commissioned work is welcomed. For additional information, please contact the artist.

Medusa, yew, 34" x 30" x 22"

Ziggurat, maple, 58" Dia., 30" H

Ron Fleming

Hearthstone Studios
4731 N. Evanston
Tulsa, OK 74130
(918) 425-9873

Ron Fleming's wooden vessels are distinctive for their flowing form, and sensual hand-carved or painted designs.

Fleming's pieces have been exhibited internationally and are represented in galleries, private collections and museums throughout the United States.

Top Left: *Pink Ivory Flora*, 11"H, 8"W
Top Right: detail, *Pink Ivory Flora*
Bottom: *Suspended Redwood Flora*, 10"H, 10"D, 21"W

Barbara F. Fletcher

88 Beals Street
Brookline, MA 02146
(617) 277-3019

Barbara Fletcher creates cast-paper wall and pedestal pieces. Wet paper pulp is air-dried in plaster casts which are made from clay forms. One-of-a-kinds or multiples can be made with this process. The pieces are painted with procion dyes to give a wonderful luminosity. The paper is made in many layers for durability and then coated with a protective acrylic, making it appropriate for commercial as well as residential space.

Fletcher's pieces are unique for their intense color, texture and whimsicality. Her work has been exhibited nationally and is included in many private collections including the collection of writer Stephen King.

Prices range from $200–$1000. Slides are available upon request. Commissions are accepted.

Top: *Elephant Mask,* 30" x 20" x 12"
Below: animal masks, similar installations include Harvard Community Health Bldg., Kenmore Square, Boston and Burlington, MA

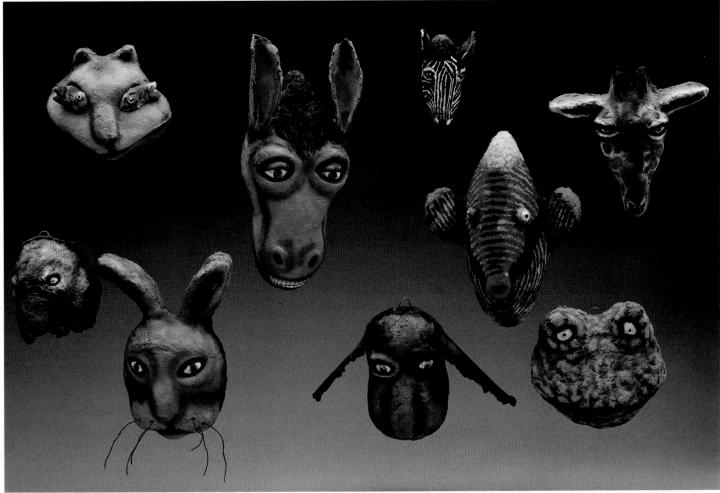

Logan Fry

2835 Southern Road
Richfield, OH 44286
(216) 659-3104

While walking through the forest, Logan Fry looks for faces, figures and forms hidden within the natural grain and contour of fallen wood. He collects this wood, and accentuates the features with twigs, nails, paint and other materials.

Adaptable to both office and home interiors, the resulting work is appropriate to collectors who like to work, live and play in relaxed, intellectually-stimulating and slightly unconventional surroundings.

Prices start at $1,250. Inquiries are invited.

Top: *Spirit of the Woodland Garden*, Exhibition History: Seventy-First Annual May Show, The Cleveland Museum of Art, Cleveland, OH 1990; All Ohio, 1990, The Canton Art Institute, Canton, OH, 10"W x 23"H x 9"D.

Bottom: *Easy ZZ*, Exhibition History: Best of 1991, Ohio Designer Craftsman, Columbus & Portsmouth, OH; Sixth Annual Holiday Exhibition, Gallery 500, Elkins Park, PA, 1991, 9"W x 14"H x 20"D.

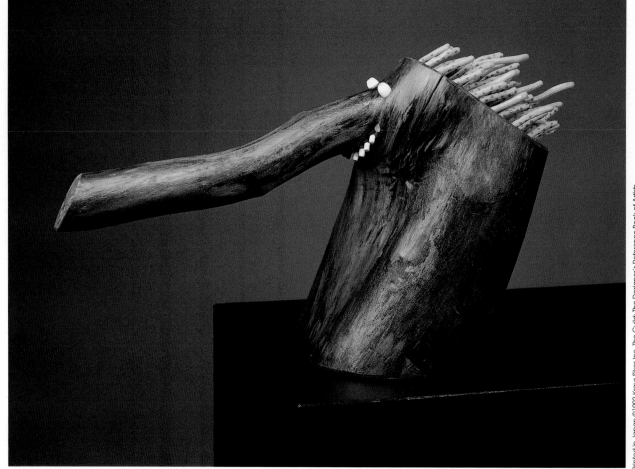

Susan J. Geissler

636 Mountain View Drive
Lewiston, NY 14092
(716) 285-5640
(800) 473-1237
FAX (716) 285-1237

Susan sculpts with affection, joy, and good humor. Her wonderfully warm pieces are unique, sturdy, and mainly one-of-a-kind creations of copper, wire, claycrete, and acrylic paint. The finished exposed wire pieces are either chrome-plated or painted with colored epoxies.

Her work is suitable for a wide range of environments from cozy to commercial.

Prices range from $700–$15,000 retail, depending on size and complexity. Allow three months and up for delivery, installation or shipping. Susan will collaborate on ideas.

Please inquire for more information.

All photos: Denise Wood, Niagara Falls, NY.

Top Left: *Blue Monday-Dog*, 8"H x 47"L x 27"W
Top Right: *Bob*, 55"H x 38"L x 26"W
Bottom Left: *Sir Charles-Lion*, 30"H x 54"L x 24"W
Bottom Right: *Scorpion Fish*, 14"H x 14"L x 14"W

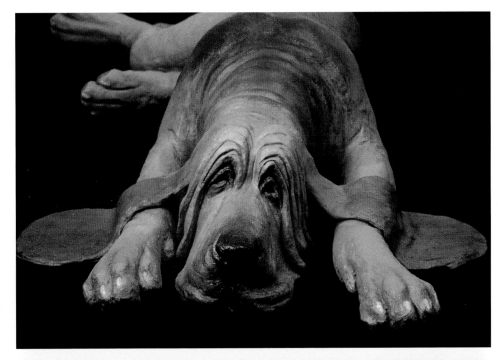

Wright E. Harris III

G3 Enterprises
P.O. Box 69115
St. Louis, MO 63169-0155
(314) 741-4445
FAX (314) 741-4445

Wright E. Harris III has designed and hand-produced unique sculptural objects since 1971 for individuals, institutions and shows. His pieces derive from visionary experiences, cross-cultural impacts and mystical events and are aimed at future generations as indicators of our legacy as the "melting pot" in this time-cycle.

His primary medium is wood; clay or bronze can be requested. All work is by commission. The chess sets are an on-going maquette series for up-sizing at later date. (Chess board, 28" x 28" x 14"; Pieces, 6"; Pawns, 3".)

Top: detail, black bishop/black knight
Bottom: full chess set

Joel Hotchkiss

Hotchkiss Mobiles
1015 22nd Avenue
Oakland, CA 94606
(510) 436-7202

Joel Hotchkiss broke from the boundaries of commercial art to enter the creative arena of mobile making in 1978.

He has since made numerous original mobiles, including limited editions, commissioned pieces, as well as a full line of mobile designs sold in contemporary galleries and museums such as the Guggenheim Museum in NYC.

From his knowledge of the unique characteristics of mobiles involving the interaction of shapes, materials, color, size, balance, and movement, Joel is able to create exciting mobiles for both private and corporate clients.

Call or write for current information and prices.

Below: *Grand Tri-Lumen*, 96"W x 48"D, $750

HOY Design Studio

Bruce S. Haughey
12246 South 44th Street
Phoenix, AZ 85044
(800) 594-4931
FAX (602) 893-6034

Bruce Haughey (pronounced HOY), totally handmakes one-of-a-kind polyresin fountains, planters, and tablebases. Each piece is virtually indestructible, lightweight and weatherproof. A variety of colors and textures including copper, silver and gold leaves, classic marbles, and granites are offered.

Planters will not crack, break or leach through. All can withstand worldwide temperature differentials. Because the fountains do not splash, they can be used inside and on carpet. Simply fill with water and plug in.

Custom finishes are available. Most pieces ship UPS. Dealer prices range from $175 to $1600. A color catalog is available upon request.

Bruce was graduated from Montana State University in fine art and has been creating since 1967.

Pamela Joseph

Metal Paintings
RR3 Box 140
Pound Ridge, NY 10576
(914) 764-8208
(914) 764-5732
FAX (914) 764-8215

Karakal, Mountain of the Blue Moon, is a recent departure for the artist. Known for her public art commissions, current painting/sculptures combine wood, metal and a stone aggregate inscribed with pictographic images.

Since 1976, the artist has specialized in providing imaginative solutions for specific sites.

Selected collections include Smithsonian Institution, Fairfield University, Schein Pharmaceutical, Danbury Pharmacal, Philadelphia's Piccoli Playground, Croton Falls Baptist Church and The Embassy of the Hungarian People's Republic.

All photos: *Karakal,* 1990, wood, pigment, metallic powders, 37" x 26" x 14"

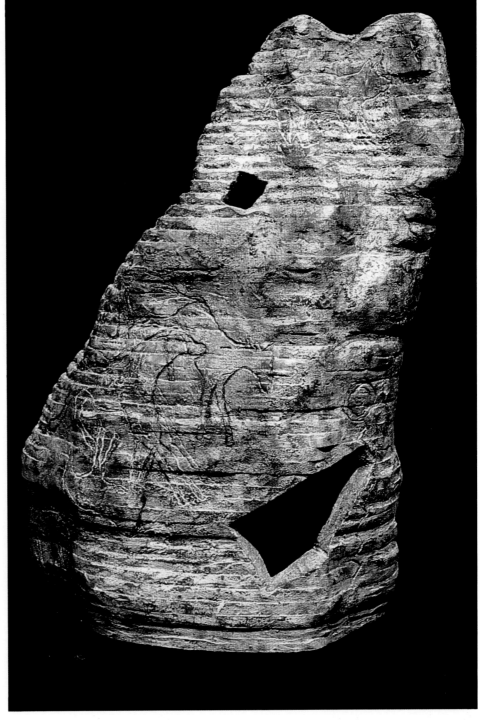

Carol Kropnick

135 Eastern Parkway
Brooklyn, NY 11238
(718) 638-4909

Whimsical, provocative, mystical, and sensuous, the masks of Carol Kropnick represent a singular art form. Shaped from such diverse materials as antique textiles, leather, exotic feathers, bone, and vintage beads, these works take one month to finish and are surprisingly durable.

Kropnick has created her masks for over 14 years. They have been exhibited in national museums and galleries, displayed in art books worldwide, and commissioned for theater, film, interior design, and by private collectors.

More examples of her work can be seen in *THE GUILD 5.* A brochure and slides are available upon request.

Prices range from $750–$2,000.

Mask for Winter Solstice, leather, bone, horse hair, and paint, 14"W x 14"H x 7"D

Printed in Japan ©1992 Kraus Sikes Inc. The Guild: The Designer's Reference Book of Artists

Anne Mayer Meier

Creative Textures
169 Sandalwood Way
Longwood, FL 32750
(407) 332-6713

Meier's "Ancestors"© are sculptural figures evoking man's primitive past using contemporary design and fabrication. Although fictional in nature, each one-of-a-kind "Ancestor"© provides mystical, spiritual, and folkloric concepts open to the viewer's interpretation.

Retail prices range $60–$1,000. Contact the artist for information.

Top Left: "Ancestor," mixed media, 22"H
Top Right: "Ancestor," mixed media, 22"H
Bottom Left: Spirit Sticks, clay, 14"–18"H
Bottom Center: "Ancestor," *Clan of the Pueblos,* mixed media, 36"H
Bottom Right: "Ancestor," *Clan of Journey,* mixed media, 24"H

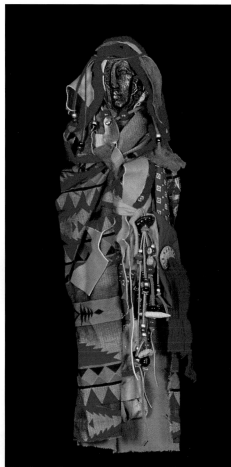

Anne Mayer Meier

Creative Textures
169 Sandalwood Way
Longwood, FL 32750
(407) 332-6713

Anne Meier has been producing a broad
range of contemporary baskets to
complement residential and corporate
settings since 1979.

Meier's sculptural and decorative vessels,
incorporating original design concepts and
superior craftsmanship, derive from classical
forms and are embellished with unique
juxtapositions of line and color.

Meier's one-of-a-kind story baskets explore
the structure of the non-functional vessel
and are then hand painted with tiny
patterns, all part of Meier's personal
symbol system.

Meier's work is collected internationally.
Prices range from $200–$2500. Contact
artist for information.

Top Left: *Primary Bowl,* 12" x 14"
Top Right: *The Red Zone,* 36" x 12"
Bottom: *Good Morning, America, Part II,*
  36" x 34"

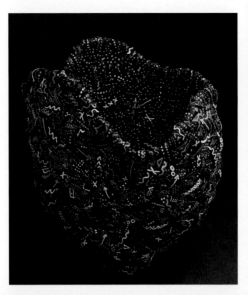

Eva S. Walsh

P.O. Box 2266
Winter Park, FL 32790
(407) 628-0422

Eva Walsh's one-of-a-kind sculptures, fashioned from gourds, provide a dramatic focal point for home and office. Their glowing colors are produced by leather dyes, sealed and protected by satin finish. She has created over a dozen designs and a number of larger pieces. They are exhibited in private collections, in galleries, and home furnishings showrooms.

Private and corporate commissions welcome. Retail prices $80–$1000.

Top (left to right): *Birds on a Nest, Birds,* and *Turtle,* gourds, edged with palm bark, broomcorn and palm ribs
Bottom Left: *Spirits Rising,* 11" gourd cut into sections and rebuilt with palm ribs, reed and twisted paper stand
Bottom Right: *My Cup Runneth Over,* gourd adorned with a beaded bib, *Captured Spirit,* gourd with twined pine needles

S.M. Warren

Vermont Paperworks
Box 7, Middletown Road
Grafton, VT 05146
(802) 843-2369
FAX (802) 843-2585

Paper pieces such as these seductively textured, organically shaped vessels have been exhibited across the country in juried shows as well as private galleries for the past 20 years. While these are suitable on a pedestal or desktop, other pieces from Warren's *Archeological Artifact Series* range in size from 6"H sculptures to 15' wallpieces and mobiles.

Prices from $400–$4,000 for commissioned works. Resume and slides upon request. Custom color available.

Top: *Four Bundles in Burned Basket,* cloth, paper and raffia, 6"H x 14"Dia.
Bottom Left: *Second Sister's Soul,* handmade paper, 86"H x 9"Dia.
Bottom Right: *Coil Pot with Cover,* handmade paper, 6"H x 10"D x 10"W

Photo: Greg Bolosky

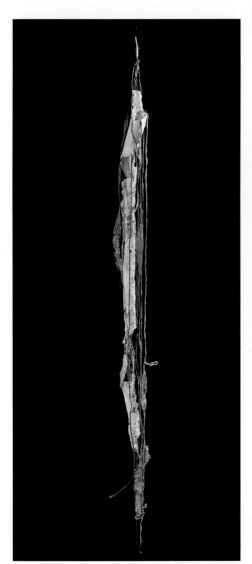

Photo: Greg Bolosky

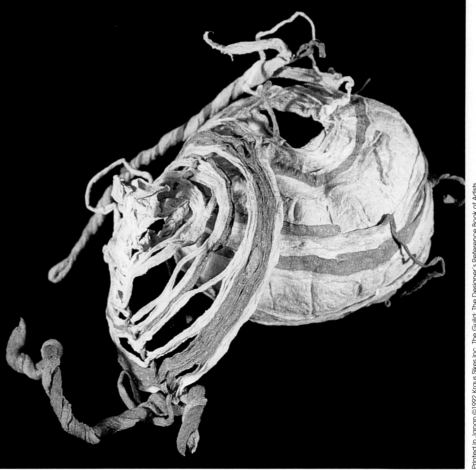

Photo: Richard A. Warren

Nancy Young
Allen Young

11416 Brussels NE
Albuquerque, NM 87111
(505) 299-6108

The Youngs design and produce original three-dimensional works. Sculpture is available in cast marble for exterior pieces. Interior pieces include wood or cast marble free-standing pieces or mixed media wall pieces. Color preferences and commissions accepted.

Prices range from $200–$2900 retail, depending on size and complexity. Allow 4–8 weeks from design approval and contract to completion. Shipping FOB Albuquerque.

Selected collections include IBM, American Express, and AT&T.

Left: *Cloud Dreamers*, 57"H x 16"W x 3"D
Right: *The Gathering*, sculpture ranges from 5'6"H x 8"W x 8"D to 8'H x 16"W x 8"D

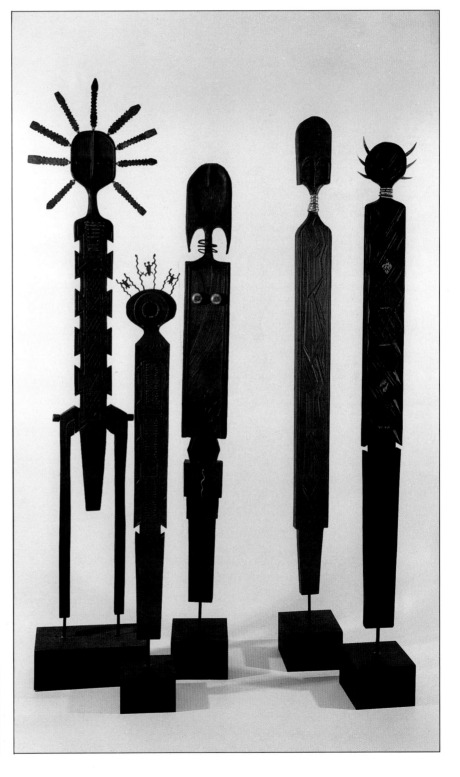

Photo Credits

Gallery Resources
Introduction

Interested in seeing original artwork by the artists within the previous pages? The following Gallery Resources section provides a way to do just that. Included is a state-by-state listing of over 150 galleries, retail stores and showrooms that carry the work of artists featured in THE GUILD.

This is not intended to be a comprehensive list of galleries in North America. In fact, the only galleries included are those recommended by one or more artists. It is, however, a way for the innovative buyer to see firsthand the work of artists who are found in THE GUILD.

The new, expanded format for this section includes information that designers need when searching for specific types of work for their clients. The listing accommodates basic designer contact information, as well as details on the type of work carried and gallery specialties. (See Gallery Resources, A Sample Listing, page 250.)

Galleries and showrooms play a vital role in marketing hand-crafted objects, and are increasingly involved in working with design professionals. The article on the following pages, "Using the Gallery as a Resource," describes the services generally available to the trade.

As you continue on into the wonderful world of one-of-a-kind, commissioned work, these galleries make exciting and inspirational stops along the way.

Using the Gallery as a Resource
An Orientation for Designers

by Leslie Ferrin

When it comes to finding a specific object to complete a space or a certain artist with a particular skill, working with a gallery is a lot like using THE GUILD -- the gallery is a resource.

Like THE GUILD, a gallery is a resource center and like THE GUILD, you can browse for ideas or come prepared with your own. Like chapters in THE GUILD, most galleries have a specialty. And just like everyone involved in a creative pursuit, each gallery has a personality which is expressed through the choice of artists represented and the mode of operation. Every gallery has its own broad range of sources drawing from years of experience and a library of magazines, books, and slides. Like all relationships, when the chemistry is right, working with a gallery can result in great collaborations. For you, the unofficial partnership can become a part of the services you offer to clients.

DEFINING YOUR IDEAS. As middlemen, galleries provide credibility for you and your projects when they recommend or introduce you to an artist or an artist's work. If they help to negotiate a project or fees, their ability to communicate with an artist can save time; they may be able to speak more frankly or directly with you and with the artist. Galleries can be especially helpful in steering you away from artists who might not be available or appropriate because of prior commitments, problems with deadlines or the requirements of your project. If the budget is pre-determined or limited, a gallery can also identify less well-known artists whose work is not as expensive.

If you have an idea of what it is you are looking for, it will be easier to identify which galleries you should be contacting. Are you searching for a certain type of object? What scale? What style? What price range? Are you seeking an artist who has a specific skill or uses a certain technique? Do you want an artist known for their ideas or style, or are you looking for someone to breathe life into your ideas?

The answers to these questions will help determine which artists a gallery might recommend. Some artists only work from the client's ideas while others are only interested in creating from their own ideas. Most projects will fall somewhere in between. Once an idea is explored, the artist creates an object to fit a client's needs, balancing creative expression with the requirements of the site.

FINDING A GALLERY. In your area, the yellow pages probably have a listing like 'Art or Craft Galleries.' Often, one street or neighborhood can be identified and a quick visit will provide an overview of the offerings. Be prepared to find a wide range of work because often the word 'gallery' is used to describe everything from a framing shop to a retail store. A true gallery presents changing exhibits and represents a 'stable' of artists, but other venues such as showrooms and stores have much to offer as well.

Local galleries tend to have special knowledge of the area's artists. Working with a local or regional artist can often save you time and money by eliminating travel and shipping costs. In addition, supporting a regional community of artists may be desired by private clients; it can also be a positive statement for a local business to make.

Working with nationally known galleries outside your area opens up specialties of a different sort. Finding a gallery in the country with strong ties to a particular medium can result in accessing artists unavailable except through their primary gallery. Additionally, a gallery's knowledge may save time in identifying the most appropriate artists for a project. These galleries generally have strong relationships with the artists they represent, and the relationships may prove helpful in gaining cooperation and avoiding problems.

HOW TO BEGIN. Once you have located the galleries you would like to approach, identify the appropriate contact person (designated as 'Designer Contact' in THE GUILD's Gallery Resources) and make an appointment to meet in person or talk on the phone. It is as much this person's job to talk with you as it is your job to seek them out. Whether to the trade or the public, the gallery's role is the same -- to present an artist's work, talk about it, explain the techniques involved and the artistic statement expressed, and through this process, to sell an existing object or create a commission opportunity.

Once you have identified the artists you are interested in, you might want to set up a time to bring in your client. Sometimes seeing actual objects is the best way to introduce the concept of working with an artist or purchasing art work. If this is not possible, ask for printed materials such as color cards, articles on the artist, resumes, statements or slides of existing pieces or installations.

The gallery may not have all of these materials on hand, especially when the most current material is needed. If the project's timeline permits, the gallery can contact the artist for appropriate materials. If time is short, the gallery will probably allow you to take a polaroid snapshot of the object you have in mind. Just keep in mind that a snapshot can quickly provide an image, but if the client is not familiar with reading quality into a polaroid, the first impression might be better if you wait for more prepared materials to arrive from the artist.

COST STRUCTURES. The price of a piece of work depends upon a variety of factors: the time involved in design and production, the degree of difficulty of the process used, the cost of materials and studio overhead, how well known an artist is, and the price he or she can command for current work. Most people are surprised to discover just how wide the range of prices is for works they consider comparable. You should definitely ask gallery personnel to explain what you're looking at and why it costs what it does; you're likely to get a terrific education in hand-crafted work. Also tell them if you need to stay within a certain budget. That will simplify your search.

LOCATING THE RIGHT GALLERY. There are thousands of galleries in the United States and Canada, and each one is unique in terms of the work it carries and the artists it represents. Many will specialize by craft media (ceramics and glass are the most common specialties); some galleries focus on regional work, such as Southwestern art, and others represent artists from a particular ethnic group. Give some thought to the type of work the gallery generally carries, and you will be able to focus your search. Such factors as price range will indicate whether the gallery specializes in one-of-a-kind works, limited editions, or production pieces.

ONE-OF-A-KIND WORKS. Artists tend to consider one-of-a-kind pieces their most important or most innovative work. Naturally, these are more expensive than works produced in multiples. Craft artists who make things in the one-of-a-kind category generally will not repeat a design, but might be willing to create a variation of it to your specifications.

LIMITED EDITIONS. Another category of craft production is limited editions, which means that a small number of pieces (6, 12, 30, 100) are made in a series. There are usually at least slight variations between limited edition objects created by an artist or small studio. Sometimes the variations are much more than slight. A piece that you order may be similar to a sample, but not identical. If your client understands that these variations are not only unavoidable, but are really quite interesting and desirable, then chances are that you will both be pleased with the results. Prices will be appropriately lower.

PRODUCTION. Objects designed for production in unlimited quantities include such things as chairs, woven throws, glass or ceramic vases. If you order a production piece from a gallery, you should still expect variations within a series, although the piece you get will pretty much resemble the sample. Keep in mind that production quantities in crafts are much more limited than in mass produced items with which most people are familiar. The biggest production facilities in the crafts field are still small businesses.

THE GALLERY RESOURCES listings in THE GUILD, beginning on page 251, provide information on galleries that carry the work of GUILD artists. If you have any questions, call the gallery --

If you identify several possibilities that you feel would interest your client, it may be possible to take a number of objects on an approval basis. I've found that once placed in the site, an object can sell itself or definitely prove to be the wrong choice. Our gallery asks that the borrower take full responsibility for an object's retail value which is guaranteed through a credit card number. (Even slight damage like a chip or a tear would result in a purchase.) Although we have insurance, the deductible is very high and no one really wants to make claims. The timing on 'borrowing' work should be clearly determined. Taking a piece from an exhibit overnight might be possible, but if lengthier arrangements are necessary, the loan will probably not be possible until the show is over.

Ask if the gallery has a standard system of working with the trade; this should set everyone at ease from the beginning. With our gallery, if someone approaches us who is actively working to 'sell' our artists work to their client, we feel it only fair to share the sales commission. Assuming that the gallery is working on a 50/50 relationship with artists, and the selling is equally shared between you and the gallery, the arrangement could be made to split the sales commission evenly. If the gallery is more involved through making presentations, site visits, billing, etc., the commission to you might be as a 'referral' or around 10%.

If your project requires the actual commissioning of site-specific work, customized financial arrangements will be necessary. Establishing how the gallery would like to work with you ahead of time will prevent any misunderstandings at a later date.

EVERYONE CAN WIN. Every gallery and each person you encounter are going to have different offerings and ways of working and not every gallery is set up to work with the trade. There are no rules and there are no set systems. Each artist, gallery, and client will find their own ways of working together and likewise, the results will be unique collaborations. When the chemistry is right -- the artist makes a great piece, you place it in the right setting, and all concerned get paid fairly and promptly -- what could be better? Everyone wins.

Leslie Ferrin is co-owner of the Ferrin Gallery in Northampton, MA.

249

Gallery Resources
A Sample Listing

Gallery Name & Owner's Name •

MINDSCAPE GALLERY
Owners: Ron Isaacson, Deborah Farber

Address, Telephone & FAX Number •

**1506 Sherman Avenue
Evanston, IL 60201
(708) 864-2660
FAX (708) 864-2815**

Information about the year the gallery was established,
the total sq. footage of gallery or showroom space,
whether the gallery is open to the public
or to the trade only, and whether the gallery
offers a discount to design professionals. •

**Established in 1974
Total sq. footage: 10,000
Open to the public
Trade discount available**

Listing of specific media carried by the gallery,
including the gallery's specialization,
and the percentage of one-of-a-kind work featured
(See definition of one-of-a-kind on page 248). •

**Type of work: Ceramics, Glass, Wood, Fiber,
Mixed media
90% one-of-a-kind work
Specialty: Contemporary American fine crafts**

'Commissions welcome' indicates that the gallery provides
assistance to designers in locating and commissioning
original crafts for their clients. (See "Using the Gallery
as a Resource," pages 246–249 for more information
on the commissioning process.) Also listed is the
name of the person to contact if you have questions. •

**Commissions welcome
Designer contact: Carole Richey**

GUILD artists represented by the gallery are listed
along with page numbers for easy reference to
their full color pages in this edition, or, where
noted, in the 7th edition of THE GUILD:
The Architect's Source of Artists and Artisans. •

**GUILD artists represented:
Lucinda Carlstrom, see pg. 54
Bruce Howdle, see pg. 114, Architect's Source
Candace Kreitlow, see pg. 44
Steven Maslach, see pg. 208
Nina Paladino, Michael K. Hansen, see pg. 205
Vincent & Carolyn Lee Tolpo, see pg. 99**

This is an opportunity for the gallery to provide additional
information about the work they represent and the
services they provide to designers and architects. •

**Statement
One of the nation's oldest and largest craft
galleries, Mindscape, located just 25 minutes
north of the Merchandise Mart in Evanston, has
long been a resource for Chicago-area and
Midwestern designers. The gallery represents
over 350 contemporary artists and craftspeople
throughout the U.S., including both established
masters and emerging talents. Media regularly
displayed are studio art glass; decorative and
functional ceramics; sculpture; metals and
mobiles; jewelry; paper and fiber wall pieces;
wooden accessories and one-of-a-kind furniture.**

Gallery Resources
State Listings

• ALABAMA

MARALYN WILSON GALLERY
Owner: Maralyn Wilson

2010 Cahaba Road
Birmingham, AL 35223
(205) 879-0582
FAX (205) 870-3022

Established in 1973
Open to the public
Trade discount available

Type of work: Ceramics, Glass,
Metal, Paper, Mixed media
65% one-of-a-kind work
Specialty: Fine art paintings, Crafts

Designer contact: Maralyn Wilson

GUILD artists represented:
Timothy Weber, see pg. 197

• ARIZONA

EL PRADO GALLERIES, INC.
Owners: Don & Elyse Pierson

Tlaquepaque Village
P.O. Box 1849
Sedona, AZ 86336
(602) 282-7390
FAX (602) 282-7578

Established in 1976
Total sq. footage: 15,000
Open to the public
Trade discount available

Type of work: Ceramics, Glass,
Metal, Wood, Leather, Paper,
Mixed media, Baskets
95% one-of-a-kind work
Specialty: Oils, Acrylics, Watercolors,
Mixed media, Sculptures

Commissions welcome
Designer contact: Don H. Pierson

GUILD artists represented:
Martha Chatelain, see pg. 55

GALLERY THREE
Owner: Sherry Manoukian

3819 North Third Street
Phoenix, AZ 85012
(602) 277-9540

Established in 1969
Total sq. footage: 2,200
Open to the public
Trade discount available

Type of work: Ceramics, Metal,
Paper, Fiber, Mixed media
80% one-of-a-kind work
Specialty: Contemporary,
Contemporary Southwest artwork

Commissions welcome
Designer contact: Sherry Manoukian,
Helen Petersen

GUILD artists represented:
Vincent & Carolyn Lee Tolpo, see pg. 99

**JOANNE RAPP GALLERY/
THE HAND AND
THE SPIRIT GALLERY**
Owner: Joanne Rapp

4222 North Marshall Way
Scottsdale, AZ 85251
(602) 949-1262

Established in 1972
Total sq. footage: 3,000
Open to the public
Trade discount available

Type of work: Ceramics, Glass,
Metal, Wood, Fiber
50% one-of-a-kind work

Commissions welcome
Designer contact: Louise Roman

GUILD artists represented:
Steven Maslach, see pg. 208
Junco Sato Pollack, see pg. 46

• CALIFORNIA

**THE AESTHETICS COLLECTION,
INC.**
Owners: Annette Ridenour

1060 17th Street
San Diego, CA 92101
(619) 238-1860
FAX (619) 231-4704

Established in 1980
Open to the trade only

Type of work: Glass, Metal, Wood,
Paper, Fiber, Mixed media

Commissions welcome
Designer contact: Annette Ridenour

GUILD artists represented:
Marilyn Forth, see pg. 167
Alexandra Friedman, see pg. 27
Anna Karesh, see pg. 61

AGNES BOURNE, INC.
Owner: Agnes Bourne

Two Henry Adams St., Suite 220
San Francisco, CA 94103
(415) 626-6883
FAX (415) 626-2489

Established in 1983
Total sq. footage: 4,400

GUILD artists represented:
David J. Marks, see pg. 129

ART BY DESIGN GALLERY
Owner: Susan Street

5889 Oberlin Drive, Suite 103
San Diego, CA 92121
(619) 452-8586
FAX (619) 452-1213

Established in 1984
Open to the public
Trade discount available

Type of work: All
75% one-of-a kind work
Specialty: Sculpture, Paper, Paintings

Commissions welcome:
Designer contact: Susan Street

GUILD artists represented:
Archie Held, see pgs. 162–163,
Architect's Source

**THE ART CENTER
EUREKA ART CENTER, LTD.**
Owner: Anne Pierson

211 G Street
Eureka, CA 95501
(707) 443-7017

Established in 1972
Open to the public

Gallery Resources

Type of work: Ceramics, Glass,
Wood, Paper
50% one-of-a-kind work
Specialty: Local artwork, Paintings,
Photos, Ceramics

Commissions welcome
Designer contact: Mary Ann Testagrossa

GUILD artists represented:
Victor Jacoby, see pg. 31

THE ART COLLECTOR
Owner: Janet Disraeli

4151 Taylor St.
San Diego, CA 92110
(619) 299-3232
FAX (619) 299-8709

Established in 1971
Total sq. footage: 4,500
Open to the public
Trade discount available

Type of work: Ceramics, Glass, Metal,
Wood, Paper, Fiber, Mixed media
Specialty: All types

Commissions welcome
Designer contact: Janet Disraeli

GUILD artists represented:
Martha Chatelain, see pg. 55
Marie-Laure Ilie, see pgs. 42–43
Deborah E. Love Jemmott, see pg. 174

BANAKER GALLERY
Owners: Nancy Barry, Era Cherry

1373 Locust Street
Walnut Creek, CA 94596
(510) 930-0700

Established in 1987
Total sq. footage: 2,500
Open to the public
Trade discount available

Type of work: Ceramics, Metal, Wood,
Fiber, Mixed media, Furniture, Baskets
98% one-of-a-kind work

Commissions welcome
Designer contact: Nancy Barry

Guild artists represented:
Nancy Moore Bess, see pg. 228
Tom McFadden, see pg. 147
Jean Neblett, see pg. 19
Junco Sato Pollack, see pg. 46
Gary Upton, see pg. 149
Scott Wynn, see pg. 152

BAY ARTS
*Owners: Hoshang Mostofizadeh,
Claudia Mostofizadeh*

309 Sutter Street
San Francisco, CA 94108
(415) 399-9925

Established in 1991
Open to the public

Type of work: Ceramics, Glass,
Metal, Wood, Fiber, Mixed
media, Furniture, Lighting, Baskets
90% one-of-a-kind work
Specialty: Bay area, Greater San
Francisco area

Commissions welcome
Designer contact: Hoshang or Claudia
Mostofizadeh

GUILD artists represented:
Scott Wynn, see pg. 152

BRAVO GALLERY
*Owners: Judith P. Redman,
Lauren B. Becker*

302 Island Avenue, Suite 101
San Diego, CA 92101
(619) 232-0396

Established in 1989
Total sq. footage: 1,500
Open to the public
Trade discount available

Type of work: Ceramics, Glass,
Metal, Fiber, Mixed media
100% one-of-a-kind work
Specialty: San Diego artists

Commissions welcome
Designer contact: Judith P. Redman,
Lauren B. Becker

GUILD artists represented:
Craig Houx, see pg. 123

CEDANNA
Owners: Cedric Koloseus, Zoe Koloseus

400 Main Street
Half Moon Bay, CA 94019
(415) 726-6776

Established in 1987
Total sq. footage: 2,400
Open to the public
Trade discount available

Type of work: Ceramics, Glass,
Metal, Wood, Furniture, Lighting
50% one-of-a-kind work
Specialty: Contemporary metal & wood,
Folk art, Furniture & furnishings,
Contemporary decorative
& functional craft

Commissions welcome
Designer contact: Cedric Koloseus,
Mimi Haas

GUILD artists represented:
Jeanine Guncheon, see pg. 120
Marcia Stuermer, see pg. 145

CEDANNA
Owners: Cedric Koloseus, Zoe Koloseus

1925 Fillmore Street
San Francisco, CA 94115
(415) 474-7152
FAX (415) 474-7157

400 Main Street
Half Moon Bay, CA 94019
(415) 726-6776

Established in 1987
Total sq. footage: 2,400
Open to the public
Trade discount available

Type of work: Ceramics, Glass,
Metal, Wood, Furniture, Lighting
50% one-of-a-kind work
Specialty: Contemporary metal & wood,
Folk art, Furniture & furnishings,
Contemporary decorative
& functional craft

Commissions welcome
Designer contact: Cedric Koloseus,
Mimi Haas

GUILD artists represented:
Jeanine Guncheon, see pg. 120
Marcia Stuermer, see pg. 145

CHAPSON ARTSVISION LTD.
Owner: William Quan

Showplace Design Center
2 Henry Adams Street, # 489
San Francisco, CA 94103
(415) 863-2117
FAX (415) 863-6553

Established in 1988
Total sq. footage: 475
Open to the public
Trade discount available

Type of work: Ceramics, Glass,
Metal, Wood, Furniture, Lighting
100% one-of-a-kind work
Specialty: Furniture and decorative
accessories by California artists

Commissions welcome
Designer contact: William Quan

GUILD artists represented:
Gary Upton, see pg. 149

COMPOSITIONS GALLERY
Owner: Siegfried H. Ehrmann

2801 Leavenworth (The Cannery)
San Francisco, CA 94133
(415) 441-0629
FAX (415) 931-4068

Established in 1980
Total sq. footage: 600
Open to the public

Type of work: Glass, Wood
90 % one-of-a-kind work
Specialty: Contemporary glass art,
Designs in wood

Commissions welcome
Designer contact: Siegfried H. Ehrmann

GUILD artists represented:
Latchezar Boyadjiev, see pg. 202

CROCK-R-BOX CRAFT GALLERY
Owner: John Wenzell

73425 El Paseo
Palm Desert, CA 92260
(619) 568-6688

Established in 1979
Total sq. footage: 1,100
Open to the public
Trade discount available

Type of work: Ceramics, Glass,
Metal, Wood, Fiber
75% one-of-a-kind work
Specialty: Decorative and functional
ceramics, Jewelry

Commissions welcome
Designer contact: John Wenzell

GUILD artists represented:
Linda Brendler, see pg. 77

DEL MANO GALLERY
Owners: Jan Peters, Ray Leier

11981 San Vicente Boulevard
Los Angeles, CA 90049
(310) 476-8508
FAX (310) 471-0897

Established in 1973
Total sq. footage: 3,000
Open to the public
Trade discount available

Type of work: Ceramics, Glass,
Metal, Wood, Fiber
75% one-of-a-kind work
Specialty: Fine contemporary crafts
of all media

Commissions welcome
Designer contact: Kevin Wallace

GUILD artists represented:
Boris Bally & ROY, see pg. 217
William C. Richards, see pg. 81
Vincent & Carolyn Lee Tolpo, see pg. 99
Glenn Elvig, see pg. 87

DEL MANO GALLERY
Owners: Jan Peters, Ray Leier

33 E. Colorado Boulevard
Pasadena, CA 91105
(818) 793-6648

Established in 1973
Total sq. footage: 2,500
Open to the public
Trade discount available

Type of work: Ceramics, Glass,
Metal, Wood, Fiber
75% one-of-a-kind work
Specialty: Fine contemporary crafts
of all media

Commissions welcome
Designer contact: Ray Leier

GUILD artists represented:
Boris Bally & ROY, see pg. 217
William C. Richards, see pg. 81
Vincent & Carolyn Lee Tolpo, see pg. 99
Glenn Elvig, see pg. 87

FEINGARTEN GALLERIES
Owner: Gail Feingarten

Pacific Design Center
Archives, B206
8687 Melrose Avenue
Los Angeles, CA 90069
(213) 652-4748
FAX (310) 274-4255

Established in 1945
Total sq. footage: 7,000
Open to the public

Type of work: Ceramics, Metal,
Wood, Paper, Mixed media
90% one-of-a-kind work
Specialty: Modern and contemporary
paintings and sculpture

Commissions welcome
Designer contact: Gail Feingarten,
Stephanie Linden

GUILD artists represented:
James T. Russell, see pg. 171,
Architect's Source

FERRARI OF CARMEL
Owner: Linda G. Ferrari

P.O. Box 3273
San Carlos, between 5th & 6th
Carmel, CA 93921
(408) 624-9677

Established in 1986
Open to the public
Trade discount available

Type of work: Ceramics, Glass, Metal,
Mixed media, Furniture
Specialty: 23K gold ceramic vases and
sculptures; Fauna collection, Blown glass

Commissions welcome
Designer contact: Linda G. Ferrari

GUILD artists represented:
Ray Lewis, see pg. 127

FLUSH, INC.
Owner: Rosemary Klebahn

245 11th Street
San Francisco, CA 94103
(415) 252-0245
FAX (415) 252-0354

Established in 1991
Open to the public

Type of work: Glass, Leather,
Paper, Furniture
5% one-of-a-kind work
Specialty: Glass, Painted furniture

Commissions welcome
Designer contact: Chuck Winslow

GUILD artists represented:
Marcia Stuermer, see pg. 145

GALLERY EIGHT
*Owners: Ruth Newmark,
Barbara Saltman*

7464 Girard Avenue
La Jolla, CA 92037
(619) 454-9781

Established in 1978
Total sq. footage: 1,600
Open to the public
Trade discount available

Type of work: Ceramics, Glass,
Metal, Wood, Furniture
40% one-of-a-kind work
Specialty: Ceramics

Commissions welcome
Designer contact: Ruth Newmark

GUILD artists represented:
Greg Mesmer & Diane Bonciolini,
see pg. 209

Statement
Dedicated to providing a forum for the
best in contemporary crafts, Gallery
Eight represents American artists
whose innovative design and fine
craftsmanship range the full spectrum
from functional to decorative art.
Continuous ever-changing exhibits
feature work in clay, glass, wood,
metal, fiber, and jewelry.

GALLERY OF FUNCTIONAL ART
Owner: Lois Lambert

2429 Main Street
Santa Monica, CA 90405
(310) 450-2827
FAX (310) 450-4831

Established in 1988
Total sq. footage: 2,000
Open to the public
Trade discount available

Type of work: Ceramics, Glass, Metal,
Wood, Furniture, Lighting, Baskets
50% one-of-a-kind work
Specialty: Contemporary

Commissions welcome
Designer contact: Lois Lambert

GUILD artists represented:
Peter Mangan, see pg. 178

HUMAN ARTS GALLERY
Owners: Stan Katz, Hallie Katz

310 E. Ojai Avenue
Ojai, CA 93023
(805) 646-1525

Established in 1974
Total sq. footage: 500

Designer contact: David Willis

GUILD artists represented:
Marcia Stuermer, see pg. 145

INTERNATIONAL GALLERY
Owner: Stephen Ross

643 G Street
San Diego, CA 92101
(619) 235-8255

Established in 1985
Total sq. footage: 4,000
Open to the public
Trade discount available

Type of work: All
99.9% one-of-a-kind work
Specialty: Contemporary craft,
Folk & primitive art

Commissions welcome
Designer contact: Stephen Ross

GUILD artists represented:
Barbara Fletcher, see pg. 231
Anne Mayer Meier, see pgs. 239–240

Gallery Resources

I. WOLK GALLERY
Owners: Ira Wolk, Lynne Wolk

1235 Main Street
St. Helena, CA 94574
(707) 963-8800
FAX (707) 963-8801

Established in 1991
Total sq. footage: 1,800
Open to the public
Trade discount available

Type of work: Ceramics, Glass, Metal, Wood, Paper, Mixed media
75% one-of-a-kind work
Specialty: American contemporary paintings, Works on paper, Sculpture

Commissions welcome
Designer contact: Ira Wolk

GUILD artists represented:
Jim Gangwer, see pgs. 36 & 84, Architect's Source

KURLAND/SUMMERS GALLERY
Owners: Ruth T. Summers, Gloria Soloman Kamm

8742-A Melrose Avenue
Los Angeles, CA 90069
(310) 659-7098
FAX (310) 659-7263

Established in 1982
Total sq. footage: 2,200
Open to the public
Trade discount available

Type of work: Glass, Paper, Furniture
95% one-of-a-kind work
Specialty: Glass

Commissions welcome
Designer contact: Ruth T. Summers

GUILD artists represented:
Susan Stinsmuehlen-Amend, see pg. 72, Architect's Source

PRIMAVERA GALLERY
Owner: Khaled Al-awar

214 E. Ojai Avenue
Ojai, CA 93023
(805) 646-7133
FAX (805) 646-0500

Established in 1983
Total sq. footage: 1,000
Open to the public

Type of work: Ceramics, Glass, Mixed media
80% one-of-a-kind work
Specialty: Blown glass and one-of-a-kind jewelry

Commissions welcome
Designer contact: Khaled Al-awar

GUILD artists represented:
Latchezar Boyadjiev, see pg. 202

PUBLIC ART SERVICES
Owner: Scott C. Griesbach

1242 Crescent Heights
Los Angeles, CA 90046
(213) 650-3709

Established in 1988
Open to the trade only

Type of work: Ceramics, Glass, Metal, Wood
100% one-of-a-kind work
Specialty: 19th and 20th century public art commissions

Commissions welcome
Designer contact: Scott C. Griesbach

GUILD artists represented:
James E. Barnhill, see pg. 153, Architect's Source

SCULPTURE GARDENS GALLERY
Owner: Dr. Jerome Rowitch

1031 Abbot Kinney Boulevard
Venice, CA 90291
(310) 396-5809
FAX (310) 476-6618

Established in 1980
Total sq. footage: 1,000
Open to the public
Trade discount available

Type of work: Ceramics, Metal, Wood, Mixed media
90% one-of-a-kind work
Specialty: Patio sculpture

Commissions welcome
Designer contact: Jerome Rowitch

GUILD artists represented:
Martin Sturman, see pg. 222

THE SEEKERS COLLECTION & GALLERY
Owners: Michael Glade Adelson, Lynda Olsen Adelson

4090 Burton Drive
Cambria, CA 93428
(805) 927-8626
FAX (805) 927-5984

Established in 1981
Total sq. footage: 2,800
Open to the public
Trade discount available

Type of work: Ceramics, Glass, Wood
100% one-of-a-kind work
Specialty: Contemporary American glass art

Commissions welcome
Designer contact: Michael Glade Adelson

GUILD artists represented:
David Van Noppen, see pg. 214

SUSAN CUMMINS GALLERY
Owners: Susan Cummins, Beth Changstorm

12 Miller Avenue
Mill Valley, CA 94941
(415) 383-1512

Established in 1983
Total sq. footage: 3,000
Open to the public

Type of work: Mixed media
100% one-of-a-kind work
Specialty: Contemporary mixed media and sculpture

Commissions welcome
Designer contact: Susan Cummins

GUILD artists represented:
Bonnie Brown, see pg. 24, Architect's Source

SUSAN STREET FINE ART
Owner: Susan Street

5889 Oberlin Drive, Suite 103
San Diego, CA 92121
(619) 452-8586
FAX (619) 452-1213

Established in 1985
Total sq. footage: 1,800
Open to the public
Trade discount available

Type of work: Ceramics, Glass, Metal, Paper, Mixed media
75% one-of-a-kind work
Specialty: Corporate art, abstract and traditional

Commissions welcome
Designer contact: Susan Street

TERCERA GALLERY
Owner: Seb V. Hamamjian

24 North Santa Cruz Avenue
Los Gatos, CA 95030
(408) 354-9484
FAX (408) 354-0965

Established in 1978
Total sq. footage: 3,600
Open to the public
Trade discount available

Type of work: Ceramics, Metal, Wood, Mixed media, Furniture
80% one-of-a-kind work
Specialty: Fine art, Furniture

Commissions welcome
Designer contact: Seb V. Hamamjian, Diane Rogalski

GUILD artists represented:
David J. Marks, see pg. 129
Gary Upton, see pg. 149

VIRGINIA BREIER
Owner: Virginia Breier

3091 Sacramento Street
San Francisco, CA 94115
(415) 929-7173

Established in 1981
Total sq. footage: 1,500
Open to the public
Trade discount available

Type of work: Ceramics, Glass,
Metal, Fiber, Furniture
100% one-of-a-kind work
Specialty: Contemporary American
crafts

Commissions welcome
Designer contact: Virginia Breier

GUILD artists represented:
Bonnie Brown, see pg. 24,
Architect's Source
Marc D'Estout, see pg. 113
Peter Mangan, see pg. 178

VICTOR FISCHER GALLERIES
Owner: Victor L. Fischer

1333 Broadway, Suite 100 Plaza
Oakland, CA 94119
(415) 777-0717

Established in 1981
Total sq. footage: 9,000
Open to the public
Trade discount available

Type of work: Metal, Wood, Paper,
Mixed media, Furniture
95% one-of-a-kind work
Specialty: Sculptural

Commissions welcome
Designer contact: Linda Fischer

GUILD artists represented:
Phillip Levine, see pg. 167,
Architect's Source

VICTOR FISCHER GALLERIES
Owner: Victor L. Fischer

350 Steuart Street
San Francisco, CA

Established in 1981
Total sq. footage: 9,000
Open to the public
Trade discount available

Type of work: Metal, Wood, Paper,
Mixed media, Furniture
95% one-of-a-kind work
Specialty: Sculptural

Commissions welcome
Designer contact: Linda Fischer

GUILD artists represented:
Phillip Levine, see pg. 167,
Architect's Source

VILLAGE ARTISTRY
*Owners: Geraldine L. McFall,
Kathy McFall-Burnell*

Dolores, between Ocean & 7th
P.O. Box 5493
Carmel By The Sea, CA 93921
(408) 624-7628
FAX (408) 626-8683

Established in 1970
Total sq. footage: 2,300
Open to the public
Trade discount available

Type of work: Ceramics, Glass,
Paper, Fiber, Mixed media

Commissions welcome
Designer contact: Geraldine McFall

GUILD artists represented:
Martha Chatelain, see pg. 55

ZOO GALLERY INC.

9632 Santa Monica Blvd.
Beverly Hills, CA 90210
(310) 278-3873
FAX (310) 278-6041

Established in 1989
Total sq. footage: 1,200
Open to the public
Trade discount available

Type of work: Ceramics, Glass,
Wood, Mixed media, Furniture
40% one-of-a-kind work
Specialty: Animal themed work

Commissions welcome
Designer contact: Yvette Silvera

GUILD artists represented:
Barbara Fletcher, see pg. 231

• COLORADO

HIBBERD MCGRATH GALLERY
*Owners: Martha Hibberd,
Terry McGrath*

101 North Main
Breckenridge, CO 80424
(303) 453-6391

Established in 1982
Total sq. footage: 700
Open to the public
Trade discount available

Type of work: Ceramics, Glass,
Metal, Wood, Paper, Fiber,
Mixed media, Furniture, Baskets
99% one-of-a-kind work
Specialty: Ceramics, Paper,
Baskets, Folk art

Commissions welcome
Designer contact: Martha Hibberd,
Terry McGrath

GUILD artists represented:
Robin Renner, see pg. 192

TOH-ATIN
*Owners: Jackson Clark II,
Antonia Clark*

145 W. 9th Street
Durango, CO 81301
(303) 247-8277
FAX (303) 259-5390

Established in 1957
Total sq. footage: 4,000
Open to the public
Trade discount available

100% one-of-a-kind work
Specialty: Navajo weavings

Commissions welcome
Designer contact: Carol Martin-Hatch

GUILD artists represented:
Robin Renner, see pg. 192

• CONNECTICUT

BROOKFIELD CRAFT
CENTER, INC.
Owner: Non-profit corporation

Route 25
Brookfield, CT 06804
(203) 775-4526

Established in 1954
Total sq. footage: 600
Open to the public

Type of work: Ceramics, Glass, Metal,
Wood, Leather, Paper, Fiber, Mixed
media, Furniture, Baskets
90% one-of-a-kind work
Specialty: American handmade

Commissions welcome
Designer contact: Judith T. Russell

GUILD artists represented:
Thomas Masaryk, see pg. 128,
Architect's Source

BROOKFIELD SO NO GALLERY
Owner: Non-profit corporation

127 Washington Street
Norwalk, CT 06854
(203) 853-6155

Established in 1984
Total sq. footage: 1,000
Open to the public

Type of work: Ceramics, Glass,
Metal, Wood, Leather, Paper,
Fiber, Mixed media, Furniture, Baskets
90% one-of-a-kind work
Specialty: American handmade

Commissions welcome
Designer contact: Amy Barrett Patrick

GUILD artists represented:
Thomas Masaryk, see pg. 128,
Architect's Source

Gallery Resources

MENDELSON GALLERY
*Owners: Carol Mendelson,
Mike Mendelson*

Titus Square
Washington Depot, CT 06794
(203) 868-0307

Established in 1986
Total sq. footage: 3,000
Open to the public

Type of work: Ceramics, Wood
100% one-of-a-kind work
Specialty: Ceramics, Turned wood

Commissions welcome
Designer contact: Carol Mendelson

GUILD artists represented:
Linda Brendler, see pg. 77

SILVERMINE GUILD GALLERIES
Owner: Non-profit organization

1037 Silvermine Road
New Canaan, CT 06840
(203) 966-5617
FAX (203) 966-9700

Established in 1922
Open to the public

Type of work: Ceramics, Glass
90% one-of-a-kind work
Specialty: Fine art and crafts,
Paintings, Prints, Sculpture

Commissions welcome

GUILD artists represented:
Marjorie Tomchuk, see pg. 65

• FLORIDA

ALBERTSON-PETERSON GALLERY
*Owners: Judy Albertson,
Louise Peterson*

329 Park Avenue South
Winter Park, FL 32789
(407) 628-1258
FAX (407) 628-0596

Established in 1984
Total sq. footage: 1,500
Open to the public

Type of work: Ceramics, Glass, Wood,
Paper, Fiber, Mixed media, Furniture
99% one-of-a-kind work
Specialty: Southeastern artists

Commissions welcome
Designer contact: Judy Albertson,
Louise Peterson

GUILD artists represented:
Georgina Holt, see pg. 75

ART BY THE PARK GALLERY
*Owners: Caloosahatchee River
Partnership*

2030 West First Street
Fort Myers, FL 33901
(813) 337-7300
FAX (813) 337 7474

Established in 1991
Total sq. footage: 4,000
Open to the public
Trade discount available

Type of work: Ceramics, Metal,
Wood, Paper, Mixed media
30% one-of-a-kind work
Specialty: Corporate art, Primitive art,
Limited edition prints

Commissions welcome
Designer contact: Cynthia Kucera

GUILD artists represented:
Frank A. Colson, see pg. 183

ART GLASS
ENVIRONMENTS, INC.
Owner: Bill Klug

174 Glades Road
Boca Raton, FL 33432
(407) 391-7310
FAX (407) 391-8447

Established in 1979
Total sq. footage: 800
Open to the public
Trade discount available

Type of work: Glass, Furniture
80% one-of-a-kind work
Specialty: Architectural art glass,
entry ways, screens, tables

Commissions welcome
Designer contact: Bill Klug

GUILD artists represented:
Bill Klug, see pg. 126

CLAYTON GALLERIES
Owner: Cathleen C. Clayton

4105 S. MacDill Avenue
Tampa, FL 33611
(813) 831-3753

Established in 1986
Total sq. footage: 2,000
Open to the public
Trade discount available

Type of work: Ceramics, Glass, Metal,
Wood, Paper, Mixed media
100% one-of-a-kind work
Specialty: Florida artists

Commissions welcome
Designer contact: Cathleen C. Clayton

GUILD artists represented:
Michele Tuegel, see pg. 66

CHRISTY TAYLOR GALLERIES
Owners: Jack Nicks, Susan Nicks

410 Plaza Real
Boca Raton, FL 33486
(407) 750-7302
FAX (407) 394-3981

Established in 1987
Total sq. footage: 2,600
Open to the public

Type of work: Glass
100% one-of-a-kind work
Specialty: Functional & sculptural
glass

Commissions welcome
Designer contact: Carrie Marie

GUILD artists represented:
Latchezar Boyadjiev, see pg. 202

Statement
Christy Taylor Galleries represents
contemporary sculptural and
functional glasswork by internationally
acclaimed artists. Consulting services
are available for private and corporate
collections. Slide and video presentations of recent and current exhibitions
are available upon request. Courtesy
discounts to the design trade may be
available on certain pieces.

FLORIDA CRAFTSMEN, INC.
Owners: Michele Tuegel, David Bewley

235 Third Street South
St. Petersburg, FL 33701
(813) 821-7391
FAX (813) 821-7391

Established in 1986
Total sq. footage: 1,400
Commissions welcome
Designer contact: David Bewley

GUILD artists represented:
Frank A. Colson, see pg. 183
Shirley Edidin, see pg. 166

GALLERY FIVE
Owners: Paul & Paula Coben

363 Tequesta Drive
Tequesta, FL 33469
(407) 747-5555

Established in 1982
Total sq. footage: 1,400
Open to the public
Trade discount available

Type of work: Glass, Metal, Wood
Specialty: Wearable art

Commissions welcome
Designer contact: Paula Coben

GUILD artists represented:
Carol Adams, see pg. 173
Barbara Fletcher, see pg. 231
Ken & Julie Girardini, see pgs. 177
and 189

HEARTWORKS GALLERY
Owner: Elaine Wheeler

820 Lomax
Jacksonville, FL 32204
(904) 355-6210

Established in 1987
Total sq. footage: 1,000
Open to the public
Trade discount available

Type of work: Ceramics, Glass, Metal,
Wood, Fiber, Mixed media, Furniture,
Lighting, Baskets
70% one-of-a-kind work
Specialty: Glass, Art furniture
Commissions welcome
Designer contact: Elaine Wheeler

GUILD artists represented:
Shirley Edidin, see pg. 166
David Ponsler, see pg. 90,
Architect's Book

KOUCKY GALLERY
*Owners: Charles J. Koucky, Jr.,
Nancy Riggs Koucky*

1246 Third Street South
Naples, FL 33940
(813) 261-8988
FAX (813) 261-8576

Established in 1990
Total sq. footage: 1,500
Open to the public

Type of work: Ceramics, Glass,
Wood, Mixed media, Furniture
75% one-of-a-kind work
Specialty: Contemporary American
designer crafts and fine art

Commissions welcome
Designer contact: Mike Fulkerson

GUILD artists represented:
Joel & Sandra Hotchkiss, see pg. 235

TIMOTHY'S GALLERY
Owner: Carolyn Luce

232 Park Avenue North
Winter Park, FL 32789
(407) 629-0707

Established in 1989
Total sq. footage: 2,000
Open to the public

Type of work: Ceramics, Glass,
Wood, Mixed media, Furniture
25% one-of-a-kind work

Commissions welcome
Designer contact: Jill Daunno

GUILD artists represented:
Anne Mayer Meier, see pgs. 239–240
Michele Tuegel, see pg. 66

• GEORGIA

CONNELL GALLERY/ GREAT AMERICAN GALLERY
*Owners: Martha Stamm Connell,
Pat Connell*

333 Buckhead Avenue
Atlanta, GA 30305
(404) 261-1712

Established in 1982
Total sq. footage: 6,400
Open to the public

Type of work: Ceramics, Glass, Metal,
Wood, Paper, Fiber, Mixed media,
Furniture, Lighting
100% one-of-a-kind work

Commissions welcome
Designer contact: Martha Stamford
Connell, Pamela Blume Leonard

GUILD artists represented:
Gloria E. Crouse, see pg. 165
Therese May, see pg. 18
Raymond Tomasso, see pg. 64

VESPERMANN GLASS AND CRAFT GALLERIES
Owners: Paul & Seranda Vespermann

2140 Peachtree Road
Atlanta, GA 30309
(404) 350-9698
FAX (404) 350-0046

Established in 1984
Total sq. footage: 4,000
Open to the public
Trade discount available

Type of work: Ceramics, Glass,
Wood, Furniture
80% one-of-a-kind work
Specialty: Art glass and other media

Commissions welcome
Designer contact:
Seranda Vespermann

GUILD artists represented:
Steven Maslach, see pg. 208

Statement
Vespermann Galleries represents
museum-quality art glass in the
glass gallery as well as flat-glass
commissions by Mrs. Vespermann.
The craft gallery boasts a delectable
selection of hand-made American
crafts in many media. The Corporate
Showroom also provides a unique
opportunity for special choices for
the corporate client. Vespermann's
offers consulting services, lighting
assistance and a source of education
in art glass for its many clients.

• ILLINOIS

CHIAROSCURO
Owners: Peggy Wolf, Ronna Isaacs

750 N. Orleans
Chicago, IL 60611
(312) 988-9253

Established in 1987
Total sq. footage: 2,700
Open to the public
Trade discount available

Type of work: Ceramics, Glass, Metal,
Wood, Paper, Mixed media, Furniture
95% one-of-a-kind work
Specialty: Contemporary American
crafts & paintings

Commissions welcome
Designer contact: Peggy Wolf

GUILD artists represented:
Jeanine Guncheon, see pg. 120

CORPORATE ART SOURCE, INC.
Owner: Kathleen Bernhardt

900 North Franklin, Suite 200
Chicago, IL 60610
(312) 751-1300
FAX (312) 751-1331

Established in 1978
Total sq. footage: 4,000
Open to the public
Trade discount available

Type of work: Ceramics, Glass,
Paper, Fiber, Mixed media
70% one-of-a-kind work
Specialty: Corporate art

Commissions welcome
Designer contact: Kathleen Bernhardt,
Elizabeth Grigoropoulos

GUILD artists represented:
Victor Jacoby, see pg. 31

MERRILL CHASE GALLERIES
Owner: Fine Arts Group Ltd.

1090 Johnson Drive
Buffalo Grove, IL 60089
(708) 215-4900
FAX (708) 215-4976

Established in 1965
Open to the public
Trade discount available

Type of work: Ceramics, Glass,
Metal, Wood, Leather, Paper, Fiber,
Mixed media
50% one-of-a-kind work

Commissions welcome
Designer contact: Meryl Stone

GUILD artists represented:
Thomas Lollar, see pg. 78
Nina Paladino, Michael K. Hansen,
see pg. 205

MINDSCAPE GALLERY
*Owners: Ron Isaacson,
Deborah Farber*

1506 Sherman Avenue
Evanston, IL 60201
(708) 864-2660
FAX (708) 864-2815

Established in 1974
Total sq. footage: 10,000
Open to the public
Trade discount available

Type of work: Ceramics, Glass,
Wood, Fiber, Mixed media
90% one-of-a-kind work
Specialty: Contemporary American
fine crafts

Commissions welcome
Designer contact: Carole Richey

GUILD artists represented:
Lucinda Carlstrom, see pg. 54
Bruce Howdle, see pg. 114,
Architect's Source
Candace Kreitlow, see pg. 44
Steven Maslach, see pg. 208
Nina Paladino, Michael K. Hansen,
see pg. 205
Vincent & Carolyn Lee Tolpo,
see pg. 99

Gallery Resources

Statement
One of the nation's oldest and largest craft galleries, Mindscape, located just 25 minutes north of the Merchandise Mart in Evanston, has long been a resource for Chicago-area and Midwestern designers. The gallery represents over 350 contemporary artists and craftspeople throughout the U.S., including both established masters and emerging talents. Media regularly displayed are studio art glass; decorative and functional ceramics; sculpture; metals and mobiles; jewelry; paper and fiber wall pieces; wooden accessories and one-of-a-kind furniture.

PIECES—ART AND ARTWEAR
Owners: Louise Shulkin, Lynn Komessar

644 Central Avenue
Highland Park, IL 60035
(708) 432-2131

Established in 1985
Total sq. footage: 4,000
Open to the public
Trade discount available

Type of work: Ceramics, Glass, Metal, Wood, Mixed media
75% one-of-a-kind work
Specialty: Contemporary crafts

Commissions welcome
Designer contact: Louise Shulkin

GUILD artists represented:
Beverly Plummer, see pg. 63

SCHNEIDER—BLUHM LOEB GALLERY, INC.
Owners: Martha Schneider, Barbara Bluhm

230 W. Superior Street
Chicago, IL 60610
(312) 988-4033
FAX (312) 642-5169

Established in 1982
Open to the public
Trade discount available

Type of work: Ceramics, Metal, Fiber, Mixed media, Baskets
100% one-of-a-kind work
Specialty: Ceramics, Jewelry

Commissions welcome
Designer contact: Elsie Loeb

GUILD artists represented:
Carolyn Dulin, see pg. 184

SUNRISE ART GALLERY
Owners: Cathy O'Keefe, Thomas O'Keefe

227 South Third Street
Geneva, IL 60134
(708) 232-0730

Established in 1987
Total sq. footage: 850
Open to the public
Trade discount available

Type of work: Ceramics, Metal, Wood, Leather, Mixed media
60% one-of-a-kind work
Specialty: Contemporary Southwest, American Indian art

Commissions welcome
Designer contact: Cathy O'Keefe

GUILD artists represented:
Robin Renner, see pg. 192

• LOUISIANA

ARIODANTE CONTEMPORARY CRAFT GALLERY
Owner: Larry S. Potts

535 Julia Street
New Orleans, LA 70130
(504) 524-3233

Established in 1990
Total sq. footage: 850
Open to the public

Type of work: Ceramics, Glass, Wood, Furniture, Lighting
50% one-of-a-kind work
Specialty: Fine contemporary crafts

Commissions welcome
Designer contact: Larry S. Potts

GUILD artists represented:
Gloria E. Crouse, see pg. 165

THE BATON ROUGE GALLERY, INC.
Owner: Artist's Cooperative

1442 City Park Avenue
Baton Rouge, LA 70808-1037
(504) 383-1470

Established in 1966
Total sq. footage: 1,300
Open to the public

Type of work: Ceramics, Glass, Metal, Wood, Paper, Fiber, Mixed media, Furniture
100% one-of-a-kind work
Specialty: Contemporary fine art

Commissions welcome
Designer contact: Anne Boudreau

GUILD artists represented:
Craig McCullen, see pg. 52,
Architect's Source

WYNDY MOREHEAD FINE ARTS
Owner: Wyndy Morehead

603 Julia Street
New Orleans, LA 70130
(504) 568-9754

Established in 1989
Total sq. footage: 1,200

Designer contact: Wyndy Morehead

GUILD artists represented:
Frank Barham, see pg. 218

• MAINE

ABACUS GALLERY
Owners: Russell Dana Heacock, Sal Scaglione

8 McKown Street
Boothbay Harbor, ME 04538
(207) 633-2166

Established in 1971
Total sq. footage: 3,000
Open to the public

Type of work: Ceramics, Glass, Metal, Wood, Fiber, Mixed media, Furniture, Lighting
15% one-of-a-kind work
Specialty: American crafts

Commissions welcome
Designer contact: Joyce Dolley

GUILD artists represented:
Ellen Kochansky, see pg. 17
Ray Lewis, see pg. 127
Jeanne L. Stevens-Sollman, see pg. 221

ABACUS GALLERY
Owners: Russell Dana Heacock, Sal Scaglione

36 Main Street
Freeport, ME 04032
(207) 772-4880

Established in 1971
Total sq. footage: 2,200
Open to the public

Type of work: Ceramics, Glass, Metal, Wood, Fiber, Mixed media, Furniture, Lighting
15% one-of-a-kind work
Specialty: American crafts

Commissions welcome
Designer contact: Joyce Dolley

GUILD artists represented:
Ellen Kochansky, see pg. 17
Ray Lewis, see pg. 127
Jeanne L. Stevens-Sollman, see pg. 221

ABACUS GALLERY
Owners: Russell Dana Heacock, Sal Scaglione

44 Exchange Street
Portland, ME 04101
(207) 772-4880

Established in 1971
Total sq. footage: 2,200
Open to the public

Type of work: Ceramics, Glass, Metal, Wood, Fiber, Mixed media, Furniture, Lighting
15% one-of-a-kind work
Specialty: American crafts

Commissions welcome
Designer contact: Joyce Dolley

GUILD artists represented:
Ellen Kochansky, see pg. 17
Ray Lewis, see pg. 127
Jeanne L. Stevens-Sollman, see pg. 221

ELEMENTS GALLERY
Owner: Bill Robertson

19 Mason Street
Brunswick, ME 04011
(207) 729-1108

Established in 1989
Total sq. footage: 750
Open to the public
Trade discount available

Type of work: Ceramics, Glass, Metal,
Wood, Paper, Fiber, Mixed media,
Furniture, Lighting, Baskets
60 % one-of-a-kind work
Specialty: Maine and New England
contemporary craft and alternative art

Commissions welcome
Designer contact: Bill Robertson

NANCY MARGOLIS GALLERY
Owner: Nancy Margolis

367 Fore Street
Portland, ME 04104
(207) 775-3822
FAX (207) 775-3822

Established in 1975
Total sq. footage: 2,000
Open to the public
Trade discount available

Type of work: Ceramics, Glass,
Metal, Wood, Furniture
20% one-of-a-kind work
Specialty: Ceramics

Commissions welcome
Designer contact: Penny Coit

GUILD artists represented:
David Van Noppen, see pg. 214

• MARYLAND

MARGARET SMITH GALLERY
*Owners: Margaret Smith,
James T. Smith*

8090 Main Street
Ellicott City, MD 21043
(410) 461-0870

Established in 1987
Total sq. footage: 1,400
Open to the public
Trade discount available

Type of work: Ceramics, Glass, Metal,
Wood, Paper, Mixed media
65% one-of-a-kind work
Specialty: Original print media

Commissions welcome
Designer contact: Margaret Smith

GUILD artists represented:
Ken & Julie Girardini, see pgs. 177 & 189

TOMLINSON CRAFT
COLLECTION, INC.
Owner: Ginny Tomlinson McKechnie

711 W. 40th Street
Baltimore, MD 21211
(410) 338-1572

Established in 1972
Total sq. footage: 1,200
Open to the public
Trade discount available

Type of work: Ceramics, Glass,
Metal, Wood, Fiber
95% one-of-a-kind work
Specialty: American ceramics

Commissions welcome
Designer contact: Ginny Tomlinson
McKechnie

GUILD artists represented:
Carol Kropnick, see pg. 238

ZYZYX

Festival at Woodholme
1809 Reisterstown Road
Baltimore, MD 21208
(410) 486-9785
FAX (410) 486-9787

Established in 1991
Total sq. footage: 3,000
Open to the public

Type of work: Ceramics, Glass, Metal,
Wood, Paper, Fiber, Mixed media,
Baskets
40 % one-of-a-kind work
Specialty: Judaica

Designer contact: Jeanette Hazel
Greenstein

GUILD artists represented:
Ken & Julie Girardini, see pgs. 177 & 189
Timothy Rose, see pg. 223

• MASSACHUSETTS

FERRIN GALLERY
Owners: Leslie Ferrin, Mara Superior

**179 Main Street
Northampton, MA 01060
(413) 586-4509
FAX (413) 586-4509**

**Established in 1979
Total sq. footage: 1,100
Open to the public**

**Type of work: Ceramics, Metal, Wood,
Mixed media, Furniture
80% one-of-a-kind work
Specialty: Contemporary ceramics**

**Commissions welcome
Designer contact: Diane Nelson**

**GUILD artists represented:
William B. Sayre, see pg. 150**

**Statement
Ferrin Gallery features a large
selection of functional and sculptural
contemporary ceramics and furniture.
The Gallery presents regular group
and one-person exhibits specializing
in artists from the area and featuring
others from throughout the country.
Customized slide and video presentations, curatorial and consulting
services are available with referrals
and discounts offered to the trade.**

SIGNATURE
Owners: Arthur Grohe, Donna Grohe

Dock Square, 24 North Street
Boston, MA 02109
(617) 227-4885
FAX (508) 539-0509

Established in 1978
Open to the public
Type of work: Ceramics, Glass,
Metal, Wood, Lighting
50% one-of-a-kind work
Specialty: Contemporary glass

Commissions welcome
Designer contact: Erin Huggard

GUILD artists represented:
Steven Maslach, see pg. 208

SIGNATURE
Owners: Arthur Grohe, Donna Grohe

The Mall at Chestnut Hill
Chestnut Hill, MA 02167
(617) 332-7749
FAX (508) 539-0509

Established in 1978
Open to the public
Type of work: Ceramics, Glass,
Metal, Wood, Lighting
50% one-of-a-kind work
Specialty: Contemporary glass

Commissions welcome
Designer contact: Priscilla Merritt

GUILD artists represented:
Steven Maslach, see pg. 208

SIGNATURE
Owners: Arthur Grohe, Donna Grohe

10 Steeple Street
Mashpee, MA 02649
(508) 539-0029
FAX (508) 539-0509

Established in 1978
Open to the public
Type of work: Ceramics, Glass,
Metal, Wood, Lighting
50% one-of-a-kind work
Specialty: Contemporary glass

Commissions welcome
Designer contact: Liz Nelson

GUILD artists represented:
Steven Maslach, see pg. 208

Gallery Resources

TEN ARROW CONTEMPORARY AMERICAN CRAFTS
Owner: Elizabeth R. Tinlot

10 Arrow Street
Cambridge, MA 02138
(617) 876-1117

Established in 1972
Total sq. footage: 1,000
Open to the public

Type of work: Ceramics, Glass, Metal, Wood, Furniture

Commissions welcome
Designer contact: Elizabeth R. Tinlot

GUILD artists represented:
Elinor Steele, see pg. 34

• MICHIGAN

ARTFINDERS OF MICHIGAN
Owner: Jeanne A. Willette

107 Washington
Grand Haven, MI 49417
(616) 847-9150

Established in 1989
Total sq. footage: 1,000
Open to the public

Type of work: Glass, Paper, Mixed media, Baskets
95% one-of-a-kind work
Specialty: Works of Michigan artists and craftspersons

Commissions welcome
Designer contact: Jeanne A. Willette

GUILD artists represented:
Fred Blackwood, see pg. 108,
Architect's Source

BELL ROSS FINE ART GALLERY
Owners: Diane & Craig Bell, Linda Ross

257 East Main Street
Harbor Springs, MI 49740
(616) 526-9855

Established in 1986
Total sq. footage: 1,100
Open to the public

Type of work: Glass, Metal, Paper, Mixed media, Furniture
95% one-of-a-kind work
Specialty: Contemporary fine art, Wall art sculpture, and Museum quality crafts

Commissions welcome
Designer contact: Diane Bell

GUILD artists represented:
Michele Tuegel, see pg. 66

CAROL/JAMES GALLERY
Owners: Carol Ann Foster, James F. Accuso

301 South Main Street
Royal Oak, MI 48067
(313) 541-6216

Established in 1988
Total sq. footage: 2,000
Open to the public

Type of work: Ceramics, Glass, Metal, Wood, Fiber
25% one-of-a-kind work

Commissions welcome
Designer contact: Carol Foster

GUILD artists represented:
Carolyn Dulin, see pg. 184

HABATAT GALLERIES, INC.
Owner: Ferdinand Hampson

32255 Northwestern Hwy. #45
Farmington Hills, MI 48334
(313) 851-9090
FAX (313) 851-9720

Established in 1972
Open to the public

Type of work: Glass
100% one-of-a-kind work
Specialty: International glass

Commissions welcome
Designer contact: Ferdinand Hampson

GUILD artists represented:
Warren Carther, see pg. 25,
Architect's Source
John Kuhn, see pg. 207
John Gilbert Luebtow, see pg. 169,
Architect's Source

KOUCKY GALLERY
Owners: Charles & Nancy Koucky

319 Bridge Street
Charlevoix, MI 49720
(616) 547-2228

Established in 1986
Open to the public

Type of work: Ceramics, Glass
75% one-of-a-kind work
Specialty: Contemporary American designer crafts and fine art

GUILD artists represented:
John D. Hubbard, see pg. 58

POSNER GALLERY
Owners: Madeline Posner, Karen Posner

32407 N. Western Highway
Farmington Hills, MI 48332
(313) 626-6450

Established in 1989
Total sq. footage: 1,800
Open to the public
Trade discount available

Type of work: Ceramics, Glass, Metal, Mixed media, Baskets
80% one-of-a-kind work
Specialty: Glass, Metal

Commissions welcome
Designer contact: Madeline Posner, Karen Posner

GUILD artists represented:
Shawn Athari, see pgs. 85 & 201

TAMARACK CRAFTSMEN GALLERY
Owners: David Viskochil, Sally Vickochil

5039 North West Bay Shore Dr. (M22)
Omena, MI 49674
(616) 386-5529

Established in 1972
Total sq. footage: 2,160
Open to the-public

Type of work: Ceramics, Glass, Wood, Paper, Fiber, Mixed media, Furniture
80% one-of-a-kind work
Specialty: Contemporary folk art and painted furniture

Commissions welcome
Designer contact: David Viskochil

GUILD artists represented:
Deborah Hecht, see pg. 74

• MINNESOTA

JAVIER PUIG DECORATIVE ARTS
Owner: Bill Puig

118 N. 4th Street
Minneapolis, MN 55401
(612) 332-6001

Established in 1989
Total sq. footage: 1,800
Open to the public
Trade discount available

Type of work: Ceramics, Glass, Metal, Furniture
Specialty: Full range of crafts by U.S. artists

Commissions welcome
Designer contact: Bill Puig

GUILD artists represented:
Kevin Earley, see pg. 116

MJL IMPRESSIONS, INC.
Owners: Jerome Luloff, Marlene Luloff

International Market Square
275 Market Street, #162
Minneapolis, MN 55405
(612) 332-4295
FAX (612) 332-2876

Established in 1975
Total sq. footage: 4,000
Open to the public

Type of work: Ceramics, Glass, Paper, Fiber, Mixed media
40% one-of-a-kind work
Specialty: Painting, Monoprints and original prints, Custom framing

Commissions welcome
Designer contact: Jerome Luloff

GUILD artists represented:
William C. Richards, see pg. 81

SAYRE STRAND SHOWROOM INC.
Owner: Roger E. Sayre

275 Market Street
Minneapolis, MN 55405-1604
(612) 375-0838
FAX (612) 375-9464

Established in 1979
Total sq. footage: 6,000
Open to the public
Trade discount available

Type of work: Ceramics, Metal, Wood,
Furniture, Lighting, Baskets
15% one-of-a-kind work

Commissions welcome
Designer contact: Roger E. Sayre

GUILD artists represented:
Robert Walsh, see pg 138

TEXTILE ARTS INTERNATIONAL, INC.
Owner: Ellen Wells

400 First Avenue North, Suite 340
Minneapolis, MN 55408
(612) 338-6776
FAX (612) 338-6885

Established in 1981
Total sq. footage: 2,060
Open to the public

Type of work: Paper, Fiber,
Mixed media, Baskets
100% one-of-a-kind work
Specialty: Textile artwork, mostly
contemporary

Commissions welcome
Designer contact: Phil Hewett

GUILD artists represented:
Doris Bally, see pg. 25

• MISSOURI

GB DESIGN
Owner: Glynn Brown

420 W. 7th Street
Kansas City, MO 64105
(816) 842-2115
FAX o(816) 474-7482

Established in 1990
Total sq. footage: 1,200
Open to the public

Type of work: Ceramics, Glass, Leather,
Mixed media, Furniture, Lighting
40% one-of-a-kind work
Specialty: Artwork

Commissions welcome
Designer contact: Kathy Beggs

NUSSBAUM MCELWAIN, FINE ART SERVICES
Owners: William Nussbaum, Mary McElwain

5595 Pershing Avenue
St. Louis, MO 63112
(314) 361-3701
FAX (314) 361-3423

Established in 1984
Open to the public

Type of work: Ceramics, Paper,
Fiber, Mixed media
90% one-of-a-kind work
Specialty: Corporate Art Advisors

Commissions welcome
Designer contact: Mary McElwain

GUILD artists represented:
Michele Tuegel, see pg. 66

PORTFOLIO GALLERY INC.
Owner: Portfolio Inc.

3514 Delmar Boulevard, Suite B
St. Louis, MO 63103
(314) 533-3323

Established in 1989
Total sq. footage: 2,500
Open to the public
Trade discount available

Type of work: Ceramics, Wood,
Paper, Fiber, Mixed media
100% one-of-a-kind work
Specialty: African-American art
produced by Missouri artists

Commissions welcome
Designer contact: Robert A. Powell

GUILD artists represented:
Wright E. Harris III, see pg. 234

• NEW HAMPSHIRE

MOLLY GRANT DESIGNS— LEATHER DESIGNS
Owner: Molly Grant

112 State Street
Portsmouth, NH 03801
(603) 436-7077

Established in 1991
Total sq. footage: 500
Open to the public
Trade discount available

Type of work: Ceramics, Wood, Leather,
Mixed media, Furniture
75% one-of-a-kind work
Specialty: Leather handbags

Commissions welcome
Designer contact: Molly Grant

• NEW JERSEY

ART FORMS
Owners: Charlotte T. Scherer

16 Monmouth Street
Red Bank, NJ 07701
(908) 530-4330
FAX (908) 530-9791

Established in 1984
Total sq. footage: 2,000
Open to the public
Trade discount available

Type of work: Ceramics, Glass,
Metal, Wood, Paper, Mixed media,
Furniture, Lighting
95% one-of-a-kind work
Specialty: 20th Century contemporary
American fine art

Commissions welcome
Designer contact: Charlotte T. Scherer

GUILD artists represented:
Len Eichler, see pg. 186

DESIGNS IN CRAFT
Owner: Janet Amon

2 Broad Street
Red Bank, NJ 07701
(908) 741-4699

Established in 1991
Total square footage: 1,500
Open to the public
Trade discount available

Type of work: Ceramics, Glass,
Metal, Fiber, Mixed media
50 % one-of-a-kind work
Specialty: Wall-hangings, Fiber art

Commissions welcome
Designer contact: Janet Amon

GUILD artists represented:
B.J. Adams, see pg. 37
Alexandra Friedman, see pg. 27
Marie-Laure Ilie, see pgs. 42-43

KORNBLUTH GALLERY
Owner: Sally Fowler

7–21 Fair Lawn Avenue
Fair Lawn, NJ 07410
(201) 791-3374

Established in 1965
Total square footage: 2,000
Open to the public
Trade discount available

Type of work: Ceramics, Glass,
Metal, Wood, Furniture
90 % one-of-a-kind work
Specialty: Contemporary American,
especially glass

Commissions welcome
Designer contact: Sally Fowler

GUILD artists represented:
Elinor Steele, see pg. 34

Gallery Resources

SHEILA NUSSBAUM GALLERY
Owner: Sheila Ford Nussbaum

358 Millburn Avenue
Millburn, NJ 07041
(201) 467-1720

Established in 1982
Total sq. footage: 1,800
Open to the public

Type of work: Ceramics, Glass,
Metal, Wood, Furniture
80% one-of-a-kind work
Specialty: Young, emerging artists,
Art jewelry

Commissions welcome
Designer contact: Sheila Nussbaum

GUILD artists represented:
Jeanine Guncheon, see pg. 120

WHITE GALLERY
Owner: Alice C. White

105 Pulis Avenue
Franklin Lakes, NJ 07417
(201) 848-1855
FAX (201) 891-8348

Established in 1982
Total square footage: 1,000
Open to the public
Trade discount available

Type of work: Ceramics, Glass, Metal,
Wood, Paper, Fiber, Mixed media
75% one-of-a-kind work
Specialty: Watercolor, Acrylic, Oil,
Eastern U.S landscapes

Commissions welcome
Designer contact: Alice C. White

GUILD artists represented:
Marjorie Tomchuk, see pg. 65

• NEW MEXICO

ANDREWS PUEBLO POTTERY
Owners: Helen Andrews,
Robert Andrews

400 San Felipe N.W., Suite 8
Old Town
Albuquerque, NM 87104
(505) 243-0414

Established in 1975
Total sq. footage: 1,000

Designer contact: Cathy Cauley

GUILD artists represented:
Nancy & Allen Young, see pg. 243

EL PRADO GALLERIES, INC.
Owner: Don Pierson, Elyse Pierson

112 W. San Francisco Street
Santa Fe, NM 87501
(602) 282-7390
FAX (602) 282-7578

Established in 1976
Total square footage: 15,000
Open to the public
Trade discount available

Type of work: Ceramics , Glass, Metal,
Wood, Leather, Paper, Mixed media,
Baskets
95% one-of-a-kind work
Specialty: Oils, Acrylics, Watercolors,
Mixed media, Sculptures

Commissions welcome
Designer contact: Don H. Pierson

GUILD artists represented:
Martha Chatelain, see pg. 55

HANDWOVEN ORIGINALS
Owners: J. Boles, Louise Lechner

211 Old Santa Fe Trail
Santa Fe, NM 87501
(505) 982-4118

Established in 1976
Total sq. footage: 750
Open to the public
Trade discount available

Type of work: Ceramics, Glass, Fiber,
Mixed media, Baskets
100% one-of-a-kind work
Specialty: Local hand-woven,
unique pieces

Commissions welcome
Designer contact: J. Boles,
Louise Lechner

GUILD artists represented:
Robin Renner, see pg. 192

MICHAEL WIGLEY GALLERIES, LTD.
Owners: Michael L. Wigley, A.A.A.,
Cindi Lawyer

1111 Paseo de Peralta
Santa Fe, NM 87501
(505) 984-8986

Established in 1976
Total sq. footage: 5,100
Open to the public
Trade discount available

Type of work: Metal, Wood, Leather,
Mixed media, Furniture, Baskets
98% one-of-a-kind work
Specialty: Fine American historic
paintings, Custom-made furniture

Commissions welcome
Designer contact: John Bullard,
Cindi Lawyer

GUILD artists represented:
Bruce Haughey, see pg. 236
James T. Russell, see pg. 171,
Architect's Source

NEDRA MATTEUCCI FINE ART
Owner: Nedra Matteucci

300 Garcia Street at Canyon Road
Santa Fe, NM 87501
(505) 983-2731

Established in 1986
Open to the public

Type of work: Metal, Mixed media,
Furniture, Baskets
99% one-of-a-kind work
Specialty: Representational paintings
and sculpture

Commissions welcome
Designer contact: Roberta Brashears,
Judi Landis

QUILTS LTD
Owner: Trisha Ambrose

652 Canyon Road
Santa Fe, NM 87501
(505) 988-5888
FAX (800) 445-9923

Established in 1977
Total sq. footage: 3,000
Open to the public
Trade discount available

Type of work: Leather, Paper, Fiber,
Mixed media, Furniture
40% one-of-a-kind work
Specialty: Southwestern and
traditional quilts

Commissions welcome
Designer contact: Eric & Trisha Ambrose

GUILD artists represented:
Lucinda Carlstrom, see pg. 54

RUNNING RIDGE
Owners: Robert & Barbara Grabowski,
John & Ruth Farnham

640 Canyon Road
Santa Fe, NM 87501
(800) 584-6830

Established in 1979
Total sq. footage: 1,500
Open to the public
Trade discount available

Type of work: Ceramics, Glass,
Paper, Fiber, Mixed media
90% one-of-a-kind work
Specialty: Contemporary crafts

Commissions welcome
Designer contact: Dan Appleby

GUILD artists represented:
Jeanine Guncheon, see pg. 120

• NEW YORK

AMERICAN CRAFTS MUSEUM GIFTSHOP

40 WEST 53rd Street
New York, NY 10019
(212) 956-3535
FAX (212) 459-0926

Established in 1990
Total sq. footage: 240
Open to the public

Type of work: Ceramics, Glass,
Metal, Wood, Fiber
50% one-of-a-kind work
Specialty: Contemporary American crafts

Commissions welcome
Designer contact: Valerie Patterson

GUILD artists represented:
Betsy Ross, see pg. 194

ARCHETYPE GALLERY
Owners: Iris De Mauro, Robert Gaul

137 Spring Street
New York, NY 10012
(212) 334-0100
FAX (212) 226-7880

Established in 1986
Total sq. footage: 3,200
Open to the public
Trade discount available

Type of work: Glass, Metal, Mixed media,
Furniture, Lighting
60% one-of-a-kind work
Specialty: Contemporary avante-garde
home furnishings

Commissions welcome
Designer contact: Robert Gaul

GUILD artists represented:
Peter Mangan, see pg. 178

THE CLAY POT
Owners: Bob & Sally Silberberg

162 7th Avenue
Brooklyn, NY 11215
(718) 788-6564
FAX (718) 965-1138

Established in 1968
Total sq. footage: 1,100
Open to the public
Trade discount available

Type of work: Ceramics, Glass, Metal,
Wood, Leather, Paper, Fiber, Mixed
media, Lighting, Baskets
100% one-of-a-kind work
Specialty: Wedding bands

Commissions welcome
Designer contact: Bill Bouchey

GUILD artists represented:
Linda Brendler, see pg. 77

CLOUDS GALLERY
Owner: Robert Ohnigian

1 Mill Hill Road
Woodstock, NY 12498
(914) 679-8155

Established in 1974
Total sq. footage: 1,200
Open to the public

Type of work: Ceramics, Glass,
Wood, Mixed media
90% one-of-a-kind work
Specialty: Contemporary American crafts

Commissions welcome
Designer contact: Robert Ohnigian

GUILD artists represented:
David Van Noppen, see pg. 214

THE CRAFTSMAN'S GALLERY LTD

16 Chase Road
Scarsdale, NY 10583
(914) 725-4644
FAX (914) 725-2117

Established in 1973
Open to the public

Type of work: Ceramics, Glass, Metal,
Wood, Paper, Fiber, Mixed media,
Furniture, Baskets
80% one-of-a-kind work
Specialty: One-of-a-kind ceramic art

Commissions welcome
Designer contact: Sybil Robins

GUILD artists represented:
David Van Noppen, see pg. 214
Elinor Steele, see pg. 34

CROSS HARRIS FINE CRAFTS
Owners: Rise Cross, Fredda Harris

D & D Building
979 Third Avenue, 3rd Floor
New York, NY 10022
(212) 888-7878

Established in 1988
Total sq. footage: 400
Open to the public

Type of work: Ceramics, Glass, Metal,
Fiber, Mixed media, Baskets
100% one-of-a-kind work
Specialty: Ceramics

Commissions welcome
Designer contact: Rise Cross,
Fredda Harris

GUILD artists represented:
Betsy Ross, see pg. 194

Statement

A convenient resource for designers
and architects interested in using
contemporary craft in their residential
and corporate spaces. Works can be
purchased directly from our showroom
or commissioned to individual
specification.

DAWSON GALLERY
*Owners: Shirley Dawson,
Beverly McInerny*

349 East Avenue
Rochester, NY 14604
(716) 454-6609

Established in 1982
Total sq. footage: 1,700
Open to the public
Trade discount available

Type of work: Ceramics, Glass,
Metal, Wood, Fiber,
100% one-of-a-kind work
Specialty: Upstate New York artists

Commissions welcome
Designer contact: Shirley Dawson,
Beverly McInerny

GUILD artists represented:
Junco Sato Pollack, see pg. 46

15 STEPS
Owners: Bettsie Ann Park, Ken Jupiter

171 The Commons, Center Ithaca
Ithaca, NY 14850
(607) 272-4902

Established in 1982
Total sq. footage: 1,700
Open to the public

Type of work: Ceramics, Glass,
Metal, Wood
Specialty: American handmade,
Jewelry, Glass

Commissions welcome
Designer contact: Ken Jupiter

GUILD artists represented:
Robert C. Shenfeld, see pg. 196

GAYLE WILLSON GALLERY
Owner: Gayle Willson

43 Jobs Lane
Southampton, NY 11968
(516) 283-7430

Established in 1981
Total sq. footage: 1,400
Open to the public

Type of work: Ceramics, Glass, Paper,
Fiber, Mixed media, Furniture
85% one-of-a-kind work
Specialty: Contemporary fiber, Selected
other media

Designer contact: Gayle Willson

GUILD artists represented:
Sara Hotchkiss, see pg. 168
Ellen Kochansky, see pg. 17
Carol Kropnick, see pg. 238

HELLER GALLERY
Owners: Douglas Heller, Michael Heller

71 Greene Street
New York, NY 10012
(212) 966-5948
FAX (212) 966-5956

Established in 1973
Total sq. footage: 4,500
Open to the public
Trade discount available

Type of work: Glass
99% one-of-a-kind work
Specialty: Museum quality contemporary
glass sculpture

Commissions welcome
Designer contact: Bob Roberts

GUILD artists represented:
John Kuhn, see pg. 207

Gallery Resources

HOLT HAUS FIBER ART GALLERY
Owner: Mary Ann Holthaus

7 Irma Avenue
Port Washington, NY 11050
(516) 883-8620

Established in 1984
Total sq. footage: 230
Open to the public
Trade discount available

Type of work: Ceramics, Fiber
90% one-of-a-kind work
Specialty: Contemporary tapestries and fabric art

Commissions welcome
Designer contact: Mary Ann Holthaus

GUILD artists represented:
Elinor Steele, see pg. 34

JARO ART GALLERIES
Owner: Jaro Parizek

955 Madison Avenue
New York, NY 10021
(212) 734-5475
FAX (212) 734-5475

Established in 1975
Open to the public
Trade discount available

Type of work: Glass, Wood, Paper
90% one-of-a-kind work
Specialty: Yugoslav and American naive art

Commissions welcome
Designer contact: Jaro Parizek

GUILD artists represented:
Marilyn Forth, see pg. 167

MARI GALLERIES OF WESTCHESTER, LTD.
Owner: Carla Reuben

133 E. Prospect Avenue
Mamaroneck, NY 10543
(914) 698-0008

Established in 1966
Open to the public

Type of work: All
95% one-of-a-kind work
Specialty: Contemporary works

Commissions welcome
Designer contact: Carla Rueben

MARK MILLIKEN
Owner: Mark Milliken

1200 Madison Avenue
New York, NY 10128
(212) 534-8802

Established in 1989
Total sq. footage: 1,000
Open to the public
Trade discount available

Type of work: Ceramics, Glass, Wood, Mixed media, Furniture
100% one-of-a-kind work
Specialty: Contemporary American crafts, Whimsical

Commissions welcome
Designer contact: Mark Milliken

GUILD artists represented:
Gary Upton, see pg. 149

PRITAM-EAMES
Owners: Bebe Pritnam Johnson, Warren Eames Johnson

29 Race Lane
East Hampton, NY 11937
(516) 324-7111

Established in 1981
Total sq. footage: 2,400
Open to the public

Type of work: Ceramics, Glass, Metal, Furniture
95% one-of-a-kind work
Specialty: Functional furniture, Metal, Glass, Ceramics

Commissions welcome
Designer contact: Bebe Pritnam Johnson, Warren Eames Johnson

GUILD artists represented:
Peter Handler, see pg. 135

PRODIGY GALLERY
Owner: Karen Weinert-Kim

126 W. Main Street
Endicott, NY 13760
(607) 748-0190

Established in 1986
Total sq. footage: 1,200
Open to the public

Type of work: Ceramics, Glass, Metal, Fiber, Lighting
40% one-of-a-kind work
Specialty: Contemporary crafts and Native American

Commissions welcome
Designer contact: Karen Weinert-Kim

GUILD artists represented:
Boris Bally & ROY, see pg. 217

SCOTT JORDAN FURNITURE, INC.
Owner: Scott Jordan

137 Varick Street
New York, NY 10013
(212) 620-4682

Established in 1980
Total sq. footage: 3,200
Open to the public

Type of work: Wood, Furniture, Lighting
Specialty: Solid wood furniture

Designer contact: Scott Jordan

GUILD artists represented:
Sara Hotchkiss, see pg. 168

SYMMETRY

348 Broadway
Saratoga Springs, NY 12866
(518) 584-5090

Established in 1990
Total sq. footage: 1,600
Open to the public
Trade discount available

Type of work: Ceramics, Glass, Metal, Wood, Fiber, Mixed media, Lighting
30% one-of-a-kind work
Specialty: American handblown glass

Commissions welcome
Designer contact: Diane Zack

GUILD artists represented:
Shawn Athari, see pgs. 85 & 201

WHEELER-SEIDEL GALLERY
Owners: Pat Wheeler, Neil Seidel

129 Prince Street
New York, NY 10012
(212) 533-0319

Established in 1991
Total sq. footage: 1,200
Open to the public
Trade discount available

Type of work: Ceramics, Glass, Metal, Fiber, Furniture
50% one-of-a-kind work
Specialty: Contemporary American crafts

Commissions welcome
Designer contact: Pat Wheeler

GUILD artists represented:
Thomas W. Lollar, see pg. 78
Betsy Ross, see pg. 194
Uli Schempp, see pg. 195

• NEBRASKA

LEWIS ART GALLERY
Owners: Carolyn D. Lewis, Julie Wynn

8025 West Dodge Road
Omaha, NE 68114
(402) 391-7733

Established in 1971
Total sq. footage: 5,000
Open to the public

Type of work: Ceramics, Glass, Metal, Wood, Paper, Mixed media, Furniture, Baskets
80% one-of-a-kind work
Specialty: Pottery, Fiber, Metal, Paper

Commissions welcome
Designer contact: Carolyn Lewis, Julie Wynn, Sam Carlson

GUILD artists represented:
Bruce Howdle, see pg. 114, Architect's Source

• NORTH CAROLINA

ARTEANO GALLERIES
Owner: Santiago Leon

119 E. 7th St.
Charlotte, NC 28202
(704) 372-3903
FAX (704) 357-8621

Established in 1989
Total sq. footage: 3,000
Open to the public
Trade discount available

Type of work: Ceramics, Metal, Paper,
Mixed media
50% one-of-a-kind work
Specialty: Paintings, watercolors,
drawings, prints and sculpture from
American and Latin American artists

Commissions welcome
Designer contact: Santiago Leon

GUILD artists represented:
Enrique Vega, see pg. 93,
Architect's Source

CITY ART WORKS
Owner: Alan Goldstein

2908 Selwyn Avenue
Charlotte, NC 28209
(704) 358-1810

Established in 1989
Total sq. footage: 1,500
Open to the public
Trade discount available

Type of work: Ceramics, Glass, Metal,
Wood, Mixed media,
15% one-of-a-kind work
Specialty: Ceramics, Glass

Commissions welcome
Designer contact: Alan Goldstein

GUILD artists represented:
Ellen Kochansky, see pg. 17

FINE LINES
Owner: Sandy Steele

304 S. Stratford Road
Winston-Salem, NC 27103
(919) 723-8066

Established in 1981
Total sq. footage: 2,000
Open to the public

Type of work: Ceramics, Glass,
Metal, Wood, Leather
20% one-of-a-kind work

Commissions welcome
Designer contact: Sandy Steele

GUILD artists represented:
Kathy Cooper, see pg. 164

FOLK ART CENTER

Blue Ridge Parkway
Milepost 382
Asheville, NC 28805
(704) 298-7928
FAX (704) 298-7962

Established in 1930
Total sq. footage: 6,000
Open to the public

Type of work: Ceramics, Wood, Leather,
Fiber, Baskets
50% one-of-a-kind work
Specialty: All craft mediums in both fine
traditional and contemporary styles

Commissions welcome
Designer contact: Andrew Glasgow

GUILD artists represented:
Beverly Plummer, see pg. 63

HAYDEN CRANE GALLERY
Owners: Susan Heyden, Priscilla Crane

7 South Main Street
Burnsville, NC 28714
(704) 682-2010

Established in 1991
Open to the public

Type of work: All
30% one-of-a-kind work
Specialty: North Carolina Glass Artists

Commissions welcome
Designer contact: Susan Heyden,
Priscilla Crane

GUILD artists represented:
Beverly Plummer, see pg. 63

PEDEN GALLERY II
Owner: Melissa A. Peden

132 E. Hargett St.
Raleigh, NC 27601
(919) 834-9800

Established in 1990
Total sq. footage: 1,500
Open to the public
Trade discount available

Type of work: Ceramics, Glass,
Fiber, Mixed media, Furniture
70% one-of-a-kind work
Specialty: Representing artists from
North Carolina and across the U.S.

Commissions welcome
Designer contact: Meredith A. Mugler

GUILD artists represented:
Enrique Vega, see pg. 93,
Architect's Source

RALEIGH CONTEMPORARY
GALLERIES, INC.
Owner: Rory Parnell

134 East Hargett Street
Raleigh, NC 27601
(919) 828-6500

Established in 1985
Total sq. footage: 1,200
Open to the public
Trade discount available

Type of work: Ceramics, Paper,
Fiber, Mixed media,
95% one-of-a-kind work
Specialty: Paintings, Drawings,
Limited edition prints

Commissions welcome
Designer contact: Rory Parnell

GUILD artists represented:
Marjorie Tomchuk, see pg. 65

SOMERHILL GALLERY
Owner: Joseph D. Rowand

3 Eastgate, East Franklin Street
Chapel Hill, NC 27514-5816
(919) 968-8868
FAX (919) 967-1879

Established in 1972
Total sq. footage: 9,000
Open to the public

Type of work: Ceramics, Glass,
Paper, Fiber, Mixed media
100% one-of-a-kind work
Specialty: American contemporary
art of the Southeastern U.S.

Commissions welcome
Designer contact: Joseph D. Rowand

GUILD artists represented:
Michele Tuegel, see pg. 66
Enrique Vega, see pg. 93,
Architect's Source

SOUTHERN EXPRESSIONS
GALLERY & STUDIOS
*Owners: Suellen Lankford Pigman,
Dwight M. Pigman*

2157 New Hendersonville Hwy.
Pisguh Forest, NC 28768
(704) 884-6242

Established in 1985
Total sq. footage: 1,245
Open to the public
Trade discount available

Type of work: Ceramics, Glass,
Metal, Fiber, Furniture
30% one-of-a-kind work
Specialty: Custom furniture,
Contemporary southern appalachian
handcraft

Commissions welcome
Designer contact: Dwight M. Pigman

GUILD artists represented:
Paul Caron, see pg. 108
Tom McFadden, see pg. 147

Gallery Resources

• OHIO

AMERICAN CRAFTS GALLERY
Owners: Slyvia Ullman, Marilyn Bialosky

13010 Larchmere Boulevard
Cleveland, OH 44120
(216) 231-2008

Established in 1965
Total sq. footage: 4,000
Open to the public
Trade discount available

Type of work: Ceramics, Glass,
Wood, Fiber, Furniture
60% one-of-a-kind work
Specialty: Contemporary American crafts

Commissions welcome
Designer contact: Sylvia Ullman,
Marilyn Bialowsky

GUILD artists represented:
William C. Richards, see pg. 81

AVANTE GALLERY
Owners: Tom Huck, Kim Huck

2094 Murray Hill Road
Cleveland, OH 44106
(216) 791-1622

Established in 1987
Total sq. footage: 1,000
Open to the public
Trade discount available

Type of work: Ceramics, Glass, Metal,
Wood, Mixed media, Furniture
100% one-of-a-kind work

Commissions welcome
Designer contact: Tom Huck

GUILD artists represented:
Pam & George Castaño, see pg. 141,
Architect's Source
Anne Mayer Meier, see pgs. 239–240

DON DRUMM STUDIOS & GALLERY
Owner: Don Drumm, Lisa Drumm

437 Crouse Street
Akron, OH 44311
(216) 253-6268
FAX (216) 253-4014

Established in 1960
Open to the public
Trade discount available

Type of work: Ceramics, Glass,
Metal, Wood, Leather, Paper, Fiber,
Mixed media
Specialty: American crafts and sculpture,
Graphics and other related art forms

Commissions welcome
Designer contact: Lisa Drumm

GUILD artists represented:
Don Drumm, see pg. 219

ODC GALLERY
Owner: Ohio Designer Craftsmen

2164 Riverside Drive
Columbus, OH 43221
(614) 486-7119
FAX (614) 486-7110

Established in 1980
Total sq. footage: 1,000
Open to the public
Trade discount available

Type of work: Ceramics, Glass, Metal,
Wood, Paper, Fiber, Mixed media,
Furniture, Baskets
100% one-of-a-kind work
Specialty: Ohio craft studios
exclusively

Commissions welcome
Designer contact: Hal Stevens

GUILD artists represented:
Dan McCann, see pg. 94

Statement
The Ohio Designer Craftsmen Gallery
presents significant work by professional Ohio artists. Decorative and
sculptural work for the private and
corporate collector may be reviewed
through video and slide presentations.
Consulting services are available for
private and corporate collections. The
ODC Gallery offers comprehensive
information concerning artists working
in contemporary crafts in the state of
Ohio.

RILEY HAWK GALLERIES
Owner: Tom Riley, Linda Riley

2026 Murray Hill Road
Cleveland, OH 44106
(216) 421-1445

Established in 1988
Total sq. footage: 3,500
Open to the public

Type of work: Glass
90% one-of-a-kind work
Specialty: Nationally known glass artists

Commissions welcome
Designer contact: Tom Riley

GUILD artists represented:
John Kuhn, see pg 207

• OREGON

CONTEMPORARY CRAFTS GALLERY
Owner: Non-profit

3934 S.W. Corbett Avenue
Portland, OR 97201
(503) 223-2659

Established in 1937
Open to the public
Trade discount available

Type of work: Ceramics, Glass, Metal,
Wood, Leather, Paper, Fiber, Mixed
media, Furniture, Baskets
50% one-of-a-kind work

Commissions welcome
Designer contact: Marlene Gabel

GUILD artists represented:
Howard & Kathleen Meehan, see pg. 53,
Architect's Source

GANGO GALLERY
*Owner: Debi Gango Teschke,
Jackie Gango*

205 SW First Avenue
Portland, OR 97204
(503) 222-3850
FAX (503) 228-0749

Established in 1980
Open to the public
Trade discount available

Type of work: Ceramics, Glass,
Metal, Wood

Commissions welcome
Designer contact: Debi Gango Teschke,
Jackie Gango

GUILD artists represented:
William Richards, see pg. 81

• PENNSYLVANIA

GALLERY 500
*Owners: Rita Greenfield,
Harriet Friedberg*

Church & Old York Roads
Elkins Park, PA 19117
(215) 572-1203

Established in 1968
Total sq. footage: 3,500
Open to the public
Trade discount available

Type of work: Ceramics, Glass,
Metal, Fiber, Mixed media
75% one-of-a-kind work
Specialty: Contemporary American
crafts

Commissions welcome
Designer contact: Rita Greenfield,
Harriet Friedberg

GUILD artists represented:
Carol Kropnick, see pg. 238
Peter Mangan, see pg. 178
Raymond Tomasso, see pg. 64

GLASS GROWERS GALLERY, INC.
Owners: Deb & John Vahanian

701 Holland Street
Erie, PA 16501
(814) 453-3758

Established in 1974
Total sq. footage: 2,200
Open to the public
Trade discount available

Type of work: Ceramics, Glass,
Metal, Wood, Leather
40% one-of-a-kind work
Specialty: Contemporary and
traditional American crafts

Commissions welcome
Designer contact: Deb Vahanian

GUILD artists represented:
Shawn Athari, see pgs. 85 & 201

MATERIA FINE ART/FINE CRAFT
Owner: Anne Blasko, Jo Prockop

86 W. State Street
Doylestown, PA 18901
(215) 348-7280

Established in 1991
Total sq. footage: 2,000
Open to the public
Trade discount available

Type of work: Ceramics, Glass,
Wood, Furniture, Lighting
100% one-of-a-kind work
Specialty: Contemporary

Commissions welcome
Designer contact: Anne Blasko,
Jo Prockop

GUILD artists represented:
Joan Kopchik, see pg. 62
Karen Singer, see pg. 117,
Architect's Source

OWEN PATRICK GALLERY
Owners: James Gilroy, Gary Pelkey

4345 Main Street
Philadelphia, PA 19127
(215) 482-9395

Established in 1989
Total sq. footage: 1,800
Open to the public
Trade discount available

Type of work: Ceramics, Glass, Metal,
Mixed media, Furniture
80% one-of-a-kind work
Specialty: Fine contemporary art
and design

Commissions welcome
Designer contact: James Gilroy,
Gary Pelkey

THE WORKS GALLERY
*Owners: Ruth Snyderman,
Rick Snyderman*

319 South Street
Philadelphia, PA 19147
(215) 922-7775

Established in 1965
Total sq. footage: 3,000
Open to the public
Trade discount available

Type of work: Ceramics, Glass, Metal,
Wood, Fiber, Furniture, Lighting, Baskets
75% one-of-a-kind work
Specialty: Ceramics and fiber

Commissions welcome
Designer contact: Ruth Snyderman,
Rick Snyderman

GUILD artists represented:
Peter Handler, see pg. 135
Ellen Kochansky, see pg. 17

• SOUTH CAROLINA

CAROL SAUNDERS GALLERY
Owner: Carol Saunders

922 Gervais Street
Columbia, SC 29201
(803) 256-3046

Established in 1984
Total sq. footage: 2,600
Open to the public
Trade discount available

Type of work: Ceramics, Glass,
Fiber, Lighting, Baskets

Designer contact: Carol Saunders

GUILD artists represented:
Anna Keresh, see pg. 61

THE CHECKERED MOON
Owner: Barbara F. Bothwell

208 West Street
Beaufort, SC 29902
(803) 522-3466

Established in 1991
Total sq. footage: 550
Open to the public
Trade discount available

Type of work: Ceramics, Wood, Fiber,
Mixed media, Furniture
90% one-of-a-kind work
Specialty: Functional Art, Wallpieces
and Jewelry

Commissions welcome
Designer contact: Barbara F. Bothwell

GUILD artists represented:
Margaret Story, see pg. 171

• TENNESSEE

THE AMERICAN ARTISAN, INC.
Owners: Nancy Saturn

4231 Harding Road
Nashville, TN 37205
(615) 298-4691
FAX (615) 298-4604

Established in 1971
Total sq. footage: 2,740
Open to the public
Trade discount available

Type of work: Ceramics, Glass, Metal,
Wood, Fiber, Mixed media, Furniture
20% one-of-a-kind work
Specialty: Ceramics, Jewelry by
U.S. artists

Commissions welcome
Designer contact: Nancy Saturn

GUILD artists represented:
Timothy Weber, see pg. 197

ARTISANS
Owners: Ellen Sloane-Solley, Jim Solley

10000 Research Blvd., # 258
Austin, TX 78759
(512) 345-3001

Established in 1975
Total sq. footage: 1,000
Open to the public
Trade discount available

Type of work: Ceramics, Glass, Metal,
Wood, Paper, Fiber, Mixed media,
Furniture, Lighting
40% one-of-a-kind work
Specialty: Contemporary American
fine crafts

Commissions welcome
Designer contact: Ellen Sloane-Solley

GUILD artists represented:
Gregg Mesmer & Diane Bonciolini,
see pg. 209

BELL ROSS FINE ART GALLERY
Owners: Diane & Craig Bell, Linda Ross

1080 Brookfield Road
Memphis, TN 38119
(901) 682-2189
FAX (901) 758-1590

Established in 1986
Total sq. footage: 2,600
Open to the public

Type of work: Glass, Metal, Paper,
Mixed media, Furniture
95% one-of-a-kind work
Specialty: Contemporary fine art, Wall art,
Sculpture and museum quality crafts

Commissions welcome
Designer contact: Diane Bell

GUILD artists represented:
Michele Tuegel, see pg. 66

• TEXAS

ARTABLES
*Owners: Oliver Goldesberry,
Nancy Goldesberry*

2811 Colquitt
Houston, TX 77098
(713) 528-0405

Established in 1991
Total sq. footage: 900
Open to the public
Trade discount available

Type of work: Ceramics, Glass, Metal,
Wood, Paper, Fiber, Mixed media,
Furniture, Baskets
80% one-of-a-kind work
Specialty: American ceramics

Commissions welcome
Designer contact: Oliver Goldesberry

GUILD artists represented:
Gene Hester, see pg. 40,
Architect's Source

Gallery Resources

BEVERLY GORDON GALLERY
Owner: Beverly Gordon

2404 Cedar Springs, Suite 100
Dallas, TX 75201
(214) 880-9600

Established in 1982
Total sq. footage: 3,000
Open to the public

Type of work: Ceramics, Metal, Paper,
Mixed media
75% one-of-a-kind work
Specialty: Contemporary fine art

Commissions welcome
Designer contact: Beverly Gordon

GUILD artists represented:
Raymond Tomasso, see pg. 64

CARLYN GALERIES
Owner: Cynthia W. Ray

12215 Coit Road
Dallas, TX 75251
(214) 702-0824

Established in 1972
Total sq. footage: 1,550
Open to the public
Trade discount available

Type of work: Ceramics, Glass,
Wood, Fiber, Mixed media
15% one-of-a-kind work
Specialty: American

Commissions welcome
Designer contact: Cynthia Ray,
Cynthia Wong

GUILD artists represented:
Ron Fleming, see pg. 230

WILLIAM CAMPBELL
CONTEMPORARY ART
*Owners: William Campbell,
Pam Campbell*

4935 Byers Avenue
Fort Worth, TX 76017
(817) 737-9566
FAX (817) 737-9571

Established in 1974
Total sq. footage: 2,000
Open to the public
Trade discount available

Type of work: Ceramics, Metal, Paper,
Fiber, Mixed media,
80% one-of-a-kind work
Specialty: Contemporary art especially
Texas artists

Commissions welcome
Designer contact: William Campbell,
Pam Cambell

GUILD artists represented:
Don Young, see pg. 32,
Architect's Source

• VIRGINIA

BLUE SKIES GALLERY

120 West Queens Way
Hampton, VA 23669
(804) 727-0028

Established in 1990
Total sq. footage: 1,050
Open to the public

Type of work: Ceramics, Glass,
Wood, Fiber, Mixed media,
95% one-of-a-kind work

Commissions welcome
Designer contact: Carol Conway

GUILD artists represented:
Margaret Story, see pg. 171

PENINSULA FINE ARTS
GALLERY SHOP
Owner: Fine Arts Museum

101 Museum Drive
Newport News, VA 23606
(804) 596-8175

Established in 1973
Total sq. footage: 825
Open to the public

Type of work: Ceramics, Glass,
Metal, Wood, Leather, Paper, Fiber,
Mixed media
10% one-of-a-kind work
Specialty: Art paintings and ceramics

Commissions welcome
Designer contact: Bess Coffee

GUILD artists represented:
Margaret Story, see pg. 171

RUSH RIVER COMPANY
Owner: Mary B. Simmons

Gay Street
P.O. Box 74
Washington, VA 22747
(703) 675-1136

Established in 1975
Total sq. footage: 1,100
Open to the public

Type of work: Ceramics, Glass,
Metal, Wood, Leather, Paper, Fiber,
Furniture, Baskets
Specialty: Virginia artists

Commissions welcome
Designer contact: Mary B. Simmons

GUILD artists represented:
Margaret Story, see pg. 171

• WASHINGTON

CREATIONS GALLERY
Owner: Sande Wascher-James

524 First Avenue S.
Seattle, WA 98104
(206) 624-5578

Established in 1985
Total sq. footage: 1,100
Designer contact: Sande Wascher-James

GUILD artists represented:
Gloria E. Crouse, see pg. 165

MIA GALLERY
Owner: Mia McEldowney

536 1st Avenue, South
Seattle, WA 98104
(206) 467-8283

Established in 1987
Total sq. footage: 2,300
Open to the public
Trade discount available

Type of work: Ceramics, Paper, Fiber,
Mixed media, Furniture
100% one-of-a-kind work
Specialty: Northwest American
contemporary crafts

Commissions welcome
Designer contact: Mia McEldowney,
Meg Schiffler

GUILD artists represented:
Brian Swanson, see pg. 146

PHOENIX RISING GALLERY
Owner: Maureen Pierre

2030 Western Avenue
Seattle, WA 98121
(206) 728-2332

Established in 1989
Total sq. footage: 1,800
Open to the public
Trade discount available

Type of work: Ceramics, Glass, Metal,
Wood, Lighting
40% one-of-a-kind work
Specialty: Functional contemporary art
and contemporary blown glass

Commissions welcome
Designer contact: Maureen Pierre,
Derek Schroeder

GUILD artists represented:
Tom McFadden, see pg. 147

WILLIAM TRAVER GALLERY
Owner: William Traver

110 Union Street, 2nd Floor
Seattle, WA 98101
(206) 587-6501
FAX (206) 587-6502

Established in 1978
Total sq. footage: 5,000
Open to the public
Trade discount available

Type of work: Ceramics, Glass, Metal,
Mixed media
100% one-of-a-kind work
Specialty: Contemporary glass

Commissions welcome
Designer contact: Holle Simmons,
Julie Junkin

GUILD artists represented:
Susan Stinsmuehlen-Amend, see pg. 72,
Architect's Source

• WISCONSIN

A. HOUBERBROCKEN, INC.
*Owners: Joan Houlehen,
Meri Berghauer*

230 W. Wells Street, #202
Milwaukee, WI 53110
(414) 276-6002

Established in 1988
Total sq. footage: 2,000
Open to the public
Trade discount available

Type of work: Ceramics, Glass, Wood,
Paper, Mixed media, Lighting
95% one-of-a-kind work
Specialty: Contemporary fine crafts for
the home and office

Commissions welcome
Designer contact: Joan Houlehen,
Meri Berhauer

GUILD artists represented:
Barbara Fletcher, see pg. 231

ART INDEPENDENT GALLERY
Owner: Joan L. O'Brien

623 Main Street
Lake Geneva, WI 53147
(414) 248-3612

Established in 1968
Total sq. footage: 1,650
Open to the public
Trade discount available

Type of work: Ceramics, Glass, Metal,
Wood, Paper, Fiber, Mixed media,
Furniture, Baskets
85% one-of-a-kind work
Specialty: Mixed media

Commissions welcome
Designer contact: Joan L. O'Brien

GUILD artists represented:
Beverly Plummer, see pg. 63

JURA SILVERMAN GALLERY
*Owners: Jura Silverman, Charles
Silverman*

143 S. Washington
Spring Green, WI 53588
(608) 588-7049

Established in 1986
Total sq. footage: 3,000
Open to the public
Trade discount available

Type of work: Metal, Wood, Paper,
Mixed media, Furniture
50% one-of-a-kind work
Specialty: Wisconsin artists in all
media

Commissions welcome
Designer contact: Jura Silverman

GUILD artists represented:
Candace Kreitlow, see pg. 44

Statement
The Jura Silverman Gallery represents
over 100 Wisconsin artists in all media.
The focus of the gallery is strong,
highly original, contemporary work by
emerging artists as well as established
regional artists. Exhibitions change
every 5–8 weeks. Slide presentations
of artists' work and gallery exhibitions
are available. The Jura Silverman
Gallery welcomes commissions and
offers consulting services for private
and corporate collectors. Referrals and
discounts are available to the
design trade.

KATIE GINGRASS GALLERY
Owner: Katie Gingrass

241 North Broadway
Milwaukee, WI 53202
(414) 289-0855

Established in 1974
Total sq. footage: 2,000
Open to the public
Trade discount available

Type of work: Ceramics, Glass, Metal,
Wood, Paper, Fiber, Mixed media,
Furniture, Baskets
85% one-of-a-kind work
Specialty: Contemporary American
fine art and fine craft

Commissions welcome
Designer contact: Katie Gingrass,
Pat Brophy

GUILD artists represented:
Nancy Moore Bess, see pg. 228
Junco Sato Pollack, see pg. 46

METRO I GALLERY
Owner: Linda Hardy-Armstrong

7821 Egg Harbor Road
Egg Harbor, WI 54209
(414) 868-3399

Established in 1990
Total sq. footage: 1,800
Open to the public

Type of work: Ceramics, Glass, Paper,
Mixed media, Furniture
80% one-of-a-kind work
Specialty: Contemporary art, Mixed media

Commissions welcome
Designer contact: Linda Hardy-Armstrong

GUILD artists represented:
Joel & Sandra Hotchkiss, see pg. 235

VALPERINE GALLERY
Owners: Valerie Kazamias, Petie Rudy

1719 Monroe Street
Madison, WI 53711
(608) 256-4040

Established in 1980
Total sq. footage: 3,000
Open to the public
Trade discount available

Type of work: Ceramics, Glass, Metal,
Paper, Mixed media
75% one-of-a-kind work
Specialty: Watercolor, Mixed media,
Limited editions

Commissions welcome
Designer contact: Petie Rudy

GUILD artists represented:
Candace Kreitlow, see pg. 44

• CANADA

SANDRA AINSLEY GALLERY
Owner: Sandra Ainsley

Exchange Tower
Toronto, Ontario, M5X 1C8
(416) 362-4480

Established in 1989
Total sq. footage: 1,500
Open to the public
Trade discount available

Type of work: Glass
100% one-of-a-kind work
Specialty: Glass

Commissions welcome
Designer contact: Sandra Ainsley

GUILD artists represented:
John Kuhn, see pg. 207

National Organizations and Associations

AMERICAN CRAFT COUNCIL
72 Spring Street
New York, NY 10012-4006
(212) 274-0630
Carol Sedestrom Ross

The American Craft Council (ACC) stimulates public awareness and appreciation of the work of American craftsmen through museum exhibitions and educational programs, visual aids, and publications. The American Craft Museum is an affiliate of the American Craft Council; membership is shared. The American Craft Council consists of four operating units:

1. American Craft Enterprises -- addresses the marketing needs of American craftspeople by organizing large-scale wholesale and retail fairs;

2. American Craft Association -- provides advocacy and support services for professional craftspeople and craft businesses, such as insurance, merchant services, travel services and specialized publications geared to marketers;

3. American Craft Publishing -- promotes appreciation of craft through publication of *American Craft,* a bi-monthly magazine; future projects include books, videos and other special efforts;

4. American Craft Information Center serves as the principal information and referral center for materials on 20th century American craft.

AMERICAN ASSOCIATION OF WOODTURNERS
667 Harriet Avenue
Shoreview, MN 55126-4085
(612) 484-9094
Mary Redig, Administrator

The American Association of Wood-turners (AAW) is a non-profit corporation dedicated to the advancement of woodturning. Its fundamental purposes are to provide education, information, and organization for those interested in woodturning. Members include hobbyists, professionals, gallery owners, collectors and wood and equipment suppliers.

AMERICAN SOCIETY OF FURNITURE ARTISTS
P.O. Box 270188
Houston, TX 77277-0188
(713) 660-8855
Adam St. John, Pres. & Ex. Dir.

The American Society of Furniture Artists (ASOFA) is a non-profit organization dedicated exclusively to the field of "art furniture" and to the artists who create it. Organized in 1989, ASOFA is the only national organization of such artists. The Society's nationwide scope and juried membership procedures promote the highest professional standards and provide its members with significant avenues for continued artistic and professional development.

AMERICAN TAPESTRY ALLIANCE
Route 1, Box 79-A
Goshen, VA 24439
(703) 997-5104
Jim Brown, Director

The American Tapestry Alliance was founded in 1982 to: (1) promote an awareness of, and appreciation for, tapestries designed and woven in America; (2) establish, perpetuate and recognize superior quality tapestries by American tapestry artists; (3) encourage greater use of tapestries by corporate and private collectors; (4) educate the public about tapestry (its history and technique), and to encourage them to recognize high-quality work by local and national contemporary tapestry artists; (5) coordinate national and international juried tapestry shows, exhibiting the finest quality American-made works.

ARTIST-BLACKSMITHS' ASSOCIATION OF NORTH AMERICA
P.O. Box 1181
Nashville, IN 47448
(812) 988-6919
Janelle Franklin, Executive Secretary

Artist-Blacksmiths' Association of North America (ABANA) is a non-profit organization devoted to promoting the art of blacksmithing. ABANA serves to help educate blacksmiths, acts as a central resource for information about blacksmithing, and publishes *The Anvil's Ring,* a quarterly technical journal for blacksmiths.

CENTER FOR TAPESTRY ARTS
167 Spring Street
New York, NY 10012
Birgit Spears, Executive Director

The Center for Tapestry Arts (CTA) is an independent non-profit art center focusing on interdisciplinary fiber arts. CTA provides a resource library and artists' slide file, educational programming, and thematic group and solo exhibitions.

EMBROIDERERS" GUILD OF AMERICA, INC.
335 W. Broadway, Suite 100
Louisville, KY 40202
(502) 589-6956
Judy Jeroy, President

The Embroiderers' Guild of America's (EGA) purpose is to set and maintain high standards of design, color and workmanship in all kinds of embroidery and canvaswork. EGA sponsors lectures, exhibitions, competitions and field trips; offers examinations for teaching certification; and serves as an information source for needlework in the U.S. EGA also maintains a comprehensive embroidery book and reference library for research and study, and publishes *Needle Arts,* quarterly.

GLASS ART SOCIETY
1305 4th Avenue, Suite 711
Seattle, WA 98101
(206) 382-1305
FAX: (206) 382-2630
Alice Rooney, Executive Director

The Glass Art Society (GAS) is an international non-profit organization founded in 1971 to encourage excellence and to advance the appreciation, understanding and development of the glass arts worldwide. The Society holds an annual conference and publishes the *Glass Art Society Journal,* as well as a roster of membership each year.

HANDWEAVERS GUILD OF AMERICA
120 Mountain Avenue, B101
Bloomfield, CT 06002
(203) 242-3577
FAX: (203) 243-3982
Janet Hutson, Executive Officer

The Handweavers Guild of America is dedicated to upholding excellence, promoting textile arts and preserving textile heritage. It accomplishes this by providing a forum for education, inspiration and encouragement of handweavers, handspinners and related fiber artists.

National Organizations and Associations

INTERNATIONAL
SCULPTURE CENTER
1050 Potomac Street, NW
Washington, DC 20007
(202) 965-6066
FAX: (202) 965-7318
Giovanna Dixon

The International Sculpture Center (ISC) is an independent, non-profit membership organization devoted to the advancement of contemporary sculpture. Activities of the ISC include sculpture conferences; symposia and workshops; Sculpture Source -- a computerized artists registry and referral service; *Sculpture Magazine;* exhibitions; and various other member services. Membership is open to all.

INTERNATIONAL TAPESTRY
NETWORK
P.O. Box 203228
Anchorage, AK 99520-3228
(907) 346-2392
FAX: (907) 346-2392
Helga Berry, President

International Tapestry Network (ITNET) is a not-for-profit global network of tapestry artists, teachers, curators and collectors. ITNET works to develop greater aware- ness of contemporary tapestry as an art form by sponsoring international tapestry exhibitions, educating the public about tapestry, and encouraging dialogue on an international level between people involved with tapestry. ITNET publishes a quarterly newsletter distributed worldwide. Newsletter correspondents and advisory board members search for and share news of exhibitions, educational oppor- tunities and other tapestry events.

NATIONAL COUNCIL ON
EDUCATION FOR THE
CERAMIC ARTS
P.O. Box 1677
Bandon, OR 97411
(503) 347-4394
Regina Brown, Executive Secretary

The National Council on Education for the Ceramic Arts (NCECA) is a professional organization of individuals whose interests, talents, or careers are primarily focused on the ceramic arts. Its purposes are to stimulate, promote and improve education in the ceramic arts, to gather and disseminate information and ideas that are vital and stimulating to the

teachers, studio artists and to everyone throughout the creative studies community.

NATIONAL WOODCARVERS
ASSOCIATION
7424 Miami Avenue
Cincinnati, OH 45243
(513) 561-0627
Edward F. Gallenstein, President

The National Woodcarvers Association's (NWCA) aims are to promote wood- carving, and fellowship among its members; encourage exhibitions and area get-to-gethers; list tool and wood suppliers; and to find markets for those who sell their work.

Many distinguished professional woodcarvers in the United States and abroad share their know-how with fellow members. NWCA proudly lists several internationally famous authors of carving books on its roster.

SOCIETY OF AMERICAN
SILVERSMITHS
P.O. Box 3599
Cranston, RI 02910-0599
(401) 461-3156
Jeffrey Herman, Director

The Society of American Silversmiths (SAS) was founded in April 1989 to preserve the art and history of handcrafted holloware and flatware, and to provide its Artisan members with support, networking and greater access to the market. SAS also educates the public in demystifying silversmithing techniques and the aesthetic and investment value of this art form through its free consulting service. Another aim of SAS is to assist those students who have a strong interest in becoming silver craftsmen, though supplier discounts and workshops throughout the school year. In addition to an outstanding benefits package, all members have access to SAS's technical and marketing expertise, Artisan archives and a referral service that commissions work from Artisans.

SOCIETY OF NORTH
AMERICAN GOLDSMITHS
5009 Londonderry Drive
Tampa, FL 33647
(813) 977-5326
FAX: (813) 977-8462
Bob Mitchell, Business Manager

The Society of North American Goldsmiths (SNAG) was founded in 1970 to promote contemporary metalwork and jewelry. Through its publications, services and advocacy, the Society serves the fine art and jewelry communities with publications and conferences for members, practitioners and teachers of metalwork. Professional metalsmiths, students, collectors, gallery owners and enthusiasts form the dynamic mix of the Society.

SURFACE DESIGN
ASSOCIATION
P.O. Box 20799
Oakland, CA 94620
(415) 567-1992
Charles S. Talley

The purposes of the Surface Design Association (SDA) are to stimulate, promote, and improve education in the area of surface design; to encourage the surface designer as an individual artist; to educate the public with regard to surface design as an art form; to improve communication and distribution of technical information among artists, designers, educators, and with industry; to disseminate information concerning professional opportunities in surface design through galleries, studios, workshops, small businesses, industry, and education; to provide opportunities for surface designers to exhibit their work, and to provide a forum for exchange of ideas through conferences and publications.

WOODWORKING
ASSOCIATION OF NORTH
AMERICA
P.O. Box 706, Route 3
Plymouth, NH 03264
(603) 536-3876
Sheri Roy, Managing Director

The Woodworking Association of North America (WANA) serves individuals and companies engaged in woodworking, and promotes woodworking as an artform. WANA issues a member bonus packet with plans and special offers. The Association also organizes the annual Woodworking World Show, with seminars, workshops and exhibits.

Index of Artists by Region

Index of Artists by Region

Index of Artists and Companies

Index of Artists and Companies

Index of Artists and Companies